Aesthetic Theology and Its Enemies

THE MANDEL LECTURES
IN THE HUMANITIES AT BRANDEIS UNIVERSITY

Sponsored by the Jack, Joseph and Morton Mandel Foundation

The Mandel Lectures in the Humanities were launched in the fall of 2011 to promote the study of the humanities at Brandeis University, following the 2010 opening of the new Mandel Center for the Humanities. The lectures bring to the Mandel Center each year a prominent scholar who gives a series of three lectures and conducts an informal seminar during his or her stay on campus. The Mandel Lectures are unique in their rotation of disciplines or fields within the humanities and humanistic social sciences: the speakers have ranged from historians to literary critics, from classicists to anthropologists. The published series of books therefore reflects the interdisciplinary mission of the center and the wide range of extraordinary work being done in the humanities today.

For a complete list of books that are available in the series,
visit www.upne.com

James Wood, *The Nearest Thing to Life*

David Nirenberg, *Aesthetic Theology and Its Enemies: Judaism in Christian Painting, Poetry, and Politics*

DAVID NIRENBERG

Aesthetic Theology and Its Enemies

Judaism in Christian Painting, Poetry, and Politics

* * *

BRANDEIS UNIVERSITY PRESS
WALTHAM, MASSACHUSETTS

Brandeis University Press
An imprint of University Press of New England
www.upne.com

Manufactured in the United States of America
Designed by Eric M. Brooks
Typeset in Dante by Passumpsic Publishing

Library of Congress Cataloging-in-Publication Data
Nirenberg, David, 1964– author.
Aesthetic theology and its enemies : Judaism in Christian painting, poetry, and politics / David Nirenberg.
pages cm. — (The Mandel lectures in the humanities)
Includes bibliographical references and index.
ISBN 978-1-61168-777-4 (cloth : alk. paper)—
ISBN 978-1-61168-778-1 (pbk. : alk. paper)—
ISBN 978-1-61168-779-8 (ebook)
1. Christianity and other religions—Relations—Judaism. 2. Judaism—Relations—Christianity. 3. Judaism in art. 4. Christian art and symbolism. 5. Judaism in literature. 6. Christian literature—History and criticism. I. Title.
BM535.N57 2015
700'.48296—dc23

5 4 3 2 1

FOR SOFÍA

Wisdom, Beauty, Love

That reason may not force us to commit
That sin of the high-minded, sublimation,
Which damns the soul by praising it,
Force our desire, O Essence of creation,
To seek Thee always in Thy substances,
Till the performance of those offices
Our bodies, Thine opaque enigmas, do,
Configure Thy transparent justice too.

* * *

W. H. AUDEN

"In Sickness and in Health" (1937)

CONTENTS

ACKNOWLEDGMENTS

The Mandels have long been the source of so much that is good in the world of art, Judaism, and higher education. I am grateful to their foundation, and to Ramie Targoff as director of the Mandel Center for the Humanities, for entrusting to me the first Mandel Lectures at Brandeis University. To the Brandeis faculty for their hospitality, to the audiences for their questions and insights, and to Richard Pult at the University Press of New England for publishing the resulting manuscript, my profound thanks.

Since the chapters of this book deal with different fields, each has been reared in a different village. Michael Fried and Sara Lipton first awakened my interest in the questions about art addressed in chapter 1. Though they have not yet read the resulting pages, the marks of their work are everywhere evident within them. Walking through museums with Chris Wood, Ralph Ubl, and Felipe Pereda first taught me what it means to look at a painting, and coediting *Judaism and Christian Art* with Herb Kessler, what it means to write about one. Felipe Pereda has improved every paragraph of chapter 1, and Niall Atkinson, Laura Fernández Fernández, Johannes Heil, Anthony Kaldellis, Robert Pippin, Larry Silver, Jonathan Unglaub, and the History of Art Department at the University of Chicago all offered important advice.

Chapter 2, by contrast, has been the victim of neglect. My thanks to Shadi Bartsch-Zimmer for her bibliographic suggestions. Would that I had offered it up to her and others for needed criticism! For all its remaining faults, chapter 3 was more fortunate: an earlier version was presented as the 2012 Kantorowicz Lecture at the Goethe Universtät, Frankfurt am Main, as well as at a seminar at the University of California, Berkeley. I am grateful to both faculties for their comments, and above all to Bernhard Jussen and his colleagues for the invitation to Frankfurt and for their care in preparing the resulting German publication: *"Jüdisch" als politisches Konzept: Eine Kritik der Politischen Theologie* (Göttingen: Wallstein Verlag, 2013). An expanded English version of that lecture was published with the title "'Judaism' as Political Concept:

Toward a Critique of Political Theology" in *Representations* 128 (Fall 2014). Every page benefited from the kind attention of my student Alexandra Montero Peters, who offered help in this book's final stages, and Brenda Shapiro sustained its writing with unfailing friendship from its beginning to its end.

I am increasingly aware—and not only because of my weakening memory—that the debts incurred in the writing of books are far too complex for any accounting, let alone repayment. From those many whose contributions I may inadvertently not have credited, either here or in the footnotes, I ask forgiveness. But there are some gifts that are beyond any forgetting. Isabel and Ricardo have read nearly everything I've ever written, from infant scrawls to present pages, and inspired it all. Alexander reminds me constantly why the world matters. As for Sofía, this book, and my life, are dedicated to her. *Quid plura*?

Aesthetic Theology and Its Enemies

INTRODUCTION

Troubling Transcendence

Some two to three thousand years ago, according to an influential narrative, there emerged a new teaching and a new kind of teacher. Homer and Heraclitus; Parmenides, Pythagoras, Plato, and Parshvanatha; Zarathustra, Siddhartha the Buddha, and Ezekiel; Confucius and Lao Tzu; Isaiah and Deutero-Isaiah; Jesus and his apostles: these and many others contributed to what some have called the "Great Leap of Being," others the "Rise of Transcendental Visions" or the "Age of Criticism," still others the "Axial Age."[1]

The German philosopher Karl Jaspers, who coined the last term, saw in these transformations "the spiritual foundations of humanity . . . the foundations upon which humanity still subsists today."[2] We need not agree with his generalizations, or with the details of his history of ideas, to concede that the teachers of transcendence he was pointing to had proposed a peculiar view of the world that transformed the possibilities of thought, and that still troubles the cogitations of the present.

I say peculiar because that view, at least in some of its most widespread formulations, contained two aspects that might seem to be in paradoxical relation to each other. The first is skepticism. Within the Greek philosophical tradition, to choose but one well-known example, thinkers like Socrates and Plato emphasized the immense difficulty of knowing anything true about the world or about our selves. They taught that the things of this world as we perceive them in the flesh, no matter how solid or certain they seem, provide us at best with partial, relative, transient glimpses of truths; at worst, with deeply deceiving corruptions. "Philosophy persuades the soul to withdraw from the senses in so far as it is not compelled to use them," as Plato put it in the *Phaedo* (83a).

In his *Concluding Unscientific Postscript*, the modern philosopher Søren Kierkegaard summed up well the lessons of this "Greek skepticism": "There one learns thoroughly . . . that sensate certainty, to say nothing of historical certainty, is uncertainty, is only an approximation, and that the positive and an immediate relation to it are the negative."[3]

This skepticism toward what we know through the senses—that is, toward aesthetics, from the Greek *aisthanesthai*, "to perceive by the senses"—is one of the founding commitments of the transcendental turn. Of course skepticism alone does not transcendence make: on the contrary, it is as capable of corroding the claims of transcendence as it is of creating them. Here we come to the second commitment: some of these teachers (one thinks here of Plato more than Socrates) subscribed to the further proposition that although there are no eternal and unchanging truths to be found in our physical world, such truths—Plato's Forms are the most famous example—do exist on a different plane of being, one of eternal, unchanging truth. Our world merely partakes in, or in some way imitates, or (more optimistically?) points us toward, that other transcendent "world" of eternal being and unchanging truth.

Philosophers like Plato did not necessarily think dogmatically about the realm of truth as another world, or as a heaven or afterlife, the way later religious traditions like Christianity, Islam, and rabbinic Judaism would. But in trying to convey their teachings, they could certainly deploy myths and metaphors that tended in that direction. Plato's account (in the *Phaedo* 107a–108c) of the treatment of individual souls after death according to the level of philosophical knowledge of the truth they had achieved in their past life exemplifies a pedagogy taken by some later ancient readers as a literal description of the afterlife.

Perhaps Plato meant the specifics of his descriptions of the afterlife to be no more than instructive fictions. He himself tells us that the soul's full participation in eternal truth cannot be adequately expressed because far beyond mortal ken. But he does seem to have understood the soul (the word he uses in Greek is *psychē*) to be eternal, or in some essential way less subject to change than the body. At the very least we can say that in many of his "myths" and metaphors he characterized the soul as ontologically distinct from the body and its senses, passions, and appetites. In other words, in Plato's cosmos it is not just "truth" that is split between seeming and being, between this physical world and the transcendent. It is also the human individual who is split, divided between body and soul, between the transient and the eternal.

It is impossible to overestimate the consequences of this split, of which Plato is but one precocious proponent. One way of summarizing those consequences would be to say that the transcendental turn introduced a fundamental element of alienation into the world. The soul became in some irreducible sense unlike and alienated from the body. Things in the world were distanced from their "truth" or essence. And the signs, symbols, images, and representations with which humans conceive and communicate the world became ambivalent and potentially deceitful media, divorced from the things they claimed to point to.

In order to approach truth within this alienated cosmos, specialized sciences of suspicion were developed. Philosophy is the ancient name for the queen of those sciences, and it is astounding how quickly all forms of knowledge could be subjected to her criticism. In Plato's corpus alone, we can already see topics as diverse as what we today call art, biology, economics, justice, linguistics, physics, poetry, politics, and even the gods (theology) come under her sway. Simply confining ourselves to the one dialogue we call *The Republic* (or the *Politeia*, as it was known in Greek), we can see all these topics put to the work of orienting the city-state toward transcendence: toward its "soul" (as Plato himself put it) rather than its material body.

If this were a book about the history of the soul, we might linger for a while with Plato and the other midwives of Hellenistic transcendence, devoting ourselves to the difficult but invaluable pages of works like (for example) Aristotle's *De Anima*, or *On the Soul*. Through such pages we would learn how this alienation of the soul from the material could be systematized into what would become the learned axioms of the next two millennia, capable of making sense of everything from the physics of vision to the natural history of slavery.[4]

But ours is not a general history of the soul, or of transcendence. I begin with these broad strokes only to frame one particular but very powerful culture of transcendence: or rather the large family of cultures we collectively call Christianity. That culture is full of exhortations like this one, in Jesus' words, from the Gospel of Matthew: "Do not store up treasures for yourselves on earth, where moth and woodworm destroy them and thieves can break in and steal. But store up treasures for yourselves in heaven, where neither moth nor woodworm destroys them and thieves cannot break in and steal. For wherever your treasure is, there will your heart be too" (Matt. 6:19–21).

Early Christian texts often call followers of Jesus to orient their attention toward transcendent truths and otherworldly priorities. This orientation was in some ways similar to (and influenced by) that of Hellenistic philosophical culture, and it came with similar worries. If humans are composed of a mortal body and an immortal soul, and if all our information about the world reaches the soul through the bodily senses, then how can we prevent the mortal body with its sensual appetites from misleading the soul in its quest for truth and eternity?

The Hellenistic philosophers had developed any number of pedagogies to help the lover of wisdom counter the gravitational attraction that the body and its passions exerted on the soul's attention. Their goal, as an ancient metaphor has it, was to see the world with the eyes of the soul, rather than the eyes of the body. In the passage we've just encountered from the Gospel of Matthew, Jesus continues in much the same terms: "The lamp of the body is the eye. It follows that if your eye is clear, your whole body will be filled with light. But if your eye is diseased, your whole body will be darkness. If then, the light inside you is darkness, what darkness that will be!" (Matt. 6:22–23)

For Christians the danger of misplaced attention, of seeing with the wrong eyes, is very great: nothing less than eternal damnation. Hence, much like the philosophers, the gospel attempts to teach Jesus' followers how to make healthier their sight, how to see through the outer, "fleshy" appearance of things, persons, texts, and into their "spiritual" interior. One way they do so is by creating and criticizing negative figures who repeatedly fail to make precisely that distinction. Often enough these negative examples are figures of Judaism—priests, scribes, Saducees, Pharisees, rabbis—who represent the error of preferring apparent to inner beauty, flesh to spirit, the life of this world to the life of the next.

The gospels' pedagogy is animated by an infectious theory of knowledge, an anxiety about the ease with which "Jewish" cognitive attributes can overwhelm the Christian. They summarize this theory in a biological metaphor. In Mark's words, "Then he gave them this warning, 'Keep your eyes open; look out for the yeast of the Pharisees and the yeast of Herod'" (8:15). Luke's version is more explicit, and more apocalyptic: "Be on your guard against the yeast of the Pharisees—their hypocrisy. Everything now covered will be uncovered, and everything now hidden will be made clear" (Lk 12:1–2). But it is Matthew who gives us the fullest and most terrifying example:

> The disciples, having crossed to the other side, had forgotten to take any food. Jesus said to them, "Keep your eyes open, and be on your guard against the yeast of the Pharisees and the Sadducees." And they said among themselves, "It is because we have not brought any bread." Jesus knew it, and he said, "You have so little faith, why are you talking among yourselves about having no bread? Do you still not understand? . . . How could you fail to understand that I was not talking about bread? What I said was: Beware the yeast of the Pharisees and Sadducees." Then they understood that he was telling them to be on their guard, not against yeast for making bread, but against the teachings of the Pharisees and Sadducees (Matt. 16:5–12).

Here, at the very moment Jesus warns his closest associates of the danger posed by the "pharisaic" world, they fall into the trap. Rather than understanding his statement metaphorically and spiritually, as he intends it, the disciples understand it literally and materially, in the context of their own bodily hunger.

The danger in this example seems an inescapable attribute of language itself. When speaking of "yeast," of "bread," or of "Pharisees" and "Sadducees," did the gospels' Jesus speak literally or metaphorically? Could the two forms of meaning be separated from each other, and if so, how? The relationship between the "thing" a word referred to ("yeast," for example) and the "higher meanings" (metaphorical, allegorical, spiritual) that it was capable of generating was imagined as similar to the relationship between perishable fleshy things of this world and eternal spirit. These linguistic questions could therefore encapsulate for the redactors of Matthew, Mark, and Luke (as they had earlier, in a different way, for Paul, discussed shortly) the difficulty of determining the proper relationship between the human world of signs and things, and the divine word of scripture. And at the crossroads of all these questions, representing the possibility of confusion in its purest form, stood figures of Judaism like the Pharisees.

The consequences of that pharisaic pedagogy are the subject of this book, whose basic argument is that, in Christian cultures and their heirs, "Judaism" became a key concept with which to struggle against the terrifying sense of alienation that transcendence introduced into the meaning of the cosmos. Terrors are infinite, and this book short. So I have picked only a handful of alienations, all linked to questions of communication, representation, and mediation. In a world oriented toward transcendence, the signs, symbols, and images with which humans think and communicate become ambivalent. Representation, no matter what its form, becomes potentially deceitful. All media become potentially corrupting. How can people who orient their ideals toward transcendence, but continue to live in a world in which community and communication inevitably depend on media and representation, contain these aesthetic dangers?

⋆ ⋆ ⋆

In the pages that follow, I focus on three broad domains of representation: painting, poetry, and politics. My goals are likewise threefold. The first two are intimately related: to establish some of the ways in which Christian cultures have understood these three domains as threatened by "Judaism"; and to describe how these arts of representation attempted to legitimate themselves as Christian by defending themselves against this threat of Judaism. For it is my principal contention that, from early Christianity to the present, painting, poetry, and politics have often discovered, reflected upon, and defined the possibilities for their own existence by representing their relationship to Judaism. In other words, the Christian world's understandings of representation, communication, and mediation—its aesthetic theologies—have been built by thinking about the differences between "Christian" and "Jew." As for my third and final goal, it is simply to suggest that this history matters. The peculiar entanglements between Christian aesthetic anxieties and figures of Judaism are of ongoing importance to the world today, a world with its own yearnings for transcendence, yearnings that are not independent—I want to claim—from those of the past.

These are three large goals in a book of small compass. To achieve them, each chapter will focus on one mode of representation, respectively painting, poetry, and politics. The three were not chosen arbitrarily, nor for alliteration, but because each suffered special stigmatization as "Jewish" in the histories of transcendence that concern us. Still, many other modes could have also been chosen: theater, for example, or economics and the sphere of circulation and exchange. Over the long history of Western Christian thought, there is perhaps no sphere of culture that has not at some point been Judaized. "Culture," as an Austrian parliamentarian quipped in the early twentieth century, "is what one Jew plagiarizes from another."[5]

In order to convince you that the phenomenon I am describing is a general one, each chapter will range across space and time, from early Christianity to the twentieth century. And yet of necessity, each will also dwell on particular places and periods where some of these issues burned particularly hot into the conscience and the artifacts of the age. Some of those places and periods—medieval Spain, for example, or modern Germany—will recur across the chapters, in the hope of providing some sense of historical depth and the importance of context. But in the end each example can serve only as a promissory note for further accumulation. I do not pretend that any one can stand for the whole of history, but avail myself of each, to paraphrase Friedrich Nietzsche, "as of a strong magnifying glass with which one can render visible a general but creeping calamity which it is otherwise hard to get hold of" (*Ecce Homo* 1, 7).

* * *

By way of background, a few words about how Judaism became a concept associated with aesthetic anxieties in Christian thought. We should begin by noting just how widespread those anxieties were in the many corners of what we call the Hellenistic world: that is, the many diverse cultures brought into contact through the conquests of Aristotle's contemporary Alexander the Great. His armies carried upon their shoulders not only new rulers and regimes but also a language (Greek) and a philosophical vocabulary. We have already noticed some aspects of that vocabulary: its anthropology, in which the human is divided between body and soul; and its epistemology, in which that division gets extended from the human being to all the things interpreted by the human being—that is, to the world itself. Jews were among the many peoples exposed to this language and this philosophical vocabulary, learning the difference between perceiving the perishable body or the eternal truth, between seeing the world through eyes of spirit or of flesh. They too could learn to divide the objects of their interpretation—signs, symbols, letters, words, customs, laws, even society as a whole—into perishable body and eternal soul. Thus an older contemporary of Jesus, the Jewish philosopher Philo of Alexandria, exhorted his coreligionists to read the Bible for "the hidden meaning that appeals to the few who study soul characteristics, rather than bodily forms."[6]

Philo is an example of a Jewish thinker confronting the many difficulties posed by reading God's words—that is, the scriptural signs and symbols that mediate for embodied humanity the teachings and commandments of an eternal and unchanging truth—through some of the grounding axioms of Greek philosophy. The thousands of pages that have reached us from his oeuvre testify to the scale and importance of the task, while the numerous new words he delighted in inventing in Greek (after Plato, Philo is responsible for more Greek neologisms than any other ancient writer) suggest the vast reconceptualizations the project required.[7]

Those pages are certainly marked by what I've been calling aesthetic anxiety: Philo is well aware of the difficulties involved in perceiving the "soul characteristics" of scripture, rather than its "bodily form." But his anxiety could be termed moderate in the sense that he emphasizes the importance of both body and soul, rather than attempting to minimize or eliminate the one or the other. Consider his treatment of biblical commandments like circumcision: "We should look on all these [outward observances] as resembling the body, and [these inner meanings as resembling] the soul. It follows that, exactly as we have to take thought for the body, because it is the abode of the soul, so we must pay heed to the written laws. If we keep and observe these, we shall gain a clearer conception of those things of which these are the symbols."[8]

For Philo, there was nothing particularly "Jewish" about the challenges of interpretation that confront us in the world. But a handful of years later and just over the eastern horizon from Philo's Alexandria, the followers of another teacher reached significantly different conclusions. Living before what scholars today call the "parting of the ways" between Judaism and Christianity, many of Jesus' disciples stood within both the "old Israel" and the "new," and they faced some pressing questions about the dependences and differences between the two. For example, if all of Israel was instructed by the same scriptural word of God, why had only a tiny fraction recognized and embraced Jesus as its messiah? How could Jesus' followers maintain the truth of their messiah's claims, and of their interpretations of scripture, in the face of that messiah's apparent defeat and death, and of the massive indifference (and sometimes hostility) of the vast majority of the children of Abraham to his claims? It was in part to answer these and similar questions that the earliest followers of Jesus began to map the history of Israel, God's chosen people, onto the history of aesthetics.

The letters of Saint Paul are among the earliest writings we have from a follower of Jesus, and are particularly revealing of this exploration. Given our subject, it is worth remembering that his most extended treatment of the relationship between the followers of the old covenant with Israel and the new—the Epistle to the Romans—begins as a comparative history of aesthetics. The gentiles, Paul explains in chapter 1, chose to worship created things rather than deduce from those things the existence of the true God (Rom. 1:18–20). To the Israelites, however, God had given additional information in the form of prophecy and Law, designed to teach them humanity's powerlessness to save itself by its own works from the "law of sin which lives inside my body" (7:23); and to announce the coming gift of God's love, the messiah who would redeem humanity from this impasse.

Yet when that redeemer came, most of Israel rejected him. It did so, according to Paul, because of its own errors of perception and cognition. It saw only the outside of God's gifts—their literal, carnal, and ceremonial significance—rather than their inner or spiritual meaning. It understood only the letter of God's scripture, only the fleshy humanity of Jesus. Because of this slavery to the flesh and to its senses, the bulk of Israel was cut off from God's vine, making room for the in-grafting of the gentiles. Outcast Israel was not condemned forever, for at the end of time "all Israel will be saved" (Rom. 11:26). The meaning of this passage is very obscure. But what is clear is that in the meantime, the Israelites who reject Jesus have an aesthetic role to play. They are "vessels of wrath" made for destruction, in order to make known the riches of his glory for the "vessels of mercy" (9:22–23). Their "blind eyes" and bent backs can serve as a lesson, a warning not to repeat their error of seeing only the letter of the law, the outer flesh rather than the inner spirit. Already here, in this text from the first generation after Jesus' death, we can see a potential for the Jews to become pedagogical media, exemplary artifacts through which God's teachings become visible and the Christian eye learns how to see.[9]

I say potential because Paul himself probably did not intend or prophesy this pedagogical future for his words about the Jews. But as we shall see, this potential was eventually realized, and that fact demands some explanation. After all, Jews were not the only examples of cognitive error Paul deployed in his writing. In the ringing words of the first chapter of the First Epistle to the Corinthians: "Where are the philosophers? Where are the experts? . . . Since in the wisdom of God the world was unable to recognize God through wisdom, it was God's own pleasure to save believers through the folly of the gospel. While the Jews demand miracles [literally signs, *sēmeia*] and the Greeks look for wisdom [*sophia*], we are preaching a crucified Christ: to the Jews an obstacle they cannot get over, to the gentiles foolishness."[10]

If the "errors" of the Jews became more powerfully exemplary for Christians than those of the Greeks or philosophers, it is because of their relevance to a slightly different set of questions confronted by Paul and his contemporaries. What were the obligations of Jesus' followers to the traditions from which their movement sprang? For those (many) who had themselves been born into those traditions, should they continue to observe them? And what of the gentile followers of Jesus, those who were not of Jewish stock? What was their proper relationship to the "old Israel" into which their savior had chosen to be born, and whose traditions he at times seems to have maintained?

Paul was, like Jesus and the other apostles, himself a Jew by birth (according to tradition, a Pharisee). But unlike the other apostles, his mission as he understood it was to non-Jews: that is, to the gentiles. And one of the crucial questions his mission generated concerned the relationship of these followers of Jesus to Jewish laws, ceremonies, and rituals. Did gentile converts to the gospel need to follow, for example, the Jewish laws of circumcision and diet?

The apostles disagreed sharply on this question. Paul's answer—given first in his letter to the Galatians (circa 50 AD) and revisited in his letter to the Romans—was a resounding no. And in order to arrive at that answer, he engaged in arguments closely related to the philosophical ones we've already encountered. Circumcision, he argued, was a bodily sign whose spiritual meaning was "faith." Gentile followers of Christ were already circumcised in this higher, truer spiritual sense and did not need the body of the sign. On the contrary, if they took on the bodily aspect, they were opting for the material rather than the spiritual and revealing themselves as "separated from Christ" by the "self-indulgence of the flesh" (Gal. 5:2, 4, 16–18).

In Galatians, Paul wanted to show his gentile readers how to cast off the outer body of a letter, word, symbol, or ritual and cleave instead to its inner or spiritual meaning. And since the issues at stake concerned the Jews' scripture and their commandments, he used Judaism as a whetstone with which to sharpen the distinction between body and soul. His reinterpretation of Abraham's biography from Genesis provides a good example of this pedagogy:

> Abraham had two sons, one by a slave and one by the freewoman. The son of the slave girl came to be born in the way of human nature; but the son of the freewoman came to be born through

> promise. Now this is an allegory: these women are two covenants. One is from Mount Sinai, bearing children for slavery: she is Hagar . . . she corresponds to the present Jerusalem, for she is in slavery with her children. But the Jerusalem above is free, and she is our mother. . . . But what does scripture say? "Cast out the slave and her son; for the son of the slave shall not inherit with the son of the free woman." (Gal. 4:22–30)

Paul translates Abraham's families, one slave, one free, into a chain of oppositions, a table of antinomies known in Greek philosophy as *systoichiai*. Hagar and Ishmael represent flesh and slavery, Sarah and Isaac promise and freedom. Paul associates Hagar and Ishmael, flesh and slavery, with the law given on Mount Sinai and "the present Jerusalem." Sarah and Isaac, spirit and freedom, are a new covenant and a heavenly city. In one bold stroke Paul has reversed the traditional readings of this story. The Mosaic law and the Jewish people and polity that possess it ("the present Jerusalem") are not the heirs of God's promise to Abraham but are condemned as "of the flesh," sentenced to slavery and exile. This terrestrial Jerusalem is to be cast out, replaced by the spiritual Jerusalem, set free by faith in Jesus. And the entire revolution is achieved by a type of interpretation that he calls "allegory," literally "other-speak" in Greek, presented here as the spiritual rather than the bodily voice of the text.[11]

Paul presented the danger confronting the Galatians as one of *mistaken aesthetic priorities*: a preference for the bodily meaning of scripture over its spiritual one, and for the bodily sign of circumcision over its spiritual significance. The danger is great, and Paul will give repeated warnings. To set the mind on the flesh is death, but to set the mind on the spirit is life and peace, he tells us in Romans 8:6. Or in his lapidary phrase from 2 Corinthians 3:6, "For the written letters kill, but the Spirit gives life." In theory, this is a danger that confronts all embodied humanity, a universal difficulty without ethnic distinction, a state in which—to borrow a phrase from Galatians—"there is neither Jew nor Greek." But in fact, Paul himself gave the danger a Jewish face. In Galatians 2:14, after calling Peter a hypocrite and accusing him of precisely this misplaced priority, he coined a verb to describe the danger: to Judaize (Lt. *iudaizare*, Gk. *ioudaïzein*).[12]

With this one verb, from one of the earliest texts of the Jesus movement, we are ready to begin our history of the anxieties about "Judaism" that assail Christian aesthetics. But before we do so, we should notice the target of Paul's verb. It is not the Jews or the Jewish followers of Jesus who "Judaized" by observing dietary laws or being circumcised.[13] "Judaizing" for Paul—and this is too often and too easily forgotten—had little to do with the actions of "real" Jews. Instead, it designated the damning displacement of a *gentile* believer's attention away from Jesus' spiritual message and toward the literal commandments of the Jewish tradition within which Jesus was born and taught. By analogy, it quickly came to signify the *Christian*'s erroneous orientation of attention away from the spirit and toward the flesh, the letter of scripture, and the material things of this world, all loosely associated with or mapable onto "Judaism" through the analogies and polarities available to the age.

Over time the repeated application of this type of analogy turned thinking about "Judaism" and Judaizing into a basic resource for Christian self-definition and self-critique, an important part of the conceptual tool kit with which Christians could make sense of their world. This thinking with "Judaism" did not require any knowledge of what real Jews believed or did. Nor did anxieties about Judaizing require the presence of any "real" Jews. A potential "Jew" exists within every Christian, no matter how "gentile," because within the Christian logics we are exploring, "Judaism" threatens anyone making his or her hesitant way through this transitory world of flesh. That is why, to paraphrase Karl Marx, Christian culture "produces Judaism out of its own entrails." And it is also why the many pictorial, poetic, and political figures of Judaism that populate the following pages do not tell us much about living Jews or historical Judaism, even as they tell us a great deal about how countless people over many centuries have learned to think about the perils and opportunities of communication and community in a cosmos oriented toward transcendence.

Aesthetic theology is the term I've coined to describe that vast ocean of learning in its aggregate. A resonance is obviously intended with the much more ancient term *political theology*, made so relevant to twentieth-century thought by the Nazi jurist Carl Schmitt in his book by that name. His slim volume, first published in 1922 and much cited by political theorists today, claimed divine transcendence as the necessary foundation for all (European, at least) politics. My claim is both much broader and much more modest. Broader, in that it encompasses not only politics but all forms of representation, all embodied knowledge, all aesthetics. And more modest, in that I speak only of history, of habits of thought that humanity has forged for itself, not of eternal truths or of necessity.

It is true that a yearning for transcendence yawns beneath so much of our aesthetics, past and present, but that does not mean we should embrace it uncritically. On the contrary, precisely because that yearning has learned to project figures of Jewish enmity into the world, it is crucial that we not do so. And here we come to another resonance with other titles and other authors. One of these is (again) Carl Schmitt, whose *The Concept of the Political* of 1927/1932 made all politics dependent on an enemy. Again, my claim is more modest. The enemy may not be necessary for politics. But historically, Christian politics and Christian aesthetics, as well as their secularized heirs, have produced their own enemies and given them a distinctive form. They retain the potential to do so, even as they understand themselves to be striving toward peace, love, and justice. Can a political theology love its enemies? Can an aesthetic theology overcome the alienations it itself produces? These are the most basic questions of this book.[14]

CHAPTER ONE

Painting between Christianity & Judaism

The Lust of the Eyes

Accustomed as we are to churches and museums overflowing with Christian images, it is easy to forget that across the centuries many Christians have considered the plastic arts perilous. Their stigma was double, inherited from both Athens and Jerusalem. On the side of Jerusalem we find some well-known prohibitions:

> You shall not make yourself a carved image or any likeness of anything in heaven above or on earth beneath or in the waters under the earth. You shall not bow down to them or serve them. For I, Yahweh your God, am a jealous God. . . . (Exod. 20:4–6)

The meaning of this passage—among the most influential in the development of Jewish, Christian, and Islamic art—has been endlessly contested. Does it forbid all art, or only graven sculpture? All images, or only those of living things? Sharp differences over its interpretation have marked the long history of debate about the making of images. But the general concern is clear: God considers certain forms of human interaction with certain kinds of objects a rival form of love, and He gets jealous.

Idols are an important subcategory of these dangerous objects of attention, but they are not the only ones. Both women and wealth, for example, appear so often in Hebrew scripture as rivals for God's love that idolatry, adultery, and greed became intimately interrelated terms. The danger is even broader: any object in the world, seen or thought about in the wrong way, can constitute a rival to our love of God. Hence "the Lord also spoke to Moses and said: 'Speak to the Israelites and tell them, for all generations to come, to put tassels on the hems of their clothes and work violet thread into the tassel at the hem. You will thus have a tassel, and the sight of it will remind you of all Yahweh's orders and how you are to put them into practice, and not follow the dictates of your own heart and eyes, *going whoring after diverse things . . .*'" (Num. 15:38–40, italics my translation).[1]

The problem is not merely with images and idols, but with *how we see and think about things themselves*. In this crucial verse our eye's attraction to those things is represented in terms of inappropriate sexual intercourse (Hebrew *zonim*, whoring; Vulgate's Latin *fornicantes*, fornicating). The fringes that God ordained for their garments were meant to teach Israel's children how to look at other objects, helping them know things chastely by disciplining their sight. Though at first blush this commandment may seem more cultic than philosophical, the potential for a vast aesthetic critique is spun into its blue threads. Much later Christian readers would recognize and develop that potential, as when Saint Augustine explained, circa 400, that the human "appetite for learning is called in the divine language 'the lust of the eyes.'"

It is perhaps easier for us to recognize questions of cognition in ancient Greek debates about art than in Israelite ones. It is, after all, the Greek language that gave us English speakers our own etymological complex of words derived from the root for sight—words like *idea, ideal, idol, ideology*. It does not seem a long step from Aristotle's claim that "the soul never thinks without a mental image" to John Locke's view that "the understanding of a man in reference to all objects of sight, and the ideas of them," is like a dark closet stacked with pictures obtained from the outside world of light.[2] And the reason this step seems so short is that Greek thought systematized for what we call philosophy the gap between the sensible and the real, or the real and the ideal: gaps full of consequences for how the world would come to think about art.[3]

Still, just one example suffices to suggest that the aesthetic anxieties provoked by these Hellenistic gaps could take shapes very similar to the ocular fornications of the Hebrews. As we saw in the introduction, Plato developed a fundamental distinction between the physical senses and the reasoning intellect, between the world of sensible things (literally, aesthetics) and of "intelligibles." The latter he thought immaterial, incorporeal (*asōmata*: Plato was among the earliest users of this Greek word). These incorporeal intelligibles were the truth of things—their *ideai*, or "Forms," in his specialized vocabulary, corresponding to our English "idea"—rather than of their image or mere appearance (*eidolon*, from whence our English "idol"). Theirs is the domain of the "greater mysteries": the transcendent world of metaphysics toward which Plato orients his philosophy.[4]

But although Plato sometimes imagines that our souls once dwelt in such a metaphysical world, "unsigned" and "unentombed" by the body (as he puns in the *Phaedrus*), he is aware that they no longer do. In *this* world our soul is imprisoned by the body "like an oyster by its shell," and we can only reach toward truth through the senses. The task is not easy, as Plato goes on to explain in this same passage (*Phaedrus* 250A-E), because sensible things can lead away from truth as easily as they can toward it. He uses the example of sight, "the keenest mode of perception vouchsafed us through the body," and of beauty, of all "beloved objects" the "most manifest to sense and most lovely." How does the sight of sensible beauty affect us? It can send us "after the fashion of a four-footed beast" to "beget offspring of the flesh" and "consort with wantonness" (recall the vocabulary of Num. 15). Or conversely, it can awaken our memory of beauty in that other world, the metaphysical world "that truly is," and stimulate our soul's striving toward it.

The discussion in the *Phaedrus* is about the attraction of one human being toward the beauty of another, but the ambivalence in question affects all forms of cognition that depend on sight and beauty.[5] The prisoners in the famous cave of Plato's *Republic* confront a similar problem: they know only the shadows of puppets, statues, and artifacts paraded on the wall before them. For them, "truth is nothing other than the shadow of artificial things." The prisoner who has been briefly dragged into the light—that is, the philosopher—also depends on sight for knowledge, but with this crucial difference: he knows that the sights in the cave are "idols" and "phantasms" and struggles to turn his soul's attention toward "that which is."

Plato does not present the ideal here as freedom from images, or as keenness of sight. There is no freedom from images to be had in this world: even the allegory of the cave is itself an "image," as both Socrates and his interlocutor Glaucon realize. As for keenness of sight, in the case of a vicious soul "the sharper it sees, the more evil it accomplishes." The difference between falsity and truth, according to Plato, lies not in qualities of vision but in the orientation of the soul itself, which needs to be "turned around toward the true things" and away from their mere appearance (*Republic* 514–19). It is the task of philosophy to effect this conversion of the soul's habits of attention and perception. But there are other arts, such as poetry, painting, and sculpture, that tend to effect conversions in the opposite direction. These misdirect the soul because they make their appeal directly to the world of things through the senses, rather than calling attention to the gap between appearance and reality.[6]

Mimēsis—a Greek word sometimes translated as representation, sometimes a bit more reductively as imitation, and sometimes left untranslated—is the key term here. Plato considers many arts to be mimetic in that they make things at some remove from the truth. The couch maker, for example, makes a couch, not the ideal form of a couch, and in this sense his product is but a shadow of the "real." But some artists are more mimetic than others, among them the painter and the poet, who make representations of everything. He "produces earth and heaven and gods and everything in heaven and everything in Hades under the earth." This promiscuity insults Plato's sense of the proper specialization of each art (*technē*). Worse, it means that what the painter and the poet produce are not real even in the couch's limited sense: "they look like they are; however they surely are not in truth" (596 C-E).[7]

Poets and painters stand further from the truth than other craftsmen because they are "imitators of phantoms of virtue" rather than of virtue itself. Not only do their works appeal to "the soul's foolish parts," but this gratification does not lead toward any greater knowledge of things: "The painter will make what seems to be a shoemaker to those who understand as little about shoemaking as he understands, but who observe only colors and shapes" (600E–601A). The result of this preference for the sensible over the true is that painting (like poetry) "produces a bad regime in the soul of each private man" (605C). It is the philosopher's task to produce the opposite—a good regime both for the person and the polity—by warning souls about the sensible and orienting them toward the true. Philosophy strives to make of every soul a critic of art.

Criticism need not mean elimination. Plato often insists that if oriented toward the good, the power of mimesis can be put to positive work. In the *Laws*, for example, he does prohibit certain forms of mediation and representation (such as money) that he deems irremediably corrupting to the polity. But he does not banish painting. Instead, "the Athenian" endorses a certain type of art by praising the example of Egypt, which "long ago recognized that poses . . . must be good, if they are to be habitually practiced by the youthful generation of citizens. So they drew up the inventory of all the standard types, and consecrated specimens of them in their temples. Painters . . . were forbidden to innovate on these models," with the result that "the work of ten thousand years ago . . . [and] that of today both exhibit an identical artistry" (*Laws* 656E–657A).

Plato's praise of the Egyptians was aimed directly at what he considered the misguided aesthetic fashions of his own day, which celebrated artists for feats of naturalism and delighted in their invention of techniques of illusion. Yet through his criticism, Plato was also issuing painting a passport into the age of transcendence. In a world of ideas in which matter was increasingly stigmatized and the appearance of things increasingly deemed distant from their truth, painting was at risk of becoming the enemy of philosophy. Plato outlined the reasons for that enmity and its dangers, but he also set forth the terms by which it might be overcome. If art would submit to ontology, he suggested, it could labor in the service of the good.

Of course Plato was not the only thinker about art in the ancient world. Aristotle, for example, had a very different understanding of the nature of the soul and the senses, of the relationship between the real and the ideal, and therefore of the perils and opportunities of representation. I've focused so much on Plato's criticism (and defense) of the mimetic arts because both would have such varied and influential futures in the many Hellenistic schools of thought into which Christianity expanded. By the end of Late Antiquity we might say that Neoplatonism had conquered even Aristotle, so that Peripatetic aesthetics were often read through Platonic eyes. But we need not take the long detours necessary to prove the point. Histories of ancient philosophy, like those of Israelite prophecy, concern us here only insofar as we need to be convinced that they provided the conceptual tools with which early Christians carved out their own concerns about the gap between the material and the real.

Judaizing Aesthetics

We can see both those conceptual tools being put to work already in the earliest Christian writings. Recall the brief history of humankind's knowledge of the divine provided by Saint Paul in chapter 1 of his Epistle to the Romans:

> Ever since the creation of the world, the invisible existence of God and his everlasting power have been clearly seen by the mind's understanding of created things. And so these people have no excuse. . . . While they claimed to be wise, in fact they were growing so stupid that they exchanged the glory of the immortal God for an imitation [*homoiōma*, counterfeit], for the image [*eikōon*] of a mortal human being, or of birds, or animals, or crawling things. (Rom. 1:20–23)

This astonishing passage takes the Mosaic law's concern with the worship of images and conflates it with the ontological preoccupations of Platonic philosophy to arrive at a general critique of gentile knowledge of created things in the world.

In Galatians Paul had developed a Jewish version of this error, accusing Judaizers of worshipping the outer fleshy appearance of things rather than their inner spiritual reality. In Romans he developed this theme, applying it to the nature of Judaism itself: "The real Jew is the one who is inwardly a Jew, and real circumcision is in the heart, a thing not of the letter but of the spirit" (2:29). In that epistle he also located the source of the Jews' ontological bind *in the Mosaic law itself*: "The commandment was meant to bring life but I found it brought death. . . . It is by means of the commandment that sin shows its unbounded sinful power." The law of Moses cannot free or save. At best it can make me aware that I "am a prisoner of that law of sin which lives inside my body." "Only the law of the Spirit which gives life in Jesus Christ" can set me free (7:7–25; 8:2).

Readers of Paul discovered multiple meanings in his writings about Jews, the Law, and the flesh. In the Epistle to the Romans alone, and specifically on the question of how humans relate to God through sensual perception of things in the world, they could find justification for two very different aesthetics. Chapter 1 condemned idolatry but held out the hope that through the sight of created things we can come to knowledge of the creator. Chapter 7 stressed the alienation from truth that came with embodiment and removed any hope that the law God gave to Moses could overcome the law of sin at work in our flesh. Chapter 1 would inspire those schools—sometimes called Neoplatonic because influenced by Plotinus and Porphyry's readings of Plato—that taught Christians how to ascend toward truth through things and the images of things. Chapter 7 would license those—like Marcion and other Gnostics of ancient Christianity, or Karl Barth and other crisis theologians of modernity—who preferred to emphasize the abyss between flesh and spirit, and for whom the only truth to be found in the things and images of this world was a heightened awareness of our imprisonment.

This diversity reminds us that Paul's epistles, like Plato's dialogues, could authorize very different ways of thinking about the gap between the sensible and the real, the material or corporeal and the spiritual. If in Romans the flesh is death (8:6), in 2 Corinthians it is a sheltering tent (5:1–4). And if on the one hand—in a passage with real implications for the future of Christian art—Christians (as opposed to those Jews who do not recognize Christ) "look not at the things which are seen, but at the things which are not seen" (2 Cor. 4:18), conversely the spiritual requires the physical. "If there is a physical body, there is also a spiritual body. . . . But it is not the spiritual which is first, but the physical, and then the spiritual" (1 Cor. 15:42–50). Later generations of Christians would discover the potential for these and many other positions in Paul's writings. But they also discovered in them a common language with which to debate the relative merits of their many different views about this gap: the language of Judaism.

Like Paul the gospel reflected on the dangers of this world of signs and things, and represented those dangers in terms of images, deception, and Judaism. In the introduction we encountered the example of the "yeast of the Pharisees." Since in this chapter we are concerned more with vision than with words, let's conclude our biblical survey with some examples of visual danger. Such examples are common enough, since the gospel authors developed special figures of Judaism through which to enact the fatal error of seeing only the fleshy significance, rather than the spiritual meaning, of a sign or thing (e.g., to see Jesus as the man he appears to be, rather than as the God he is; or to understand the Hebrew Bible only in its literal meaning, rather than in the spiritual sense that announces the coming of Jesus). Think again of the Pharisees: "Everything they do is done to attract attention, like wearing broader headbands and longer tassels. . . . Blind Pharisee! Clean the inside of cup and dish first so that it and the outside are both clean. Alas for you, scribes and Pharisees, you hypocrites! You are like whitewashed tombs that look handsome on the outside, but inside are full of the bones of the dead and every kind of corruption. In just the same way, from the outside you look upright, but inside you are full of hypocrisy and lawlessness" (Matt. 23:5, 26–28).

In this passage there swirls about the figure of the Pharisee—who will return in our chapters on poetry and politics—an extreme confusion between appearance and truth, beauty and meaning, material exterior and spiritual interior. Out of this confusion we can begin to see how types of Judaism will emerge in Christian thought to represent misplaced priorities, the wrong kind of attention, an absorption that focuses on the lethal delights of this world rather than seeing through them into the next.

But although the error of absorption in the world is often given Jewish form in the New Testament and in the ensuing Christian tradition, this does not mean Christians are not susceptible to the same error. On the contrary, Paul has already taught us that Judaizing is a gentile error: it is not Jews who Judaize, but Christians. And in the gospel we have seen how easily the apostles themselves could be infected by pharisaic "yeast," even when under the direct tutelage of Jesus. The founding fathers of Christian theology were perfectly aware that embodied as they are, all humans are subject to the temptations of the world and its beauty. It is precisely this universal nature of the danger that made the particular language of Judaizing so useful.

Saint Augustine, for example, taught that "to be unable to lift the eye of the mind above what is corporeal and created" is "a miserable slavery," "the death of the soul." This condition of misplaced absorption was the state of the Jews, he explained, because they had subjected their souls to the material form of the scripture's letter, just as they had earlier subjected it to the material form of the sculptor's golden calf (*De doctrina Christiana* 3.5.9). But Augustine also recognized that every embodied human being, even the most Christian, was at risk of this miserable slavery. As he put it in Book 10 of the *Confessions*, "The eyes delight in fair and varied forms, and bright and pleasing colors. . . . There is no rest from them given me. . . . But that corporeal light . . . seasons the life of the world for her blind lovers with a tempting and fatal sweetness."

Augustine did not believe anyone, however prayerful or pious, was capable of breaking this fatal attraction. "I resist the seductions of my eyes, lest my feet be entangled as I go forward in your way; and I raise my invisible eyes to you, that you would be pleased to 'pluck my feet out of the net.' You pluck them out continually, for they are easily ensnared. You pluck them out unceasingly, but I remain fast in the snares set all around me" (*Confessions* 10.34). A charming example from his own everyday life makes clear how great the danger is: "I do not nowadays go to the circus to see a dog chase a rabbit, but if by chance I pass such a race in the fields, it quite easily distracts me even from some serious thought and draws me after it . . . with the inclination of my mind. And unless, by showing me my weakness, you [God] speedily warn me to rise above such a sight and [turn] to you by a deliberate act of thought . . . then I become absorbed in the sight, vain creature that I am" (10.35).

Augustine knows that the temptation of the world's corporeal light is constant. Almost as constant is the potential to imagine that temptation in terms of Judaism or Judaizing.

When I say this potential is constant within Christian cultural critique, I do not mean to imply that its power is always the same, or that the ways in which the danger is imagined or put to work are unchanging. Quite the contrary, my claim is that precisely because the potential of Judaizing haunts Christian aesthetics, developments in that aesthetics are often accompanied by new ways of activating and deploying the potential dangers of Judaism. Which is also to suggest that transformations in Christian practices of representation can transform the possibilities of life for Jews (and Christians) of flesh and blood, just as changes in how Christians think about and experience Jews and Judaism can alter how they think about aesthetics.

Iconoclasts and Iconophiles

From their earliest emergence in Christian debates about images, figures of Judaism played many and often-opposing roles, serving Christians simultaneously as thesis, antithesis, synthesis. This should not be surprising, given the important place assigned to Judaism within what a modern theologian might call the incarnational dialectics of matter and spirit. On the question of images, for example, the Jews could provide Christians with examples of the most sublime rejection of the eye's attraction to the material object: "Thou shalt have no graven image." They could equally well model the most degraded submission to such objects, as in their worship of the golden calf. And they could even represent the incarnational bridging of the gap between spiritual and material, as when the art objects in the Hebrews' Tabernacle, understood as material dwelling-place of the divine, were interpreted typologically as a prefiguration of Jesus. So varied were these roles, so flexible this dialectic, that virtually any visual relationship to the object could be mapped onto the figure of the Jew.[8]

These diverse possibilities are already evident in 394 CE, during a debate over the decoration of churches between a relatively obscure presbyter named Nepotian and the much more famous Saint Jerome, author of what became the standard Vulgate translation of the Bible into Latin, and himself the subject of many medieval and Renaissance paintings. In an earlier letter Nepotian had apparently invoked the example of the Jews and their Temple as justification for the Christian decoration of churches with expensive materials and images. Jerome attacked precisely that point in his counterargument: "And let no one allege against me the wealth of the temple of Judea, its tables, its lamps . . . and the rest of its golden vessels." Those things of the Temple, Jerome explains, were "figures typifying things still in the future." But for Christians, who *live in that future*, "the Law is spiritual." If Christians "keep to the letter" in this, they must keep it in everything, and adopt the Jewish rituals: "Rejecting the superstition of the Jews, we must also reject the gold; or approving the gold, we must approve the Jews as well. For we must either accept them with the gold or condemn them with it." Note Jerome's infectious logic: those who choose to decorate churches must become Jews. Jerome's colleague Epiphanius of Salamis made much the same argument at much the same time, but with a slightly different vocabulary. Criticizing paintings of the saints on church walls, he reminded his readers of Paul's characterization of false priests as "whitewashed walls" (Acts 23:3). To paint a fresco on a church wall, he implied, was to become a Pharisee.[9]

We can see from this one example that invocations of Judaism could justify diametrically opposed positions toward devotional objects. Where Nepotian stressed the ongoing value of the Hebrew prophets' literal examples in order to approve of Christian decorations and devotional images, Jerome rejected both by insisting on the complete supersession of the letter by the spirit, casting any residual literalism as Judaizing. But of course the example is not exhaustive: there were countless other positions available, as many as there were ways of thinking about the relationship between the "Old Testament" and the "New." John of Damascus would assert yet a different relation in the eighth century, amid a civil war over images—the Iconoclast controversy—that shook the eastern Roman Empire (Byzantium) in the eighth and ninth centuries (730–787 and 815–843 CE). According to him, the prohibition in the Old

Testament had been addressed only to the childlike Jews, who were prone to idol worship:

> It was, therefore, for the Jews, on account of their sliding into idolatry, that these things were ordained by law. To speak theologically, however, we, to whom it has been granted, fleeing superstitious error, to come to be purely with God, and having recognized the truth, to worship God alone and be greatly enriched with the perfection of the knowledge of God, and who, passing beyond childhood to reach maturity, are no longer under a custodian, have received the habit of discrimination from God and know what can be depicted and what cannot be delineated in an image.[10]

Christians could therefore utilize images without danger, since they were mature enough to look to the spirit and not the flesh.

It is precisely because Christian questions about that relationship were so multiple, and so important to Christian understanding of the relationship between God and the material world, that Jews and Judaism came to stand at the center of Christian thinking about the dangers of aesthetics and the possibilities for art. In the Byzantine conflict over images all sides deployed Judaism as a weapon. The iconoclasts insisted that advocates of devotional art were either worshippers of the picture, in which case they were idolaters, or else they were worshippers of the image of Jesus' human body, in which case, like the Jews, they were overlooking his divinity. After all, painters could represent only the humanity of the savior, not the divine presence that had been consubstantial with that humanity. In this world (according to the iconoclasts), the only thing that could truly represent this consubstantiality of matter and divinity is the body and blood of the man-God in the consecrated bread and wine of the Eucharist. Everything else is merely matter without presence. The worship of such matter is a damning confusion of God's nature, just like the many Judaizing heresies of the past.[11]

The defenders of images attempted to turn the same weapon against their foes. According to them, iconoclasm was itself the invention of "a leader of the lawless Jews, a sorcerer and the agent of demonic soul destroyers called Tessarakontapēchys" (the name means "forty cubits tall") who convinced the Muslim caliph Yazid II to order all Christian images in his land destroyed. When some unworthy Christians heard of this, "they imitated the lawless Jews and the unbelieving Arabs, and began to insult the churches of God." This "tall tale" is not idiosyncratic. Numerous Greek iconophile sources attribute the origins of iconoclasm to a Jewish magician who falsely advises the Muslim caliph to ban images from Christian churches in his domains. These same sources generally go on to present Jews, Muslims, and Christian iconoclasts as the real "idolaters," who perceive only the outer beauty of the images themselves, without realizing that this beauty is meant to turn the inner eye toward God.[12]

According to the defenders of images, this error, which misled the Jews into crucifying Christ, now misleads the iconoclasts into destroying his image. In the words of an eighth-century text: "Formerly the impious put to the lips of Jesus a mixture of vinegar and gall; in our day, mixing water and lime and fixing a sponge to a pole, they applied it to the icon. . . . They have perpetrated the work of the Jews." The ninth-century Khludov Psalter converted the words into image, juxtaposing a drawing of two Jews tormenting the crucified Jesus with long-poled sponges of vinegar and gall with an illustration of two iconoclasts using the same instruments to whitewash an image of the savior. Within the iconophiles' logic, to deface a fresco is to become a Christ-killing Pharisee.[13]

These brief paragraphs do not pretend to account for the history of these Byzantine debates. Their only goal is to suggest that in those debates both the defense and the critique of images could be conducted in terms of Judaism. This translatability explains why, in eighth- and ninth-century Byzantium, a conflict *between Christians* over images also produced an explosion of *anti-Jewish* polemics, violence, and forced conversions of living Jews.[14] What better example of the phenomenon we are trying to discover and explain? Because of the theological centrality and dialectical utility of figures of Judaism in Christian discourses about representation, a period of heightened anxiety about representation produced heightened anxiety about Judaism.

This potential holds as true for the Western as for the Eastern reaches of Christendom. Even Pope Gregory the Great's famous letter to Bishop

Serenus of Marseilles circa 599–600 CE, ordering him to stop destroying the images in his church—"you should not break what has been placed in churches not for adoration but simply to instruct the mind of the ignorant"—might be seen in this context. My admired teacher Peter Brown has suggested, for example, that the ignorant *gentes* here were Jews, and that Gregory's letter must be read within a context in which the forced conversion of Jews and Jewish criticism of devotional images were frequently staged together. I would only add that, in this exchange, both Gregory and Serenus could well have understood themselves as in a battle against Judaism even if no Jews in the flesh were involved in their debate, since both of their positions could be represented as Judaizing with the Christian concepts available for thinking about images.[15]

It is within this context of contending Christian attitudes toward images that we should understand what may well be the first account in Latin Christian culture of a Jew as exemplary enemy of icons. Bishop Gregory of Tours (d. 594), who flourished at much the same time as Serenus of Marseilles and Gregory the Great, included in his *On the Glories of the Martyrs* the story of a Jew who snuck into a church by night and ripped off the wall a board painted with the image of Christ. The Jew took the painting home, without noticing in the dark that the image was bleeding so profusely that it had soaked his clothes in blood. The next day the Christian population of the town (unspecified, but presumably in the Greek East) noticed the bloody tracks and followed them to the Jew's home, where they discovered the crime and stoned the criminal. Stories such as these, which cast opponents of icons as murderous Jews, became quite popular among defenders of painting. A more widely circulated version promoted by iconophiles in the ninth century stipulates both church (St. Sophia) and town (Constantinople), the Jew throws the pilfered picture down a well, and the perpetrator is not lapidated but converted.[16]

In Western Europe neither Gregory the Great's letter nor Gregory of Tours's miracle ended the debates over images. It is true that the Carolingians did not experience as violent a conflict over images as their Byzantine contemporaries did, but a colder war continued for centuries.[17] Circa 1000 CE, for example, devotional practices in Western Europe began a substantial transformation whose main attribute was an increasing emphasis on the mortal birth, human body, and fleshly death of Jesus in Christian worship. This emphasis was accompanied by an explosion in the devotional uses of representations of Jesus' body, ranging from the expanding role of crosses and crucifixes in liturgy to the introduction of the freestanding religious images of the Virgin and Child that we now consider so characteristic of the Middle Ages.[18]

All of these practices were controversial, and the controversy was itself often represented as a conflict between Christian and Jew. The earliest Western medieval example I know of comes from circa 1010 CE, when Henry, a cleric in the employ of the Emperor Henry II (r. 1002–1024), penned a defense of devotional images.[19] He did so by staging an epistolary debate with one Wecelin, who had supposedly been so disturbed by the use of images in Christian devotion that he had converted to Judaism. We may never know whether Wecelin really existed and, if he did, whether he was really a convert to Judaism. Both may be fictions invented by Henry to associate critics of images with Judaism. What we do know is that Henry rebutted Wecelin with a punning credo: "We believe," he replied, "in the *crucifixum*, which for you has become a stone of offense and a rock of scandal. . . ." *Crucifixum* here means both the Crucified and the crucifix, while "stone of offense and rock of scandal" alludes to Paul's "stumbling stone for the Jews" from 1 Cor. 1:23. Those Christians who object to the new use of crucifixes thus become Jews, according to Henry, because they look at these objects like the Jews, "with the eyes of the body" rather than "with the eyes of the heart" as a Christian should.[20]

We are seeing here the emergence of new figures of Judaism produced by changes in Christian aesthetics and devotional media. It is worth stressing here that the emergence of such mediatic figures of Judaism could transform the ways in which Christians perceived and treated living Jews. Transformations in the use of Christian images in the early eleventh century produced new representations of Jews as opponents of those images, representations that were in turn projected onto Jews in the flesh. For example, it is concurrent with the new visual culture of the crucifix that ancient Byzantine stories about crucifixes that bleed when mocked and struck by Jews enter the Latin liturgy as part of the office of the "Passion of the Image" (*Passio imaginis*).[21] And only within this new visual culture do we begin hearing accusations like one reported by Adémar of Chabannes (d. 1034), who claimed that an earthquake struck Rome on Good Friday in 1020 because some Jews had mocked a crucifix, and was stilled only by Pope Benedict VIII's execution of the perpetrators.[22] Again we see how the changing ontological claims of art can violently transform the nature of the real.

Perhaps one more example from yet another century can make plausible my claim that Christians had learned to stage all angles of their debates about devotional images as polemics with Judaism.[23] The twelfth-century "renaissance," as it is sometimes known among medievalists, produced among many other things expansive (and expensive) new programs of image and architecture that we sometimes associate with the birth of Gothic style. The impresarios of this decorative program defended it in familiar terms, invoking the decorations of the Tabernacle and the capabilities of devotional art—when properly viewed with the eyes of the soul rather than those of the flesh—to orient the soul toward God.[24] Conversely, critics of images, such as Saint Bernard of Clairvaux, took a by now equally familiar tack, aligning lovers of devotional art and decorators of churches with the Jews. The true Christian, wrote Bernard, regards "all things . . . as dung." (Bernard is here echoing two critics of images we have already encountered: Saint Paul, Philippians 3:8; Saint Jerome, Letter 52.10.) Those who fill sanctuaries with material beauty are not Christians but "Jewish money-lenders" driven by "avarice, which is the service of idols." Small wonder, Bernard complained elsewhere, that many confuse churches with synagogues.[25] For Bernard, like critics of images before him, art is in close proximity to "Judaism." And the defenders of devotional art, like many advocates before them, in turn criticize Bernard's critique as literalizing and Judaizing.[26]

Painting the Enemies of Painting

Thus far we've focused on texts, exploring the efforts of Christian thinkers to address tensions between their ideals of transcendence and the materiality of devotional objects, and showing how these efforts cast both defenders and opponents of images as Jewish enemies of transcendence. But if we shift our attention from texts to the objects themselves, we will see that they could speak in their own defense. There were any number of ways in which objects could stage the choice between eyes of flesh and eyes of spirit, and thereby present themselves as catalysts for the conversion of the beholder's soul toward the divine, rather than as temptations toward the material. These might even include a pasted verbal warning onto the image, as in the mosaic of the *Maiestas Domini* in Venice's San Marco, where the makers tiled an explanatory text declaiming: "For the image teaches what God is, but it is not itself God. You see it, but you worship in spirit what is recognized in it."[27] I will focus on a very different technique for the defense: the deployment of figures of Judaism within the work in order to project onto those figures the dangers of Judaizing inherent within Christian aesthetics.

My claim, at its boldest, is that one of the most important ways in which European art discovered the conditions of possibility for its own existence was through the pictorial exploration of its relationship to Judaism. There are countless medieval examples from every region of Europe, but we will consider only one.[28] In the late thirteenth century the Castilian king Alfonso X "the Wise" actively supervised (one might even say authored) a set of illuminated manuscripts of vernacular poetry and music praising the Virgin Mary and telling of her miracles. These manuscripts, known collectively as the "Songs of Holy Mary" (*Cantigas de Santa María*), make novel claims for the power of the painter, poet, and prince to motivate divine attention and mobilize miracle. In fact many of the miracles collected in the manuscripts are themselves meant as manifestations of the Virgin's love for her troubadours, her singers and painters, for King Alfonso as impresario of the entire project, and even (as we shall see in chapter 3) for the physical manuscripts of the *Cantigas* themselves.

Often enough these manifestations are achieved by first figuring the enemies of a particular claim to transcendence and then miraculously defeating them. We will return to these manuscripts in each of our following chapters, since what is true for art is also true for poetry and

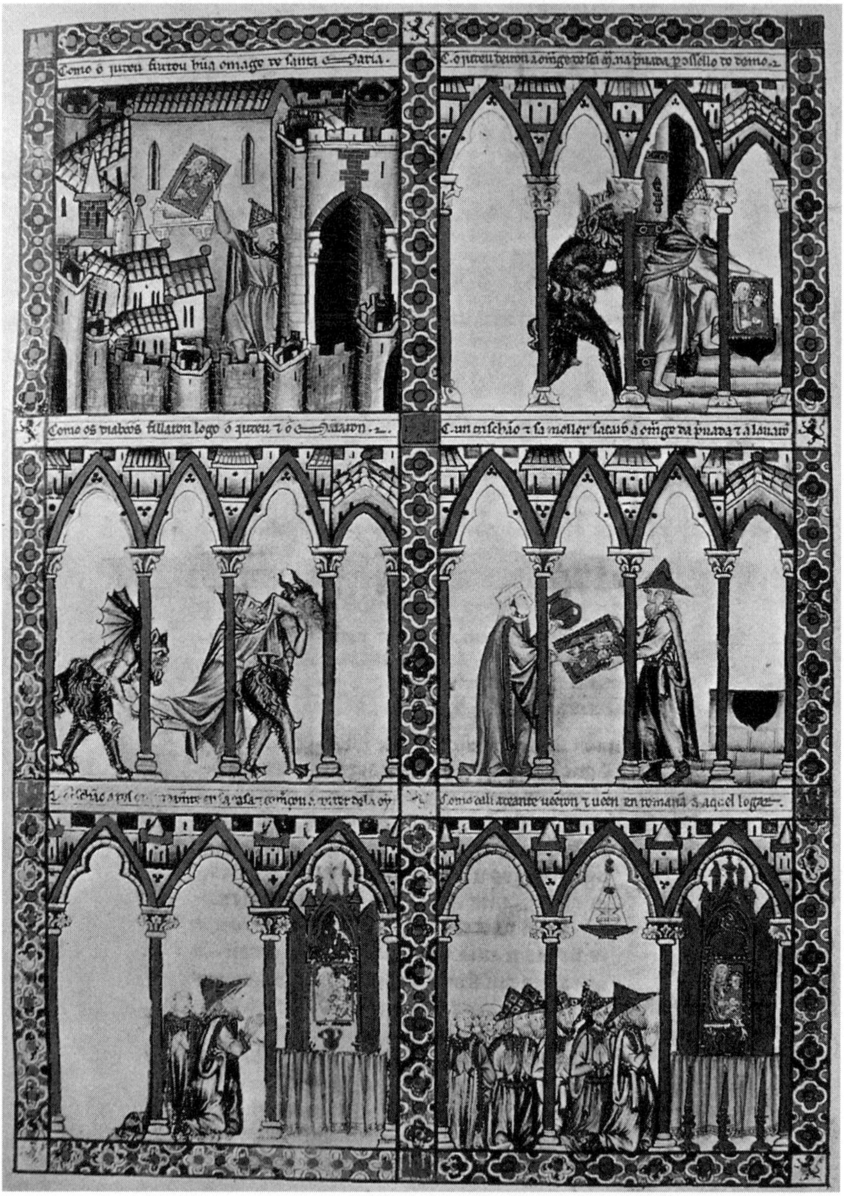

FIGURE I.1 (PLATE I)

Cantigas de Santa María, Cantiga 34, Escorial, MS. T.I.1, folio 39r.

PHOTO COURTESY OF EDILÁN-ARS LIBRIS.

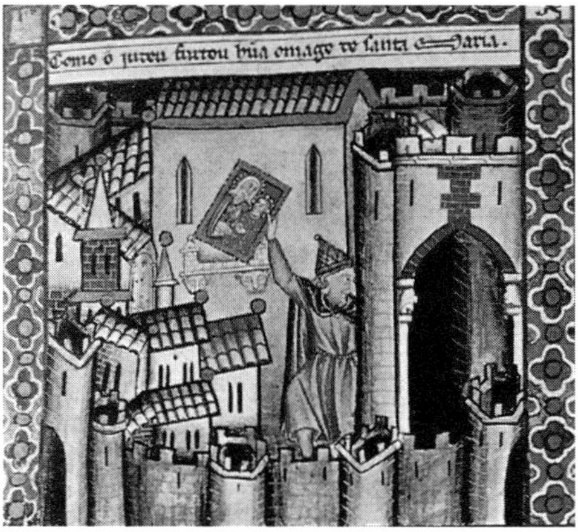

FIGURE 1.2
Detail of Cantiga 34, *Cantigas de Santa María*, Escorial, MS. T.I.1, folio 39r.
PHOTO COURTESY OF EDILÁN-ARS LIBRIS.

politics. But in this one we are concerned with visual objects of devotion, whose enemies in the *Cantigas* are played by Jews, Muslims, and Christian blasphemers of various types. In Cantiga 74 the devil himself is enlisted in defense of pictorial realism: angered by a painter who has accurately rendered his ugliness, he destroys the scaffolding upon which the artist is working on a high fresco of the Virgin. The falling painter prays to his patroness, who suspends him miraculously in midair by his brush, the instrument of his trade becoming also the instrument of his salvation.

In other songs the enemy of Christian painting is figured as a Jew. In Cantiga 34 (see figure 1.1), for example, a Jew of Constantinople steals an outstandingly beautiful (the text tells us) image of the Virgin that has been painted on a board and hung in the street. In the first scene of the illumination the illuminator makes the point starkly but artfully (see figure 1.2). A grotesque Jew in profile is juxtaposed to the painting he holds askew in his hands, already striding into a doorway whose darkness plays foil to the light color-field of wall from which the painting has been removed. The Jew here serves as an icon of the anti-iconic, the "pictoriality" of the entire scene emphasized by the accumulation of frames (bordering, city walls, and the frame of the icon itself) the illuminator has deployed. In the following scenes the Jew acts accordingly, throwing the painting down a latrine and defecating upon it. We have already encountered earlier versions of this story (in Gregory of Tours and in

Byzantium). In this one the Jew is neither stoned nor saved but executed by the devil himself. A Christian then discovers the image, which instead of stinking of feces smells sweeter than spices, balsam, and unguents, and emits henceforth a substance like oil. In the last panel we see the board itself enshrined as object of devotion. And all this, the poem tells us, the Virgin did "in order to teach" (*por dar entendimento*). The Jew here serves as an example, a "vessel of wrath" whose negative contrast allows the proper Christian attitude toward images to emerge in high relief.

These and other images of Jews acting upon images in the *Cantigas de Santa María*—such as Cantiga 12, in which Christians massacre the Jews of Toledo for attacking a wax image of Jesus—are often studied for what they can tell us about shifts in Christian relations to *Jews* in thirteenth-century Castile.[29] They tell us just as much about shifts in Christian relations to *images*. There were in fact many Jews (and Muslims) living in the Christian lands of the Iberian Peninsula, and their representations in the *Cantigas* owe a great deal to how Christians experienced or imagined this social reality. But when the Christian poets, illuminators, and editors of the *Cantigas* represented Jews (or demons or Muslims or "blasphemous" Christians) acting upon images, they were not only or necessarily describing the practices of living Jews (or demons or Muslims or Christians with views different from their own) but rather also articulating and defending their own innovative and controversial engagements with media. The Jewish figures that emerge from the defense of image making staged by the illuminators of the *Cantigas de Santa María* were neither reflections of reality nor stable stereotypes, but Christian projections of Judaism produced at the dynamic intersection of media, mental concepts, and social context.

Projecting Danger: The Fountain of Grace

It would require many pages to make this point about the *Cantigas* convincing, pages we do not have. If we want to establish the claim that this type of projection was central to art's exploration of its own potential, then we must move out of the Middle Ages and into what one art historian has famously called the "era of art." Let us jump, then, to the Low

Countries in the fifteenth and sixteenth centuries, a place and time of such rapid technical and stylistic change that it is precisely there that the same art historian placed the "discovery of painting." What role did figures of Judaism play in that discovery?[30]

A painting hanging today in the Prado Museum of Madrid seems almost explicitly to thematize our topic. *The Fountain of Grace, or the Dispute between Church and Synagogue* is attributed to Jan van Eyck or his workshop (see figure 1.3).[31] Van Eyck (c. 1385–1441) was not the inventor of oil painting, as Giorgio Vasari believed, but he was certainly a precocious master of oil and its glazes, and of the detailed realism the new techniques made possible. If we remember the Church Fathers' complaints about artists, such as Saint Isidore's Platonic quip that "when they strive to make things more real, they bring forth [more] falsehood," we might expect such realism to arouse some Judaizing anxieties: anxieties about literalism, mimetic deceit, and idolatry, among others. In *The Fountain of Grace* we can see a self-conscious rebuttal of the charge—sharpened by both aesthetic and sociological change—that it is itself, qua painting, a catalyst for conversion toward idolatry and Jewishness, rather than toward grace.[32]

The upper story of the painting is an enclosed paradise with God seated at its apex. To his right and left sit Mary and John the Evangelist, each absorbed in reading a book. A lamb lies at his feet, and a river flows from his throne through the garden: a pictorial representation of the verse from the Apocalypse "procedentem de sede Dei et Agni" (Rev. 22:1, "the river of life, rising from the throne of God and of the Lamb"). The river descends until it empties into a fountain outside the walls of paradise. Those walls, with turrets left and right, separate paradise from the painting's ground floor: the terrestrial antechamber or forecourt, so to speak, of the heavenly city.

The angel in the turret on the left reads from a book, while the angel in the right turret unfurls a scroll bearing an inscription from the Song of Songs: "Can. Fons [h]ortorum, puteus aquarum viventium" (Cant. 4:15: "Fountain of the garden, well of living water"). Only the river and the scroll—grace mediated through scripture—break the barrier between the garden and the exterior courtyard, in which two groups are

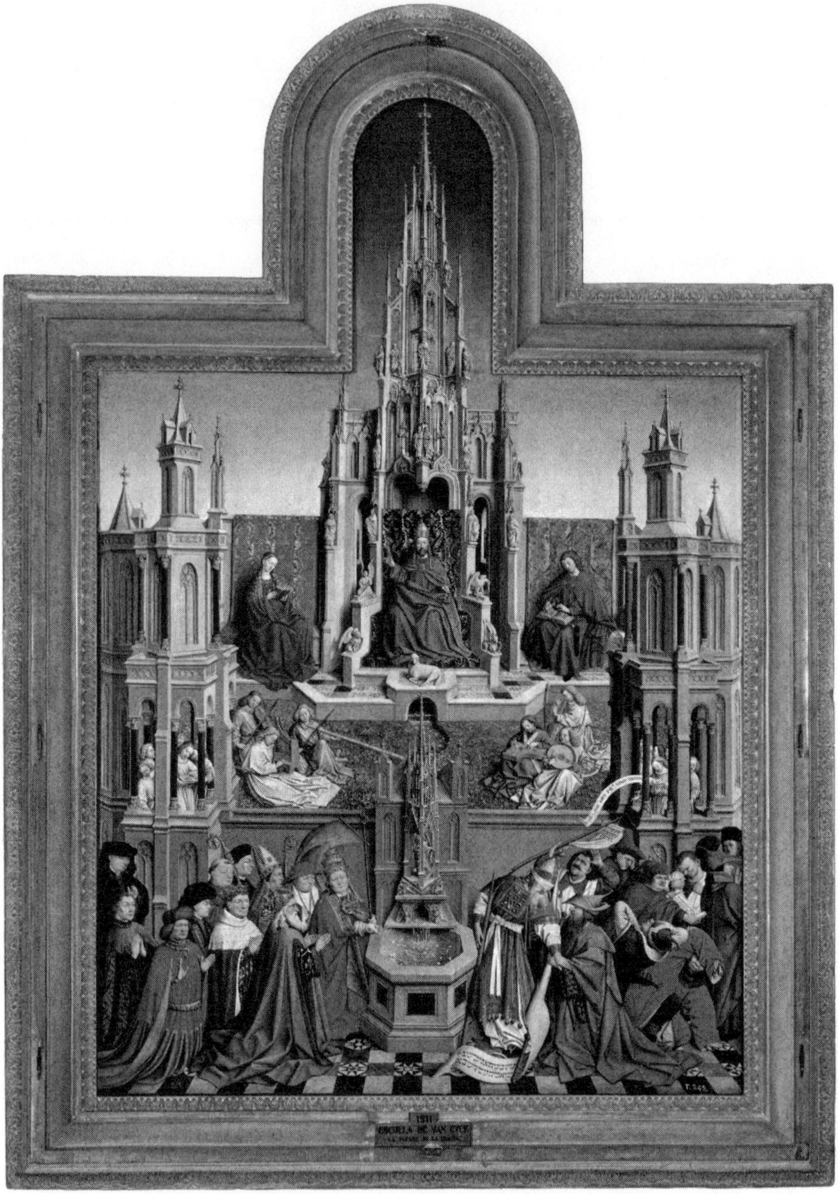

FIGURE I.3 (PLATE 2)

Jan van Eyck, *The Fountain of Grace, or the Dispute between Church and Synagogue*, workshop of Jan van Eyck, Prado Museum, Madrid.

PHOTO COURTESY OF ALBUM/ART RESOURCE, NY.

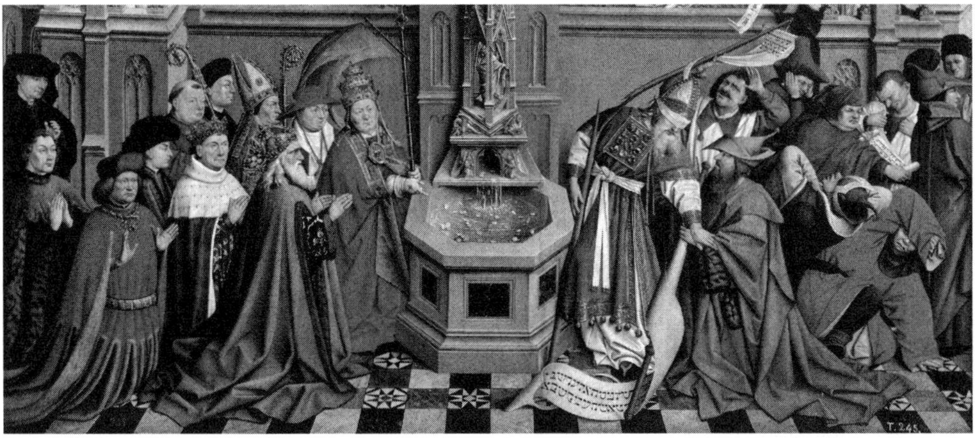

FIGURE 1.4
Detail of river and scroll, *The Fountain of Grace, or the Dispute between Church and Synagogue*, workshop of Jan van Eyck, Prado Museum, Madrid.
PHOTO COURTESY OF ALBUM/ART RESOURCE, NY.

clustered on either side of the fountain (see figure 1.4). On the left a pope stands by the fountain, surrounded by Christian clerics, cardinals, and kings; on the right a group of Jews, surrounding their high priest. The Christians gesture in rapt attention toward the fountain of grace, in which some eucharistic wafers are floating. The Jews, their high priest blindfolded, lean away from the fountain and avert their faces, vainly consulting various scrolls of Hebrew script, the largest of which lies unfurled like a fallen standard on the floor.

The painting's foregrounding of media and mediation—books and scrolls, music and the gestures of preaching, and of course, that most perfect of material media, the Eucharist—calls attention to our questions about art.[33] In fact in the artistic bravura of those watery wafers floating at the very center of attention in the painting, we should see a manifesto about the power of painting in mediating grace. But if the Eucharists in the fountain familiarly evoke the salvific potential of material mediation, the Jews and their scrolls, painted with realistic but nonsensical Hebrew script, are an equally familiar embodiment of the inability to see properly, of a carnal insistence on the fleshy aspects of the killing letter rather than its spiritual content.

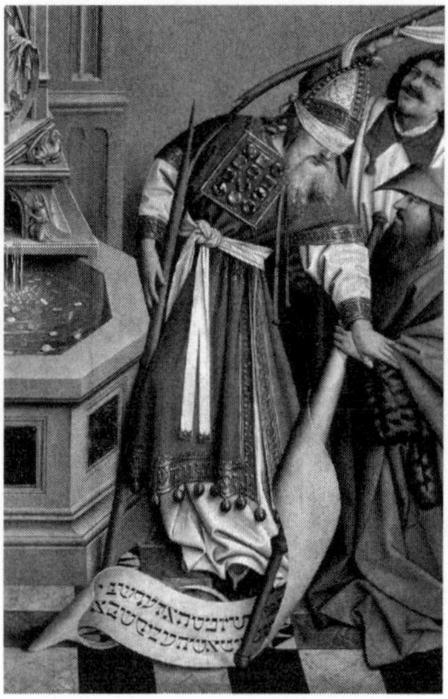

FIGURE 1.5
Detail of high priest, *The Fountain of Grace, or the Dispute between Church and Synagogue*, workshop of Jan van Eyck, Prado Museum, Madrid.
PHOTO COURTESY OF ALBUM/ ART RESOURCE, NY.

Note the double gesture here. The painting is not condemning the literal. On the contrary, it explicitly legitimates its own status through claims of literal scriptural translation—that is, the representation of biblical phrases as images, such as Revelation 22:1 and Song of Songs 4:15. Indeed the most bravura example of this strategy is also the most Jewish: I mean the depiction of the *archisynagogus* or high priest himself (see figure 1.5). In the treatment of the priest's bejeweled breastplate (*ephod*), for example, the painter reveals his meticulous attention to the letter of Exodus 39. He bases his rendering of this famously obscure ritual object on a drawing provided by the biblical commentator Nicholas of Lyra but makes slight changes in favor of an even more literal reading of the Vulgate text.[34]

Through the figure of the *archisynagogus*, the painting announces its Jewish hyperdependence on flesh and letter, on external beauty and the outer appearance of things. But the same figure, condemned and blind, also proclaims the *Christian* artwork's transcendence of that letter, and projects the dangerous Judaizing potential of literalism onto the critic of painting, that is, onto the beholder who sees only the material object and not the grace that it mediates. In other words, the painting responds to the critical viewer who would reproach the painter with an excess of literalism, realism, artifice, or materialism by placing that critic among the Jews within its frame, standing blind before the fountain of grace. The figure in a red cloak and blue headdress, furiously consulting a scroll, provides a good example. It may well be the Christian reformer Jan Hus, who a decade before was punished with death at the Council of Constance for his iconoclastic teachings on devotional art and the Eucharist.[35]

Borrowing a term from Melanie Klein, we might call this strategy "projective identification." In this case an intolerable potential in Christian painting is split off and projected outside the Christian, projected within the painting into a figure of Judaism, and into a figure of Judaism outside the painting as well, since the projection Judaizes any beholder who remains critical of the Jewishness of painting. These pictorial figures of Judaism are the product of Christian painting's reflection upon the conditions of possibility for its own existence. They constitute, so to speak, a metadiscourse with which the image can comment on the perils and possibilities it poses to maker and viewer. To put it in less positive terms: *The Fountain of Grace* provides an excellent example of how, during a period of rapid stylistic change that threatens both artist and beholder with dangers of Judaizing, anti-Jewish projection could provide new ways of channeling those dangers so as to expand the ontological space available for the creation of Christian art.[36]

Painting as Inquisition

The painting is exemplary in yet another sense: it reminds us of just how difficult it is to establish relationships between these aesthetic deployments of Judaism and "real" Jews or Judaism in a society. Van Eyck himself is unlikely to have encountered many Jews of flesh and blood in Bruges or any of the other cities of the Low Countries in which he lived. But he did visit Portugal in 1428–1429 and, during that visit, might well have made a pilgrimage to Santiago and met with the Castilian king John II.[37] There were indeed Jews living in the Iberian Peninsula, whom van Eyck might have met or heard of. But more important, these were years marked by heightened anxieties about Judaizing in Castile and the other kingdoms of Iberia, anxieties with important consequences for, among many other things, Christian art. Should we understand *The Fountain of Grace* as a response to these anxieties?

Beginning with a series of massacres in 1391 and continuing through the early fifteenth-century forced preaching campaigns of Saint Vincent Ferrer, tens of thousands of Jews living in the Iberian kingdoms had been converted to Christianity. By the time of van Eyck's visit to the peninsula, a generation more or less after these mass conversions, tensions between "Old" and "New" Christians (as they began to be called) were emerging violently in the form of riots, discriminatory legislation, and other exclusionary practices aimed at the converts and their descendants. The Inquisition, the Statutes of Purity of Blood, and even the expulsion of the remaining Jews from Spain in 1492: these were all products of the work done by discourses of Judaizing within this new context of high anxiety about how to establish differences between "Christianity" and "Judaism" in a world in which Jews of flesh and blood were disappearing, with Christians emerging in their place.

Conflict about the status of religious images was yet another product of these anxieties. Such worries were put to new kinds of work after the mass conversions, as when in 1407—in a variant of *Passio imaginis* accusations previously used against Jews—a New Christian from Lleida was accused of having desecrated a village church's crucifix while passing through on militia service. In this particular case the charge proved weak, and was dismissed when those named as witnesses by the accuser denied any knowledge of the deed. But the power of the more generalized anxiety is evident both in specific visual programs such as that of the Mallorcan chapel of San Salvador, decorated in the first half of the fifteenth century with a program of Jewish assaults upon Jesus and his images, and in heightened polemics about the virtues and vices of devotional art.[38]

First the vices: there had always been those who worried about the ways in which devotional art might misdirect the viewer's attention from the creator to the created, but such worries took on new meanings in Iberia after the mass conversions. Perhaps the best example comes from the second half of the fifteenth century, when an anonymous author invoked Saint Paul's linkage of idolatry and sodomy (in 1 Romans) in order to exhort his fellow Christians not to contaminate themselves with idols (that is, devotional art objects) nor fall into homosexual fornication. Unfortunately his warnings are transmitted only via their rebuttal, penned by Queen Isabel's confessor Fray Hernando de Talavera (who would become archbishop of Granada after that city's conquest from the Muslims). According to Talavera, the critic had warned that the more realistic and more decorated the picture, the greater the danger, a view the friar strongly condemned:

> Thinks this idiot that there is some great inconvenience in preferring to pray in front of images that are better-made and more ornamented? But there is not, and there's no fault in it, because we [i.e., the good Christians] don't do so thinking that the more beautiful image has any more virtue than the others, but because our intellect naturally enjoys more what better fits its object; and if the purpose of images is to represent what they represent, the better they do it, the more pleasure they provide, just as anyone who wants to see himself in a mirror will try to find the one that makes him look better.[39]

We do not know if this anonymous critic was a New Christian (as Talavera himself was). We cannot even be sure that he actually existed. Some converts may have brought an aversion to devotional images with them into their new faith. But there were also plenty of Old Christian critics of images to be found, such as Alfonso de Madrigal, alias "el Tostado" (1400–1445), widely admired as the most prolific scholar of his age. And even the most canonical defenders of images in Christian worship, such as Saint Thomas Aquinas, had nevertheless worried about the dangers they posed, and emphasized the viewer's responsibility to achieve the various orientations of the will necessary to view them appropriately, as signs rather than as things. It may well be that Talavera's "idiot" was, like so many other Jews in Christian debates about images, a figure of polemical thought stitched out of theological tissues rather than living flesh.[40] What we can be certain of, however, is that the social context of the mass conversions transformed the potential stakes and meanings of debates about how images could or could not mediate between the believer and the divine.

One important aspect of these transformations was precisely that it heightened the possibilities for confusion between figures of thought and figures of flesh. Critics of images, for example, could now be cast as real Jews (that is, as false converts from Judaism) rather than as the baptized Christians all participants in these debates in fact were. And the image itself could become a diagnostic tool capable of distinguishing between false Christian and true. In other words, within this Iberian context of mass conversion painting could become an even sharper weapon in the struggle to define difference between Christianity and "Judaism."

Beginning in the 1440s we can document the widening domestic use of devotional images in Iberian cities, presumably as a new way of asserting one's Christian bona fides. In polemical works with titles like "Fortress of Faith," theologians such as Alonso de Espina simultaneously sought to reinforce painting's status as a Christian medium and attack the Christianity of the converts and their descendants. In 1478 Hernando de Talavera and Pedro González de Mendoza, the archbishop of Seville, went so far as to issue an edict without analogue in medieval or early modern Europe *requiring* all Christians to keep images at home: "And because it is reasonable that the houses of faithful Christians should [honor] the memory of the passion of Our Lord Jesus Christ and of his blessed Mother, we desire and declare that every Christian should have at home the painted image of the cross where Christ was sacrificed and some painted images of the Virgin and other saints that would provoke the inhabitants, arousing them to devotion."[41]

With the 1478 establishment of the Inquisition's tribunals we begin to find New Christians confronted with charges like those against Donosa Ruiz in 1484—that she "never had nor has at home an oratory of the Virgin Mary or Jesus Christ or of the saints, such as Christians usually have to pray in front of." Others were accused of misusing the paintings they did have, turning their backs to them during prayer, or even whipping or torturing them. And not surprisingly, along with this transformation of devotional images into more or less official detectors of Judaism there came an increasing tendency to regulate the image. The archbishop of Seville's 1478 edict about images was followed, in 1480, by civic ordinances regulating Seville's workshops, controlling the quality and style of the pictures produced, and instituting a system of examinations, licenses, and inspectors for painters and paintings.[42]

What does the painting of *The Fountain of Grace* owe to this Iberian context of mass conversion? We first encounter the retable in the historical record in 1455, by which time it was already housed at the El Parral monastery in the Castilian city of Segovia. Some art historians have suggested that the retable had been specifically commissioned to commemorate the Segovian synagogue's violent transformation into a Christian church in 1412, a consecration itself occasioned by charges of Jewish image desecration. If so, then perhaps its composition reflects the painter's conscious engagement with renewed anxieties about devotional art spurred by the mass conversions.[43]

We are unlikely ever to know definitively whether or not van Eyck visited Castile, or whether *The Fountain of Grace* flowed from his own brushes or those of his followers. What we can say with certainty is that the retable vividly thematizes general Christian questions about the conversionary potential of painting—does it lead one toward transcendence and Christianness or toward literalism, materiality, and Jewishness? The context in which the painter or his studio confronted those questions and painted the painting remains in shadow. But the context in which the painting was viewed is clear (at least after 1455). Its beholders lived in a world in which mass conversions had transformed the place of painting in Christian devotion; the attributes associated with Jewishness and Christianness in Iberia; and even the meaning and the possibility of conversion itself. Within this particular context, the beholder of *The Fountain of Grace* stood in an inquisitorial tribunal of sorts, a tribunal in which the painting demanded a declaration of pictorial faith from its viewer and condemned as Judaism any resistance to its claims of transcendence.

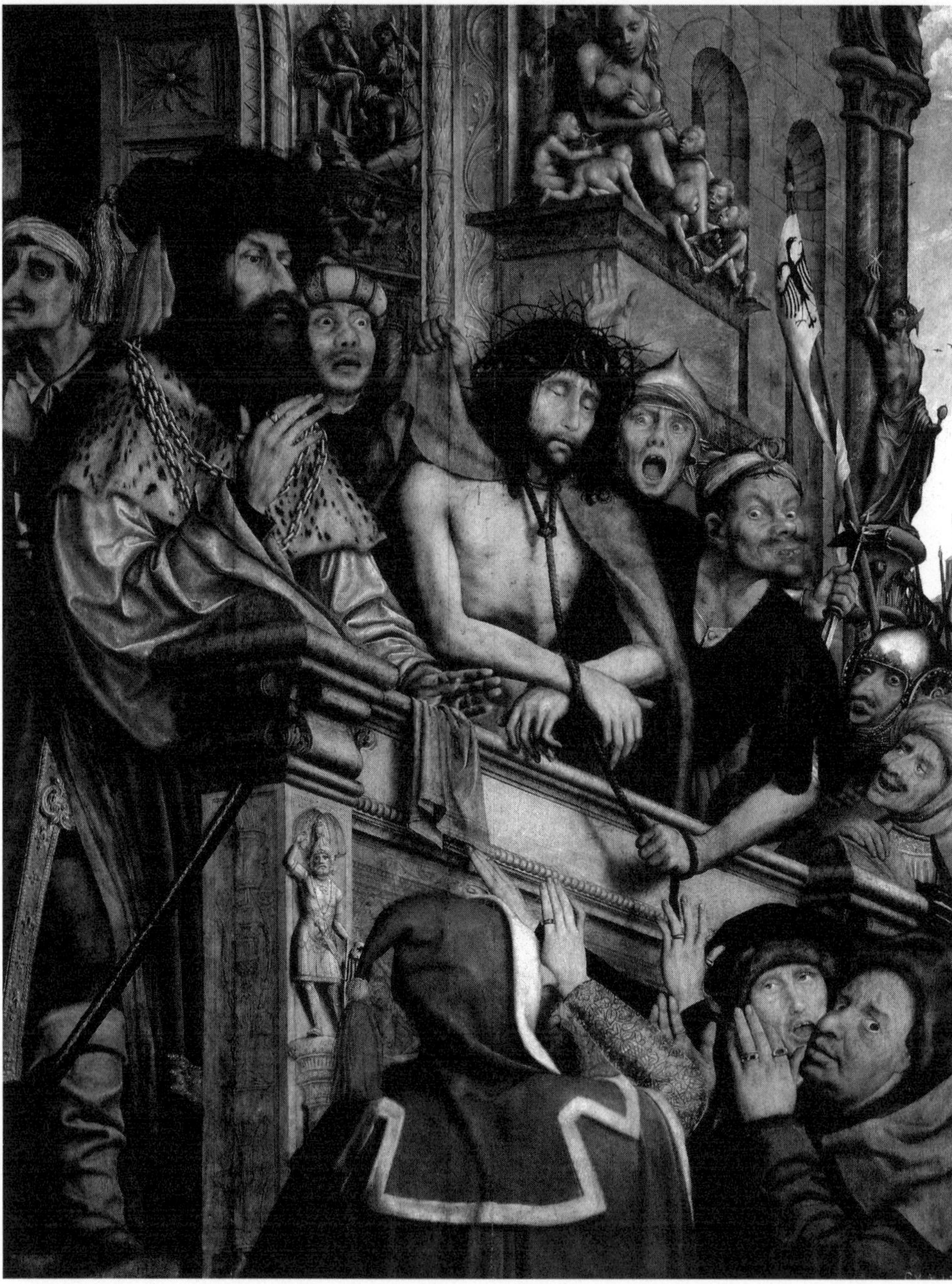

FIGURE 1.6 (PLATE 3)
Ecce Homo, Quentin Massys, Prado Museum, Madrid.
PHOTO COURTESY OF THE ART ARCHIVE AT ART RESOURCE, NY.

Painting as Ambivalence: Interrogating the Beholder

We lingered so long with *The Fountain of Grace* and its Iberian contexts because it provides such a beautiful (albeit complicated) example of how artistic style and social changes can be interrelated in ways that affect the possibilities of existence not only for painting but also for people. We would, however, be wrong to think that art's struggle with Judaism was particularly or peculiarly Spanish, that it required some sociological relation to Jews or converts from Judaism, that "projective identification" was its only strategy, or that it ended with van Eyck. For however much painters tried to project the dangers of representation onto Jews real or imagined, there was no way to escape the danger within a Christian system of thought that stigmatizes as Jewish the material forms of communication and community on which it simultaneously depends. Every representation remains potentially too material, too literal, and hence always vulnerable to the critical charge of Judaizing.

That vulnerability would become violently clear just over the historical horizon, when Protestant iconoclasts would deploy charges of Judaism against the very possibility of devotional art. But even before the earthquakes of Reformation and Counter-Reformation, artists were well aware of the need to wrestle with the Judaism of their practice, and their engagements continued to produce not only new pictorial styles but also a visual vocabulary with which to comment and reflect upon the opportunities and dangers of pictorial style itself.

Van Eyck's Flemish successors provide an exquisitely focused lens through which to make these engagements visible. Exquisite because of the precocity and the self-conscious intensity of their pursuit of style, and focused because in the Low Countries (as in much of Western Europe at the time) there were still few if any living Jews to complicate our inquiry. In these decades primarily figural Jews peopled the Flemish imagination—its sermons, proverbs, literature, and art—but these were populous indeed. Among those many let us look at just a handful appearing in one painting by Quentin Massys (1466–1530), his "Behold the Man" (*Ecce Homo*) from circa 1515 (see figure 1.6).[44]

Standing before this painting is a discomfiting experience, not least

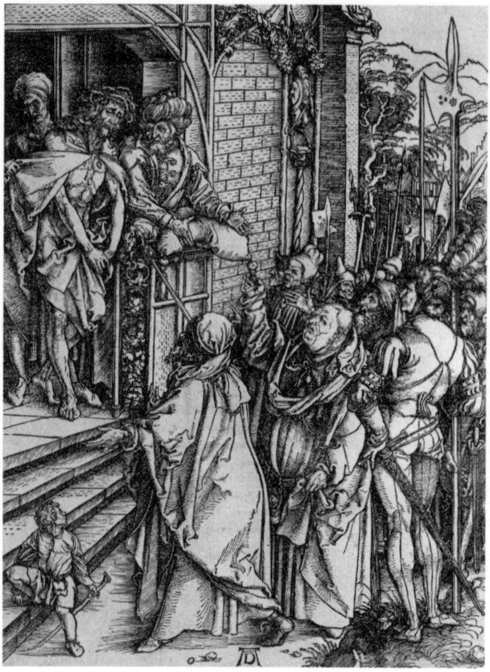

FIGURE 1.7
Ecce Homo, Albrecht Dürer,
The Passion of Christ, 1512.
PHOTO CREDIT RENÉ-GABRIEL OJÉDA, COURTESY OF RMN-GRAND PALAIS/ ART RESOURCE, NY.

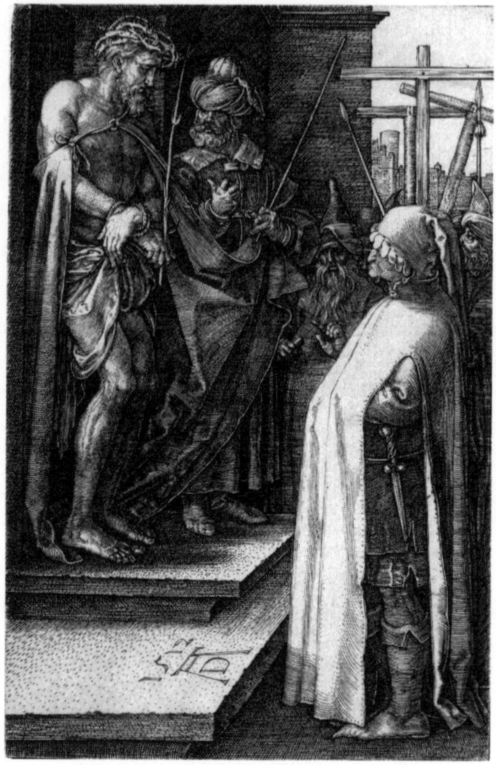

FIGURE 1.8
Ecce Homo, Albrecht Dürer,
The Great Passion, 1497–1500.
PHOTO COURTESY OF FOTO MARBURG/ ART RESOURCE, NY.

because we seem to be in the wrong place. Rather than encountering Jesus frontally as was conventional we are placed far to the side, pushed as if by the crowd away from our customary place of devotion. We find ourselves oblique to Jesus, and directly behind a figure who is clearly *not* looking where he should be looking—that is, at the savior—and whose stark profile, beard, hooked nose, and eyes blinded by his own hood all hypermark him as a figure of Judaism. In other words, the painting places us, as beholders, in uncomfortable proximity to Judaism.

This radical disposition of figures seems borrowed from Albrecht Dürer's Great Passion cycle of prints (see figures 1.7 and 1.8), but the painting's figures interact among themselves and the viewer in a way that Dürer's staging did not.[45] The Jew in front of us is addressing another, who looks out at us with interrogatory eyes, as if to make us complicit in the affair. "Hypocrite voyeur, mon semblable, mon frère!" If the Italian artist and "art critic" Leon Battista Alberti (1404–1472) could have seen this painting, he would have appreciated the pointing function of this figure's sidelong glance: "I like there to be someone in the 'historia' who tells the spectator what is going on, and either beckons them to look . . . or points to some danger or remarkable thing in the picture."[46] But note the danger being pointed to: Are you with us Jews, our figure seems to ask, who see here nothing but a man, or are you among those who see in this man both God and king? Even more dramatically than in van Eyck's painting, our status as viewers is immediately questioned. Are we Jewish beholders or Christian ones?

I suspect that the interrogatory power of this particular painting was recognized early, since the frame in which it hangs is itself inscribed along each side with a pointed question culled from the first chapter of the book of Lamentations: "O all of you who pass by on the road, attend, and see if there is any pain like my pain."[47] But the nature of the interrogation is very different from that carried out by *The Fountain of Grace*. Unlike van Eyck, Massys is not attempting to project "Judaism" out of the practice of Christian painting. On the contrary, he seems to proclaim that the potential Judaism of painting lies not only in the visual and cognitive errors of the viewer but within the medium itself.

This essential difference between Massys and van Eyck becomes more evident if we attend for a moment to another painting of van Eyck's, his *Annunciation* of 1428, hanging today in Washington's National Gallery of Art (see figure 1.9). Perhaps it was Erwin Panofsky who first noted that there seem to be two orders of representation in this painting, pointing toward Old Testament and New. Elaborating on this observation in a direction different from Panofsky's, I would suggest that in the first of these orders—represented in the personages of the Annunciation, angel, Virgin, and Holy Spirit—painting presents itself as a representation of incarnate life and truth. The second order, in this scheme, presents painting not as a representation of life but as a representation

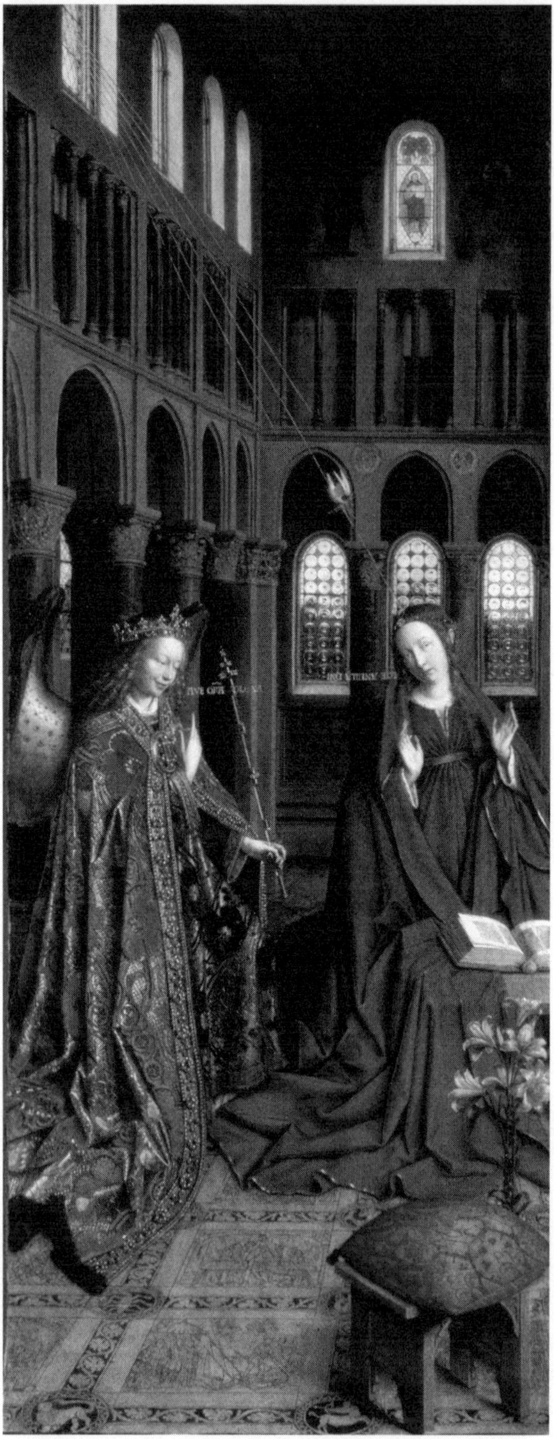

FIGURE I.9
(PLATE 4)
Annunciation,
Jan van Eyck,
National Gallery,
Washington, D.C.
PHOTO COURTESY OF HIP/
ART RESOURCE, NY.

of representation: a shadowed and (largely) colorless ekphrasis of architecture, statuary, stained glass, decorated tiles, and other media.

This second order is distinguished by painterly means, such as the use of grisaille and a nearly monochrome palate, but also by scriptural ones. Its themes, such as Samson and David killing gentiles on the tiles beneath the Virgin's feet, are drawn from the Hebrew prophets (see figure 1.10). The scriptural foundation for this play of shadow and life is the angel's announcement to Mary in the Gospel of Luke: "The power of the Most High will cover you with its shadow" (Lk 1:35: "et virtus Altissimi obumbrabit tibi"). Through this play van Eyck aligns his painterly powers with the salvific truths of the Incarnate God, while simultaneously casting other media into the shadowed teachings of the Old Testament. In other words van Eyck's painting proclaims its supersession not only of Judaism but also of sculpture, architecture, stained glass, and other rival arts.[48]

In Massys's painting the situation is dramatically reversed. This painting also has two orders manifest in its architectural organization, divided as it is into banded ranks. The top band is an explicit ekphrasis of architectural sculpture, its subjects stunningly realized but their moral value unclear. Is the man with winged headdress a pagan god? Are we to understand as an idiosyncratic representation of Roman charity the naked woman swarmed with children and impassively (or lewdly?) observed by a male figure? Is the sculptural scene of a soldier observing one man washing the feet of another meant in some way to foreshadow Jesus' example (John 13:1–17)? Sculpture here does not sit easily within any one stage of salvation history, nor is it confined to any easily legible domain of truth or untruth.

Below that uppermost sculptural register comes a band of living beings: Pilate, Jesus, and his tormentors. Here, just where one might expect some sort of mediatic separation as in van Eyck, we find quite the contrary. The figures are placed in deliberate planarity, all arrayed against an intervening wall, as if to mimic a sculptural program on a church façade. Jesus himself points to this mimicry with one extraordinary finger of his right hand, a hand that deliberately breaks the extreme planarity the wall enforces. That wall itself represents another

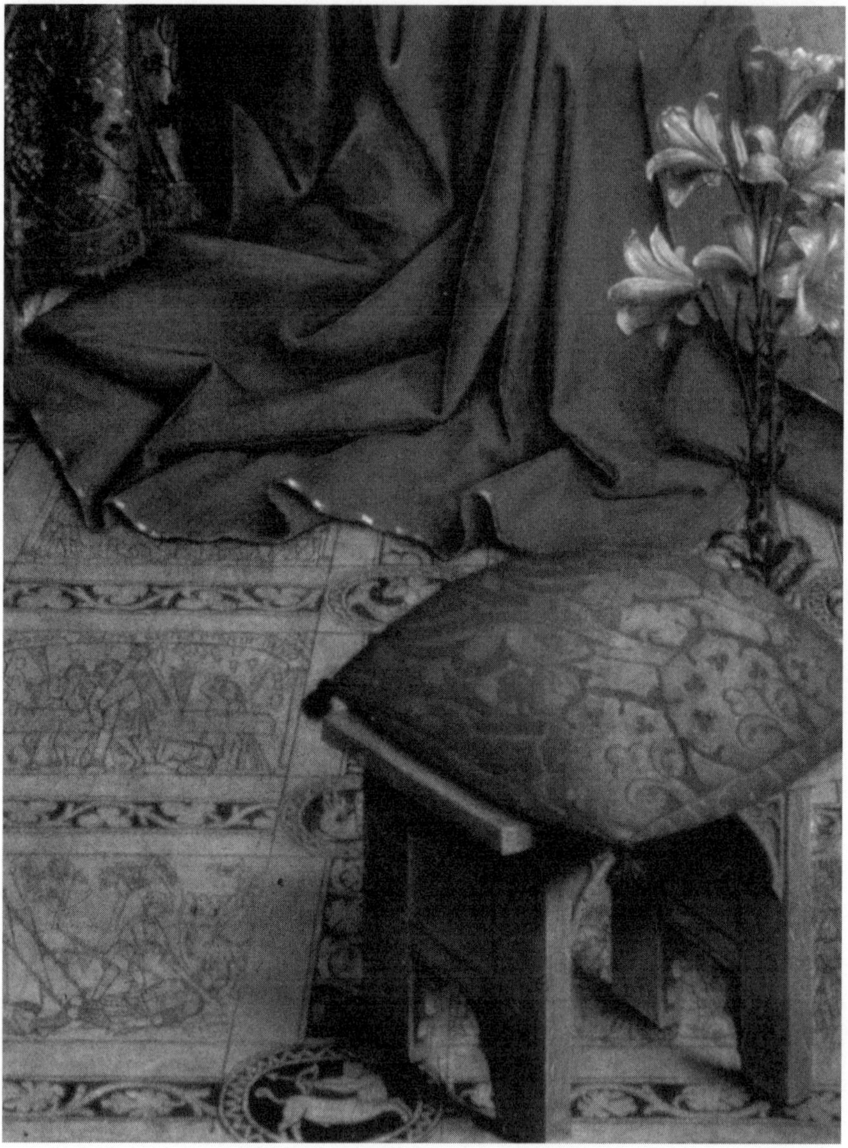

FIGURE 1.10
Detail of floor, *Annunciation*, Jan van Eyck, National Gallery, Washington, D.C.
PHOTO COURTESY OF HIP/ART RESOURCE, NY.

architectural band, also decorated with sculptures, of which, however, only one is visible. Finally, in the lowest level of the painting, there stand the three beholding figures among whom we almost find ourselves.

The sculptural and the living stand in some sort of ontological relation to each other within this painting, and Massys asks us to notice that relation by putting the two registers in conversation at the foreground of the picture. The gesture of the sculpted soldier closest to us mirrors that of the Jew who obstructs our view, even as the two are differentiated by the directionality of their attention and, above all, by color. Color here distinguishes the living from the built: nearly absent from the architectural registers, color appears at the fringes of what I'm calling the middle band, until it emerges at the center of our attention in the Jew, whose cape almost becomes a color-field, kept in the world of representation only by the shape of the figure it almost completely conceals. The concentration of color here at the bottom of the painting is made all the more striking by its absence at the center of it, in the representation of Jesus, whose body shares the shades of the sculptural figures rather than the living. Even the color of Jesus' cape barely escapes that of the architecture surrounding it.[49]

Van Eyck announced painting as the Christian fulfillment of representation by associating color and a first order of representation (painting as painting) with the covenant of the spirit, and using a second order of representation (painting as ekphrasis of architecture and other media) to point to and contain the veiled meanings of the old covenant of the flesh. In Massys's painting, however, the most vital register—and by vital here I mean not only the most colorful but also the closest to the beholder as a living being—is poured into the figure of the blind Jew. Painting as painting is placed in the pharisaic world of flesh, while the Incarnate God threatens to fade into architectural sculpture. To put it another way: Massys deploys the figure of the Jew not to project Judaism away from painting, but to remind us that not only the beholder but also the painter and the painting are caught in a Christian ontology in which our visual attention, mediated as it is through matter and flesh, can never quite escape the danger of being misplaced and therefore Jewish.

In this case the dangerous ambivalence is posed as the confused interrelation of two ontological registers: the religious one of Christian and Jew and the mediatic one of sculpture and painting. Massys poses this ambivalence repeatedly, but he does not propose to protect painting by resolving it, as van Eyck did. On the contrary, he asserts the impossibility of resolution in a striking way, by adapting one of the favored objects of Flemish artists: the mirror.[50]

Much could be and has been said about the place of mirrors in Netherlandish (and not only Netherlandish) art. For the painter David Aubert, working in the second half of the fifteenth century, that place was central: hence a mirror hangs in the middle of the illumination of his own studio that opens the manuscript of the "History of Charles Martel" that he presented to the Duke of Burgundy, Charles the Bold.[51] That mirror seems itself to be a citation of a more famous one hanging at the center of van Eyck's Arnolfini wedding portrait of 1434, today at the National Gallery, London. Mirrors surely had many functions, among them optical ones. But already in Aubert's citation we can see that they offered painters a point of reflection upon their own place in an evolving pictorial tradition. And equally important for the questions that concern us here, they provided painters an opportunity to represent—often with bravura displays of technical skill—painting's claim to be a medium capable of reflecting upon the world, and of calling upon the beholder to participate in such reflection.

What is striking in this particular painting of Massys is that this representation of reflection emerges in a very odd place: among the accouterments of Christ's tormentors. Massys chooses to celebrate the reflective powers of painting in the helmet of a soldier whose face is deformed with hate. Equally striking is the mediatic confusion of the reflecting object itself (see figure 1.11). For at the same time that the helmet proclaims the power of painting, it itself becomes sculptural, its golden rivets emerging from the picture plane (and here we come to the real limitation of reproductions) in such a way that the viewer (or at least this viewer) cannot determine without touching whether they are painted (as in fact they are) or, as was also a common practice, a gilded sculptural appliqué.

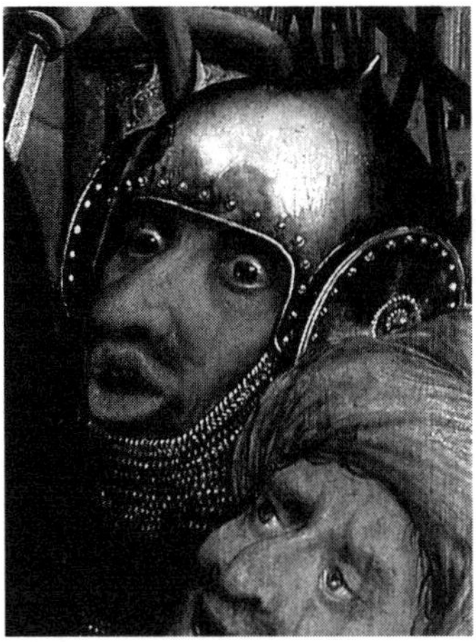

FIGURE I.II
Detail of helmet, *Ecce Homo*,
Quentin Massys, Prado Museum, Madrid.
PHOTO COURTESY OF THE ART ARCHIVE
AT ART RESOURCE, NY.

Massys's *Ecce Homo* deploys figures of Judaism in order to explore the powers of art. But rather than revel in the fantasy of art's perfection, it performs its own ambivalence. We might want to understand this strategy in art's struggle with Judaism less in terms of the "splitting" and "projective identification" we found in *The Fountain of Grace* and more—remaining with psychoanalytic terms for the sake of the comparison—with what Melanie Klein termed the "depressive position," in which polar qualities and potentials can be tolerated as part of the same object. In using these terms I am not pretending to address the subjectivity of the painter through the painting, nor implying that one strategy or another was "better for the Jews." I am merely looking for a metaphor to help clarify a difference legible in these paintings between two ways of representing Judaism *within* painting in order to address a basic anxiety about the Jewishness *of* painting.

Again, this potential Jewishness need not have anything to do with real Judaism, or with real conversion. It was a product of a Christian theology and ontology capable of representing every moment of worldly choice as Judaizing—that is, as a metaphorical conversion to Judaism. Within this ontology the beauty of painting, like any other of this world's sensual delights, presents the beholder with a moment of aesthetic choice between Jewish and Christian attention to the world. The basic task of Christian painting (and poetry and politics) is to mediate that choice.[52]

Materialism and Conversion: "The Moneychanger and His Wife"

In the previous examples this mediation was achieved by depicting explicitly Jewish figures within explicitly religious contexts, but neither was required for Christian painting to declare its relationship to transcendence. Precisely because discourses of Judaizing propelled so many of the moralizing discourses with which Christians made sense of their relationship to the material world, their breadth could animate genres of painting we might today call secular. Massys painted his first "genre" portrait of *The Moneychanger and His Wife* (see figure 1.12) at roughly the same time (1514) as his *Ecce Homo*, but in it he turned to a worldly scene and obviously "gentile" figures in order to stage the dangers of Judaizing that haunt the beholder's relation to material beauty. Here Alberti's fondness for pointing is fulfilled not by persons but by things: the scale and the mirror. Both directly address the beholder, the scale by seeming to emerge from the picture frame, the mirror by reflecting the beholder's space.

One thing these objects point to is painting itself, for as we have already seen with the mirror, they are themselves citations from works by Massys's predecessors, among them Petrus Christus's *Goldsmith/St. Eligius* of 1449 (today at the Metropolitan Museum of Art). Both objects also activate and invade the space before the painting: the space of the beholder. And they call attention to a moment of judgment and absorption: we might even want to see a proxy for the beholder in the absorbed figure reflected in the mirror. These objects draw that beholder into the drama of conversion taking place within the painting, a drama presented as a choice between two forms of attention, two directions of the gaze. In this case both forms of attention are themselves represented as paintings within the painting.[53]

The first of these paintings within the painting is the wife's illuminated book of devotions. Here the wife's choice of attention is dramatized by the shifting of her gaze away from that book and toward the gold on the green fabric of the desktop. That fabric doubles as a representation of the canvas picture plane, and its greenness doubles the

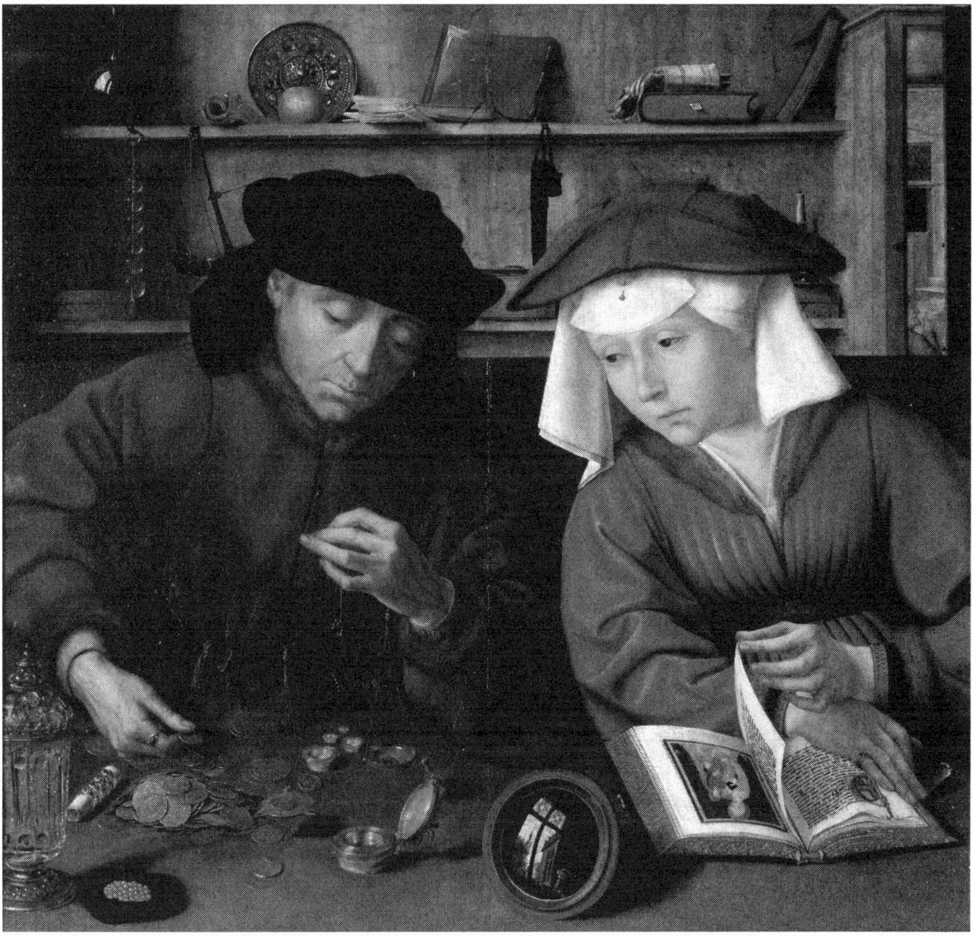

FIGURE 1.12 (PLATE 5)
The Moneychanger and His Wife,
Quentin Massys, Louvre Museum, Paris.
PHOTO COURTESY OF SCALA/ART RESOURCE, NY.

background of the sacred image abandoned by the lady's attention. The common color highlights the pairing of the competing media, the one oriented toward the spiritual, the other toward the material. The wife's pictorial conversion has been toward the material: she has made the Jewish choice. The question the scales seem to pose to the beholder is: what form of conversion does this art object catalyze for you?[54]

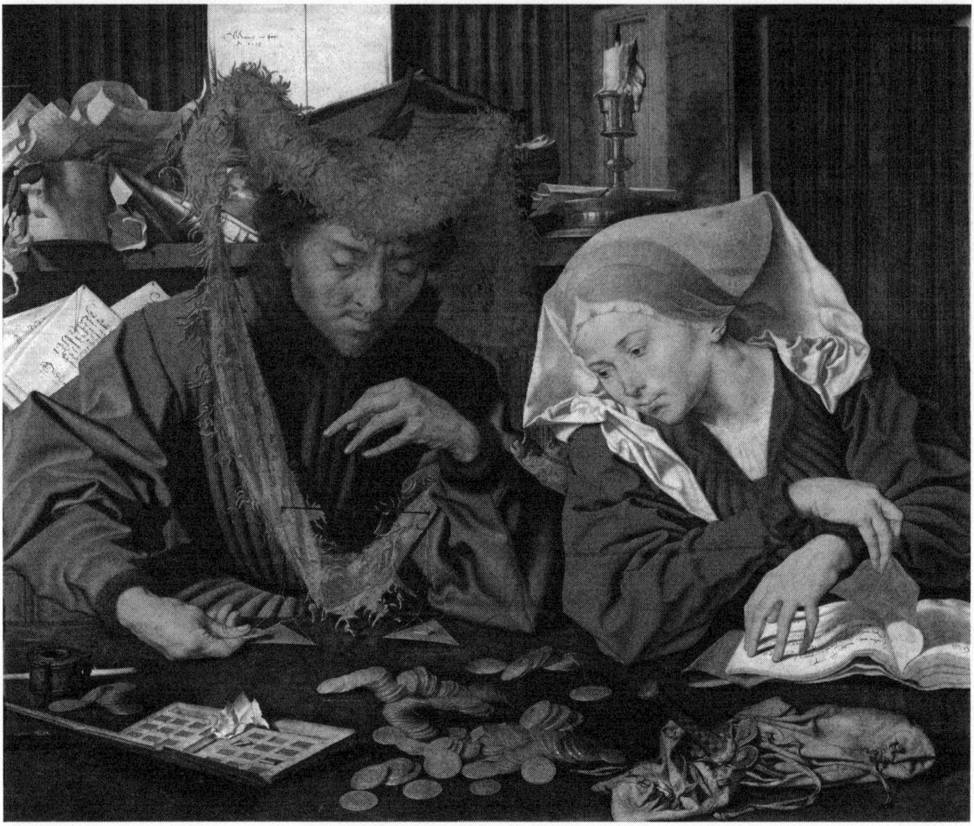

FIGURE 1.13 (PLATE 6)
The Moneylender and His Wife,
Marinus van Reymerswaele, Prado Museum, Madrid.
PHOTO COURTESY OF MUSEO NACIONAL DEL PRADO/ART RESOURCE, NY.

In this painting the choice posed to Christian beholders in their every engagement with material media is articulated as a choice between gold and a devotional image, but other forms of mediation can be just as successfully interrogated, as in a painting from the same genre but a short generation later: Marinus van Reymerswaele's (ca. 1490–ca. 1567) *The Moneylender and His Wife*, painted around 1535 (see figure 1.13).[55] In this painting the questions posed to the beholder are significantly shifted by the fact that the wife's attention is focused not on a book of prayer but of accounts, and the displays of painterly bravura are concentrated upon paper and IOUs, as well as on the extraordinary headgear of the protagonists. (The headgear reminds me of Francis Bacon's report that it was customary for moneylenders to wear Jews' hats, "orange-tawny bonnets, because they do Judaize."[56])

Here it is writing and paper, the seductive media of contract and commerce, that are the exuberant subjects of painterly ekphrasis. I am not prepared to explore the implications of this attention to the media of writing, but will simply repeat what we already saw in Massys's painting. In the cultures that produced these paintings, Judaizing represents a mistaken form of Christian attention to the signifying objects of this world. Hence painters did not need to paint Jews or sacred scenes in order to engage questions about the powers and perils of painting as a catalyst to conversion toward or away from Jewish types of attention to the material media of communication. They could simply paint the Christian making choices in the world.

And yet it is also true that the theme of conversion from Judaism sometimes permitted painters to engage these questions with particular power. In another painting of van Reymerswaele's, his *Calling of St. Matthew* from circa 1530 (see figure 1.14), the act of conversion is exuberantly dramatized by the Jew's hat that the protagonist removes from his own head as he is transformed from the Jew Levi into the Christian Matthew. The trompe l'oeil realism of the account books and paper receipts heightens the sharpness of that conversion, which is not only from Judaism to Christianity but also from an extreme of mediatic evil—receipts and IOUs—to another of mediatic good, namely the gospel. (In support of my rather Manichaean characterization I would invoke the sixteenth-century Dutch aphorism: "A usurer, a miller, a money-changer, and a tax-collector are the Devil's four evangelists."[57]) And hanging in the middle of the painting, at the apex of our visual arc, we have a hypermarked interrogation of the relationship between painting and prophecy: a framed piece of paper containing biblical citations—Matthew 9:9; Mark 2:13; Luke 5:1 (gesturing toward 5:27–32). Like van Eyck's scrolls in *The Fountain of Grace*, these are the scriptural proof-texts that provide the ontological foundations for the painting's claim that its pictorial literalism and realism point the beholder not toward error but toward truth.

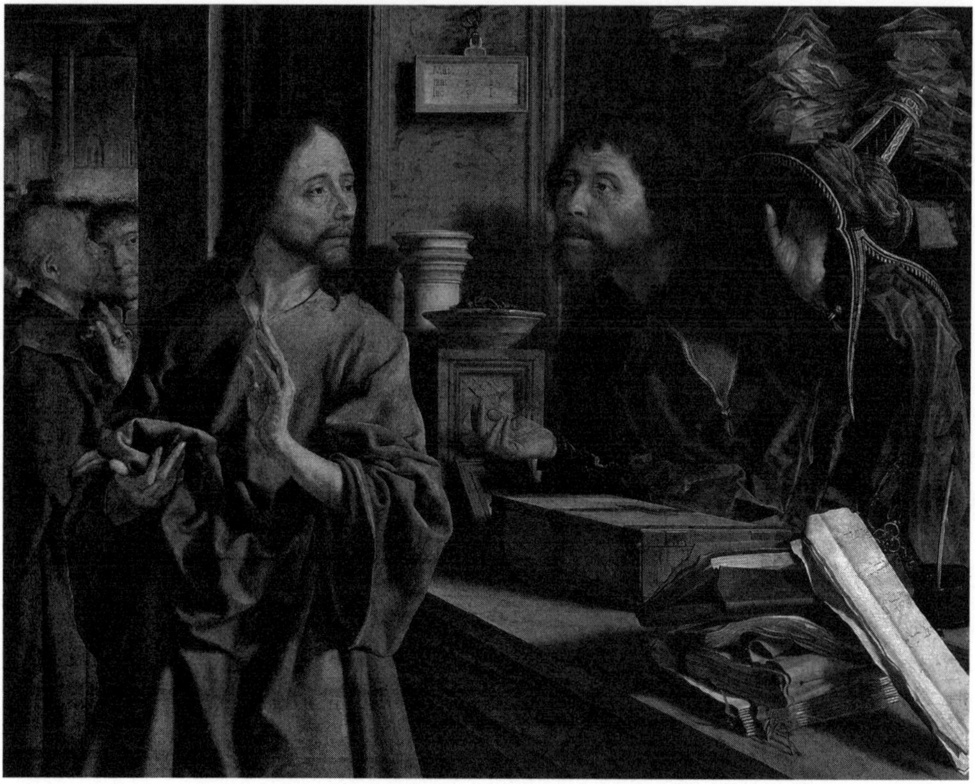

FIGURE 1.14 (PLATE 7)
The Calling of St. Matthew, Marinus van Reymerswaele,
Thyssen-Bornemisza Museum, Madrid.
PHOTO COURTESY OF HIP/ART RESOURCE, NY.

Yet what is most interesting about the painting is that, as with Massys's *Ecce Homo*, the claim is undercut the moment it is made. This painting, like Massys's, is divided by an angled barrier, in this case the moneychanger's counter, which bisects the painting into compositional registers. It is clear that the converted Matthew should emerge from the materialistic space of moneychanging and Judaism at the left side (the viewer's right side) of the painting into the space alongside Jesus at the painting's right (the viewer's left). It is less clear just how he will emerge, since the counter extends implacably beyond the pictorial frame, with no relieving opening. (Compare the less ambivalent triptych painted by

Orcagna for Florence's Exchange Guild in 1367–1368. In that painting Matthew emerges from behind the bisecting counter through an opening placed at the center of the pictorial field.[58]) But even more curious than the counter's extension is the stylistic division it effects. The "Christian" side of the counter is executed in an archaic style, as if van Reymerswaele were here imitating his famous Flemish predecessor Hans Memling (d. 1494). His own distinctive style—the triumphant illusionism of the Jew's hat and cape, the loving realism of the account books and stacks of paper, the naturalism of the wood—is poured into the Jewish side of the divide.[59]

Paintings such as these heighten the dangers of Judaism within themselves, rather than projecting those dangers outward with the goal of fantasizing their own perfection. Their goal in doing so, however, is not to surrender in the struggle against Judaism but rather to shift the field of battle. By assuming an ambivalent attitude to the seductions of its own style, the art object announces itself as an ordeal of discernment and puts the viewer on the qui vive, as if to say, like the frame on Massys's *Ecce Homo*: attend, for yours is the choice, yours the conversion, yours the spiritual consequences. From this point of view one can imagine a pressure upon the painter to push the point further. The deeper the ambivalence, the more difficult the discrimination between the material and the spiritual, the better the painting as catalyst for the beholder's critical reflection upon and choice of absorption—that is, for the beholder's choice between Christianity and Judaism.

Counter-Reformation Coda: Caravaggio

A later and more famous *Calling of St. Matthew* provides an excellent example of this stylistic strategy pushed toward its extremes: I mean, of course, Caravaggio's painting of 1599–1600. Without pretending to encompass much of what has been thought or written about Caravaggio's case in general or this painting in particular, let me just state that Caravaggio's mimetic naturalism immediately produced reactions both admiring and critical. Among the most famous of these reactions was that of Giovanni Pietro Bellori, who characterized the painter as a mindless copyist of vile life. Bellori did not call Caravaggio Jewish, but he described him in terms that should be familiar to us, as someone whose eye was peerless when it came to the plain literalism and materialism of surfaces, but who could not penetrate to "the ideal in art," nor reach the figural or inner truths. According to Bellori, Caravaggio's problem was one of character. Artists with good "prudence" (Bellori gave the example of Annibale Carraci) oriented their *disegno* toward idealism. Those with poor prudence, whose souls were governed by appetites, oriented their art toward naturalism. What could one expect, Bellori asked, from an artist like Caravaggio, who had been known to use his canvases as table linens for his supper before painting on them?

By 1672, when Bellori's criticism was published, such charges against Caravaggio were already old. Carl van Mander, Giulio Mancini, Giovanni Baglione, Francesco Scannelli: all had said similar things.[60] Caravaggio's paintings were said to be divinely real, but deeply deceptive. Ottavio Tronsarelli put the point sharply in a song he wrote circa 1634 after seeing a version of Caravaggio's *Gypsy Fortune Teller*:[61]

> The Egyptian girl in the canvas
> Makes such vivid utterances that,
> If you were to listen closely
> While she unveils fortunes,
> You would hear her voice there,
> And you would consider foolish
> Him alone, whom you see trusting her
> Incautiously.
> Here is the lady who keeps lying to all,
> Even if just painted on linen.
> She hardly lacks in deceptions,
> If she appears truthful to him, and
> Alive to you.

The poem is most revealing in its interrelation of the painting, the depicted, and the beholder. It aligns the art object itself with what is depicted within it: the beautifully deceitful fortune-teller. And it places the beholder within the painting as well, as the young gentleman, con-

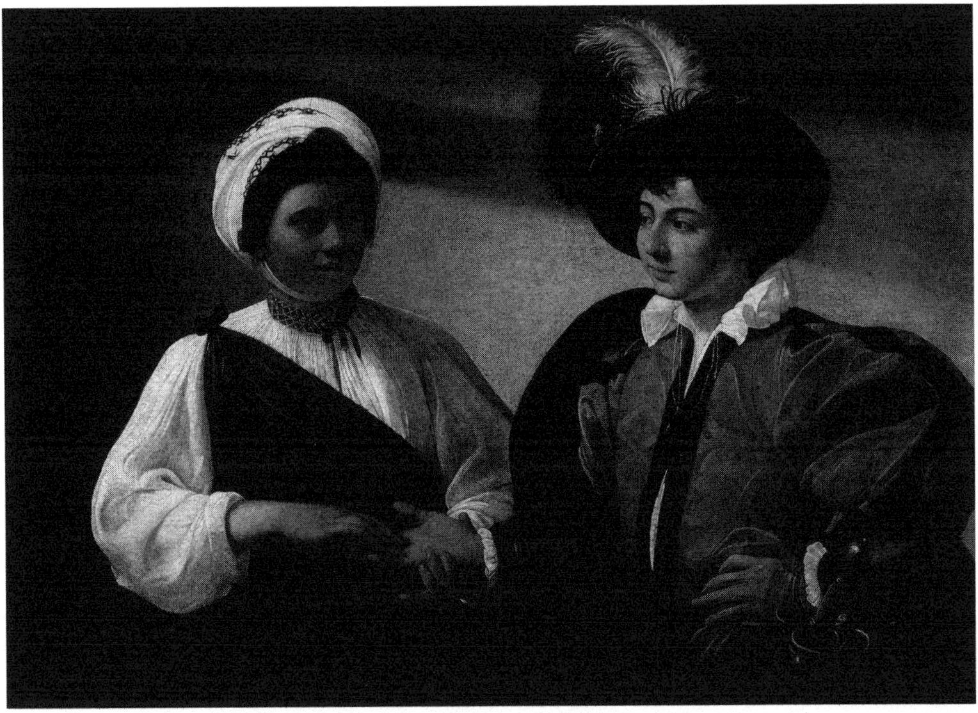

FIGURE 1.15 (PLATE 8)
The Gypsy Fortune Teller, Michelangelo Merisi (Caravaggio), Louvre Museum, Paris.
PHOTO CREDIT GIANNA DAGLI ORTI/THE ART ARCHIVE AT ART RESOURCE, NY.

fronted with choices about a claim to truth. Tronsarelli's song presents Caravaggio's painting as catalyzing entanglements among painter, object, and viewer: entanglements in which the truth status of all three are potentially at risk.

If the ontological stakes are high in *The Gypsy Fortune Teller*, they are much higher in *The Calling of St. Matthew*, where what is at risk is the relation between the deceits of painting and the truth of God. Caravaggio did not need the writings of contemporary Counter-Reformation theologians of art like Gabriele Paleotti to tell him that the attempt to portray the visibility of God in material form was the limit case for the truth claims of painting.[62] He had himself experienced the controversies that could attend such claims with his own previous commission on

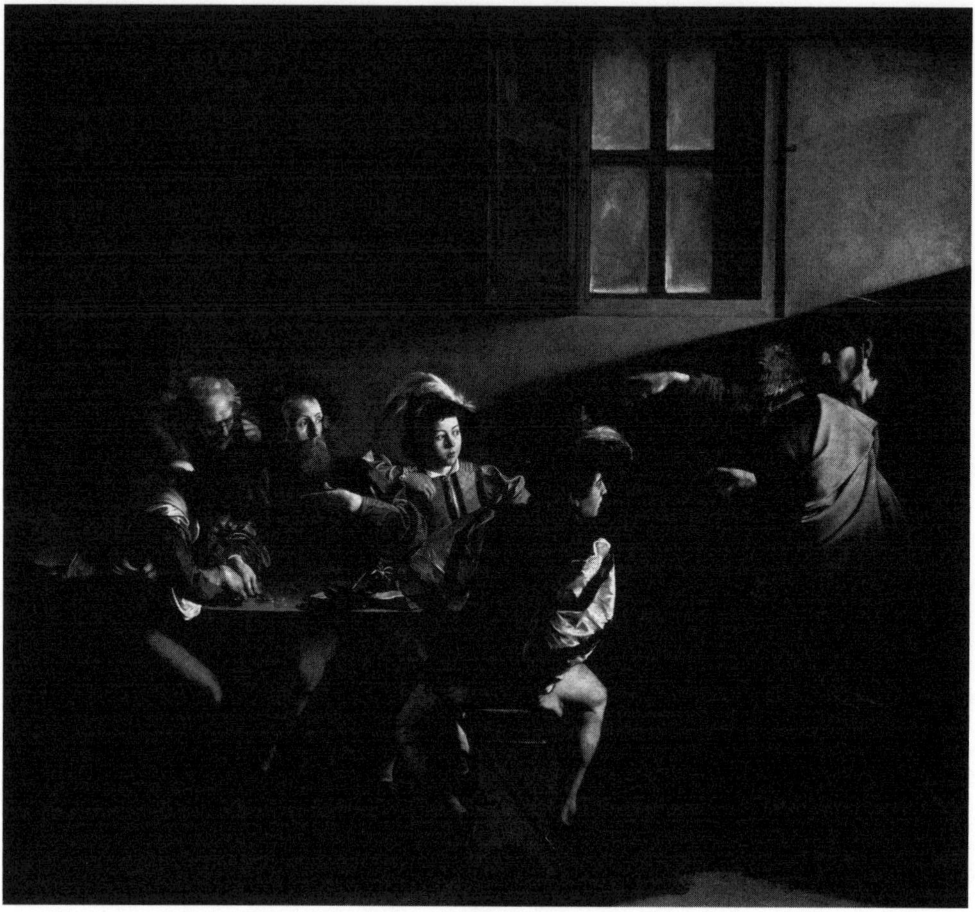

FIGURE 1.16 (PLATE 9)
The Calling of St. Matthew, Michelangelo Merisi (Caravaggio), San Luigi dei Francesi, Rome.
PHOTO COURTESY OF SCALA/ART RESOURCE, NY.

the subject of Matthew's conversion, a painting that had not pleased its patrons. In any event he indicates the problem in a way that would again have delighted Alberti: by pointing to it.

The pointer here is Jesus' arm, itself a pictorial citation: in this case to Michelangelo's Sistine Chapel. Perhaps we are meant to wonder whether the arm is that of God or of Adam. That ambivalence is interesting, but the arm also poses a different question: just which of the

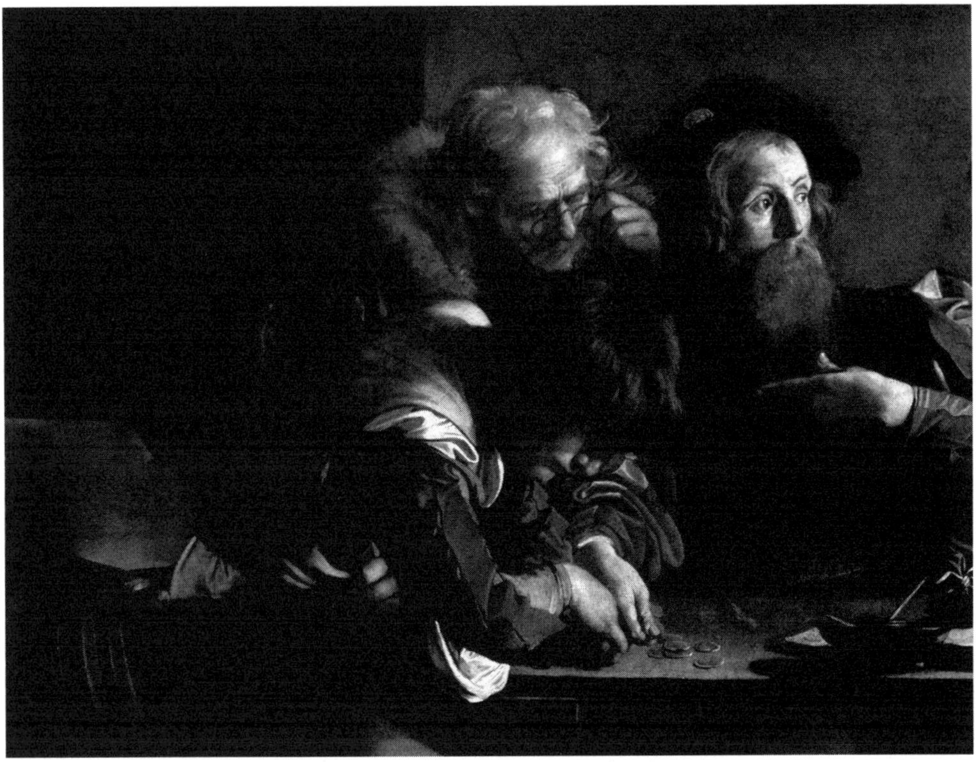

FIGURE 1.17
Detail of bearded man and absorbed youth, *The Calling of St. Matthew*, Michelangelo Merisi (Caravaggio), San Luigi dei Francesi, Rome.
PHOTO COURTESY OF SCALA/ART RESOURCE, NY.

figures in the picture is being called from Judaism by Jesus' gesture? Is Matthew the bearded man making a questioning gesture, itself equivocal? Or is he the young man entirely absorbed—like Massys's money-changer—with the coins and writing utensils on the table before him? (See figure 1.17.)

A number of art historians have noted the ambiguity and offered various explanations for it.[63] Without endorsing any one of these, what I would like to suggest is that this ambiguity itself has radical implications for the interrelation of painter, painting, and beholder. Conversion becomes difficult to read in this multiplication of picture planes, directions of absorption, and indeterminate pointing. We as beholders are left unable to say with certainty which of the figures is the apostle and which the unconverted Jew, an ambiguity that extends to us as beholders before the painting, called to choose between critically different forms of our own absorption in it—critical because a choice of life or death, salvation or damnation, Christianity or Judaism—that it turns out we can scarcely distinguish.

Caravaggio deals with the ontological knots that bind the senses in an age of transcendence by painfully tightening the bonds. Like Massys he seems to realize that no amount of anti-Jewish projection can make painting—or the sensual world—entirely safe for the Christian, and delights instead in pointing to the dangers. Others, such as van Eyck, prefer to cleave the knots, mapping some sort of spiritual legibility onto the distinction between Jew and Christian. The narrative order of my examples should not lead us to conclude that one strategy replaced the other. On the contrary, the potential for both was present in every age, and the choice between them was an important factor in painters' development of their own particular styles. On occasion we can see this process at work, in one artist's rejection of the choices of another. Hendrick ter Brugghen, for example, was a Dutch devotee of Caravaggio and paid homage to the master's Matthew in his own painting of 1621. But he could not bear the indeterminacy of the original. His painting (which may also have been influenced by van Reymerswaele: note the paper documents decorating wall and table) is easily legible (see figure 1.18). All salvific fingers point in the same direction, and it is only an ugly and easily recognizable figure of Judaism, squinting blindly through bespectacled and hooded eyes, whose attention is entirely oriented toward the coins scattered upon the damning picture-plane of the moneychanger's table.[64]

Again, I do not mean to present either strategy as victorious, or as peculiar to any one time, place, or pictorial style. It was not only "naturalism" and "realism" that were at risk of Judaism but also any thought dependent on the senses (and is there any thought that is not at some level so dependent?), any attempt by one thinking subject to represent such thought to another, which is also to say any form of communication. I will attempt to strengthen that claim in the chapters to come, on

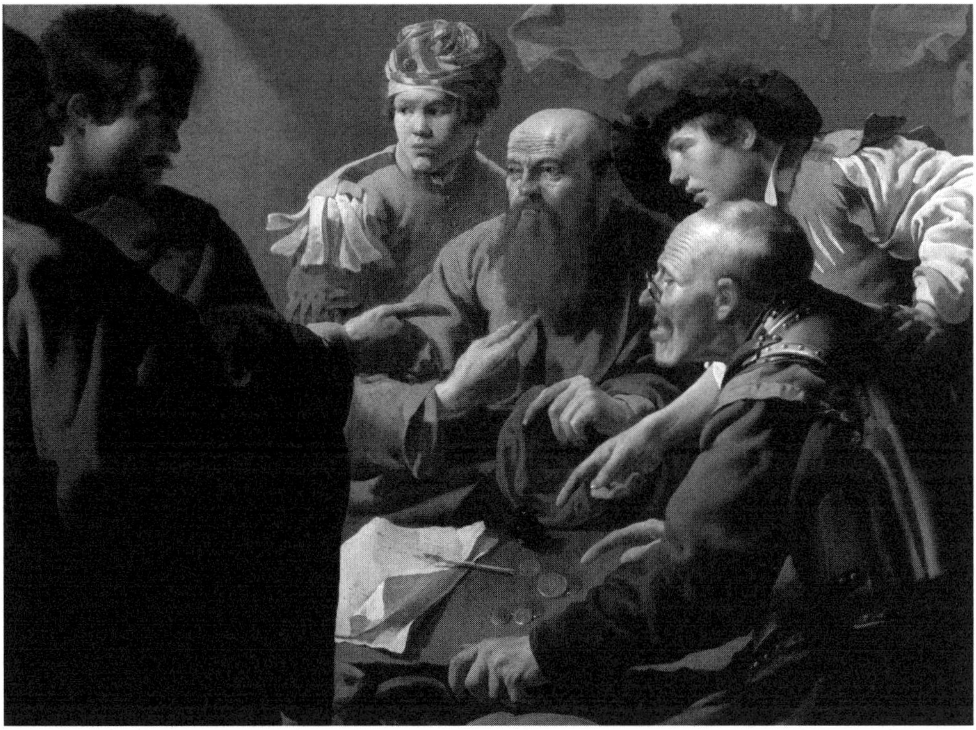

FIGURE 1.18 (PLATE 10)
The Calling of St. Matthew, Hendrick ter Brugghen, Oil on Canvas;
h 102.3 cm x w 136.9 cm; with frame 129.2 cm x 162.6 cm.
Collection of Centraal Museum, Utrecht. Purchased
with support of Vereniging Rembrandt, 1925.
PHOTO COURTESY OF CMU/ERNST MORITZ.

poetry and politics. Here I will simply suggest that the potential Judaism of art did not end with Reformation, Counter-Reformation, or Enlightenment but continued well into modernity.

"Art Has Ceased to Be the Supreme Need of the Spirit"

"We may say, in general," write Antoine Arnauld and Pierre Nicole in their *Logic, or the Art of Thought* of 1662, "that the world values most things by the exterior alone, since we find scarcely any who penetrate to the interior and to the foundations of them; everything is judged according to the fashion, and unhappy are those who are not in favor." In all forms of representation this attention to exterior "ornamentation" leads to a falsity that they describe by comparing words with stones and metal, the untruths of rhetoricians with those of sculptor or architect: "The orator . . . disposes of [the truth] as we do the stones of a building or the metal of a statue: he cuts it, lengthens it, narrows it, disguises it, as he thinks fit, in order to adapt it to that vain work of words which he wishes to make."

Michel Foucault thought that the theory of representation articulated by Arnauld, Nicole, and their Jansenist Catholic colleagues at the philosophical school known as Port-Royal marked a sharp break from a medieval and Renaissance system of knowledge to what he called the "Classical episteme." "From the Classical age," according to Foucault, "the sign is the *representativity* of the representation in so far as it is *representable*." But from the point of view of our inquiry the aesthetics of Port-Royal seem quite conventional, and their concern with the dangers posed by the "letter" and the "exterior thing" are recognizably Augustinian, even as they pushed that Augustinianism in new directions. Their goal was to minimize the distorting mediation of mimesis and representation. If, they argued, we are to approach things as conceived by God, without the distortion of human language and human interests, then we need to "present not only present things naked as they are, but also the very act of conceiving them." For this we need to strip down as far as possible the material supports of our cognition. "Too much attention to words and ornament . . . weakens the force of . . . thought. Similarly, painters have noticed that those who excel with color do not normally excel with drawing; the mind is not capable of mastering both, since one undermines the other." Whenever our cognitive tools of representation pay attention to the beauty of their own "surface," cognition is alienated from the object it seeks to apprehend. This misplaced attention was, for the Port-Royal thinkers as for so many others, essentially Jewish: "It is pharisaic to attend to the exterior before attending to the interior."[65]

The logicians could appeal so confidently to the analogy of painting in their quest to make the letter transparent because a stylistic discourse about the dangers of color in painting was already well established. That discourse was only reinforced by new physics and philosophy. Descartes's argument that objectivity is extension in space and local motion strengthened the truth claims of drawing—*dessin*, the tracing of extension in space—and reinforced the stigmatization of color, associated with the distortions of pathos and passion. It was in these terms that the *débat sur le coloris* (debate on coloring) was carried on in the mid-seventeenth century, as when the Jansenist rector of the Académie Royale, Philippe de Champaigne, warned of the moral dangers of color, which confronts us with its éclat, its exterior glitter, rather than pointing to the soul of the painting, its *dessin*. For all their dependence on the most up-to-date research, such words were not so far from the ontology underlying Saint Bernard's critique, half a millennium before, of those Judaizers who "believe more holy, what is more colorful."[66]

The great seventeenth- and eighteenth-century French debates over "modern taste" (*goût moderne*), the forays of Diderot and other Enlightenment philosophes into art criticism and theory, all were underwritten, each in its own way, by cognates of Christian aesthetics of transcendence such as these, or their secularized kissing cousins.[67] Something similar could be said of many of the great German founders of modern aesthetic theory. Since we have little space, let us focus for a page or two on the "Father of Art History," as E. H. Gombrich dubbed him: the philosopher Georg Wilhelm Friedrich Hegel (1770–1831).[68]

Hegel did not hesitate to cast his philosophy in an explicitly Christian vocabulary (however idiosyncratic), which means a Jewish one as well. This is evident already in *The Earliest System-Programme of German Idealism*, a youthful text from 1796 that was probably coauthored with his friends Friedrich Schelling and (principally) the poet Friedrich Hölderlin. The foundations of the "system" could not be more familiar: "The people without aesthetic sense are our philosophers of the letter. The philosophy of the spirit is an aesthetic philosophy." Only beauty has the power to move us from letter to spirit. This confidence in the power of beauty would disappear from Hegel's later writing, but the fundamentally Pauline antinomy of spirit and letter, with all its related pairs—"spirit and matter, soul and body, faith and intellect, freedom and necessity . . . reason and sensibility, intelligence and nature . . . absolute subjectivity and absolute objectivity," and of course Christian and Jew—endured throughout his career. Indeed Hegel understood his "speculative philosophy" as the successor to the Christian Incarnate God in the overcoming of these antinomies, a new and higher stage in the dialectical overcoming of the opposition between "the dead concept, empty within itself, and the full concreteness of life," by the unfolding Idea as it realizes itself in "the unity of concept and objectivity."[69]

History was, for Hegel, a teleological movement toward "[stripping] off the forms of dualism from its extremes, rendering the opposition in the element of Universality fluid, and bringing it to reconciliation." Within this history he assigned Judaism a familiar double role. In its recognition of the sharp difference between God and the material world Judaism represents a crucial stage in the progress of the spirit. But this difference, once discovered, should have been dialectically overcome (as the Christian Incarnation would do). Instead Judaism rejected the world in favor of total subjection to a distant God. The Jews' prohibition on images, their inability to love others, their blindness to the Incarnation—these were all symptoms of this rejection. As Hegel put it in *The Spirit of Christianity and Its Fate*, his early (1799) and long unpublished attempt to map the history of philosophy onto the history of Christianity: "The Jewish principle of opposing thought to reality, reason to sense; this principle involves the rending of life and a lifeless connection between God and the world."[70]

Like religion and philosophy, art is for Hegel an activity striving toward the unity of concept and reality. He sees "works of fine art as the first reconciling middle term between pure thought and what is merely external, sensuous and transient, between nature and finite reality and the infinite freedom of conceptual thinking." Art can achieve this mediation in a way that "immediate appearance" cannot, precisely because it calls attention (like the Christian art objects we have seen) to its own deceptiveness: "It points through and beyond itself, and itself hints at something spiritual of which it is to give us an idea, whereas immediate appearance does not present itself as deceptive but rather as real and true." "Beauty" is the name Hegel gives the successful outcome of this mediation: "When truth in this its external existence is present to consciousness immediately, and when the Concept remains immediately in unity with its external appearance, the Idea is not only true but beautiful. Therefore the beautiful is characterized as the pure appearance of the Idea to sense."[71]

Hegel's art and beauty, in other words, stood in opposition to Judaism, as one of his more famous students, Heinrich Heine (1797–1856), noted: "As the prophet of the Orient [Muhammad] called [the Jews] 'the people of the book,' so the prophet of the Occident [Hegel] . . . called them 'the people of the spirit.' . . . Their whole religion is nothing but a dialectic act by which matter is separated from spirit and the absolute is recognized solely as spirit. . . . In what a dreadful opposition they must have stood to colorful Egypt, the Temples of Joy of Astarte in Phoenicia, lovely, fragrant, Babylon, and finally to Greece, the flourishing home of art."[72] "Dreadful opposition" is not emancipation. Precisely because of this opposition, within Hegel's system the work of art's adequacy to the task of concretizing the Idea can be measured in terms of its distance from Judaism: a measurement that applies not only to the individual work but to the entire history of art itself.

Hegel provided a version of that history in his *Lectures on the Fine Arts*, given over the course of the 1820s and published after his death from notes by his students. In these lectures he presents the development of art as a progressive overcoming of oppositions that throughout his career he encoded as Jewish, so that his history of art can also be read as a chapter in the history of the human spirit's flight from Judaism. That history extends over 1,237 pages in English translation, but a brief summary may suffice to make the point:

1. The first stage of art, which Hegel called Symbolic, used natural forms to point toward the unrepresentable mystery of the divine. This art—which includes the art of the ancient Egyptians, Jews, Persians, and Hindus—was abstract and "sublime." But the enormous distance between the representation and the ideal in symbolic art (precisely the distance that led Plato to praise the art of the Egyptians!) meant that it demanded rules of interpretation. How else to

determine, for example, the ideal represented by a statue of an ibis? In Hegelian terms, symbolic art is Jewish in that it restricts the freedom of the subject by placing her under the necessity of such rules and external laws.

2. Classical art made freedom visible in the shape of individuals—for example, in the statue of a god or hero in human form. Freedom and self-sufficiency are the ideal expressed in the unity of form and content achieved by "classical beauty." "Classical beauty has for what is internal in it the free self-sufficient meaning, i.e., not a meaning of this and that but what means itself and therefore interprets itself." But classical art itself begins to discover that this aesthetic freedom is at odds with the finitude of the world in which it expresses itself, and soon Greek philosophy begins to point out art's inability to express what it might mean "for a finite, embodied human to be free." Classical art, Hegel concludes, possessed "spiritual individuality, but as a corporeal not inwardized, over which there stood the abstract necessity of fate" (607). Insofar as it was subject to this abstract necessity, it could also be understood as too Jewish.
3. A new stage of art emerged once the Incarnate God revealed the human vocation of freedom in the world. Romantic art is the art that seeks to comprehend this "infinite subjectivity" aesthetically. It is the art that has learned (from Christianity and philosophy) that the grounding assumption of art itself is false: the ideal, the true nature of reality, has no adequate sensible form. The remaining task of art is therefore to express its awareness of its own inadequacy: "Romantic art is the self-transcendence of art within its own sphere in the form of art itself" (79–80). This process of self-transcendence is unceasing: "It is the effect and the progress of art itself which, by bringing before our vision as an object its own indwelling materiality, at every step along this road makes its own contribution to freeing art from the content represented" (604). Art must not pause along the road to delight in its content, settle into a style, or linger over its materiality. In this sense Hegel's Romantic art remains, like so much of the art we've studied in these pages, in constant stylistic flight from Judaism.

4. Yet Romantic art cannot escape Judaism any more than the Christianity that birthed it can. The Jewish element of opposition remains within both of them (recall Hegel's claim that Christianity remained metaphysical, representing God as both transcendent and immanent simultaneously). Only in post-Kantian speculative and conceptual thought can the metaphysical divide between mind and world finally disappear, and with it the alienation that Hegel had formerly called Judaism (104, 176). Only at this stage of the spirit's unfolding can man be said to be free. But this stage has no correlative in religion or art. Religion comes closer than art, because although it still "has pictorial thinking as its form of consciousness," it moves away from the "objectivity of art" to "pictorial thinking in a subjective way." But only speculative philosophy "makes its own or knows conceptually what otherwise is only the content of subjective feeling or pictorial thinking." It alone achieves true freedom, "untrammelled *thinking*" (104), escaping the shadow of necessity that Hegel cast over all "pictorial thinking," a shadow that he, like so many before him, associated with Judaism.

Art, like Judaism, has been left behind by the dialectical unfolding of the spirit that it itself set in motion: "For us art counts no longer as the highest mode in which truth fashions an existence for itself. . . . The form of art has ceased to be the supreme need of the spirit" (103). To translate the point into terms more obviously relevant to our analysis: now that the spirit, aided by art, has finally been freed from Jewish opposition and necessity, it becomes clear that art itself can never achieve that freedom. This does not mean that Hegel thought art must disappear (as he thought Judaism should have). Like other norms that no longer count as the highest mode of existence (such as law, or the Christian religion) art may still have an important pedagogical or propaedeutic role in human life.[73] But it does mean that art, like those other norms, must not forget its belatedness. When it does so, it becomes deadening rather than enlivening, falling into the type of necrophilia he elsewhere associated with Judaism. "Past worldviews" cannot be resurrected. "Only the present is fresh: the rest is paler and paler" (606, 608).[74]

Degenerate Modernity

We must not give Hegel the last word, as if philosophy had really superseded art. Painters, too, wrestled with these same questions about the relationship between thought, beauty, truth, and freedom. The theoreticians of many modern artistic avant-gardes shared the worry that the self is alienated from the world by images, representation, and pictorial thought. Arnaud and Nicole's ideal that art should "not only present things naked as they are, but also the very act of conceiving them" sounds not so different from the prescriptions of Maurice Raynal, the early twentieth-century defender of Cubism: "In painting anyone who wishes to approach the truth must record only conceptions of the objects, the only things created without the aid of the senses, which are the source of inexhaustible errors."[75]

Cubists did not have a monopoly on dissatisfaction with representation. Henri Matisse (1869–1954) dreamed of an art in which painter and beholder were mediated without distortion, in which the "feelings and the soul of the painter travel without difficulty into the spirit of he who looks on." He believed (unlike the Jansenists) that color was the painter's best hope in the attempt to communicate sensations and, to that end, developed his own distinctive style. But yearnings for transparency and immediacy, worried reflections on the limits of representation: these concerns common to the long history of transcendent aesthetics were also common to modernism as a whole. Piet Mondrian's (1872–1944) desire to "dispense with all the arts"; James Ensor's (1860–1949) push toward abstraction and narrative unintelligibility in order to perform the incommunicability of private perception: these and many other very different pictorial styles were all produced (or at least understood) as attempts to engage with the alienation that transcendence had introduced into art.[76]

I say engage rather than overcome because although there were certainly artists who thought art could escape the ontological straitjacket within which transcendent ideals had confined it, others sought to explore art's stigma rather than cure it, or even to heighten the performance of the madness in order to criticize any claims to transcendence.

Not all artists shared the fantasy that art could overcome our feelings of alienation as communicative subjects in the world, nor did all painters, critics, or beholders "dream of the pure and simple absence of the frame." And even when they shared these questions and yearnings, many artists, and many critics of art, did not think of them in terms of Judaism. In modernity as in any other period covered in this chapter, Judaism was only a potential charge in thinking about art, not a necessary or inevitable one.[77]

We still know too little about the work done by categories like flesh and spirit, Judaism and Christianity, in the thought of modern painters. (Compare the case of poetry, where the antisemitism of an Ezra Pound or a T. S. Eliot is so frequently explored.) It would be fascinating, for example, to ask the poet and painter Max Jacob (1876–1944)—roommate of Picasso; friend of Braque, Modigliani, and so many others—what aesthetic convictions and desires might have motivated his conversion from Judaism to Catholicism (ca. 1909). If those questions are rarely asked of these avant-gardes, it is in part because the work done by Judaism in the aesthetics of their enemies was so much more notorious. Among those enemies, the most notable were the Nazis and their allies, who took the lives of Max Jacob and so many others.

Perhaps the most famous example of the work done by Judaism in National Socialist aesthetics is the *Entartete Kunst* (Degenerate Art) show that opened at Munich's Archaeological Institute on July 19, 1937, and then traveled throughout Germany and Austria until 1941. The exhibition—among the best attended in history—was organized by Joseph Goebbels, by then the powerful Nazi minister for propaganda and enlightenment of the folk, in conjunction with an exhibition on "Great German Art" that opened a day earlier to inaugurate a grand House of German Art. The Great German Art show was meant to showcase the "Greco-Nordic art" that the triumph of National Socialism had returned to its rightful place of honor. In Hitler's own words, albeit from 1930: "There is only one eternal art that has validity: namely Greco-Nordic art. There are no revolutions in the field of art. . . . Anything with any claim at all to the name art can only be Greco-Nordic." Or in Goebbels's echo of his master's voice, at the opening of the Reich Chamber of Culture (Reichskulturkammer) in 1933: "The laws of art can never be changed; they are eternal and draw their standards from the spaces of immortality. Only consecrated hands have the right to serve at the altar of art."[78]

Judging from Goebbels's diaries, the Nazis had a difficult time finding good products of such consecrated hands to include in the (poorly attended) Great German Art exhibit. It was apparently far easier to decide what German art *was not*: the Degenerate Art exhibition was designed with a hasty efficiency. It sought to stage the Jewish-Bolshevist-bourgeois-liberal danger that threatened the work of art and, through art, the German people. Once again this danger was not confined to living Jews, whether by confession or even by the Nazis' racial classifications. Of the approximately 112 artists condemned as degenerate by inclusion at the exhibit, only six were Jews even by the Nazi definition of race. And the most heavily represented artist in the exhibition was the champion of German Expressionism, Emil Nolde.[79]

It is worth lingering for a moment over Nolde's fate, since it makes clear the power of Judaism as an aesthetic category. On the one hand Nolde was a victim of that power. More than a thousand of his works were confiscated from German museums in the Nazis' purge of degenerate art in 1937, and his cycle The Life of Christ was the central exhibit in the Degenerate Art exhibition. In 1938 the Nazi press began to include him in its lists of prominent Jews in the arts, stressing his links to Jewish art dealers and critics during the Weimar Republic. In Goebbels's 1940 propaganda film *Der ewige Jude* (The Eternal Jew), directed by Fritz Hippler, Nolde's work was used to illustrate the Jewish corruption of German art. The voiceover explains: "The Jewish people is most dangerous whenever it is allowed to get mixed up in the most sacred things of a people, in its culture, in its religion and art, and to offer its arrogant opinions. The concept of beauty of the Nordic people is completely incomprehensible to the Jew. . . ."

To visualize the point, the image of the infant Jesus in Lucas Cranach the Elder's (ca. 1472–1553) *Madonna under the Apple Tree* is transformed by a wipe (in the rough shape of a Star of David) that replaces it frame by frame with the "unnatural, grotesque, perverse [and] pathological" face of Emil Nolde's painting *Eve*, while the sound track changes from Bach's Toccata in D Major into African rhythms. The following year Nolde was among the German artists entirely banned by the Reich's Chamber of the Fine Arts from "any further professional activity." Henceforth he painted only watercolors, which after the war he called his "unpainted pictures."

And yet Nolde was certainly not Jewish by race or religion. He was a member of the Nazi Party, and a painter whom Goebbels had approached soon after the party's rise to power in 1933 about the directorship of the Vereinigte Staatliche Kunstschule (Unified State Art School) in Berlin. Nolde was keen on the job and, in letters to friends, expressed himself willing to do that or anything else within his power for "the cause," for this "forcefully executed and beautiful rising of the German people." In his eagerness for the position he even denounced a potential rival — Max Pechstein, his former friend and colleague in the German Expressionist movement known as "Die Brücke" (The Bridge) — as a Jew. (Nolde was nevertheless disappointed: the post went to a longtime party member.) At numerous points throughout his career — and most notably in *Jahre der Kämpfe* (Years of Struggle), the revealingly entitled second volume of his autobiography written in 1934—Nolde presented himself as the lonely and brave defender of German art against the "Jewish pack" (the phrase is from an admiring article defending Nolde in the Nazi newspaper *Völkischer Beobachter*), often attacking painters like Max Liebermann and the dealer and critic Paul Cassirer in explicitly antisemitic terms.[80]

In what sense, then, was his art — or that of any other condemned artist — degenerate and Jewish? We cannot answer that question in terms of "real" Judaism. Even the concept of cultural *Entartung* itself was not, in its early formulations, particularly tied to Judaism. Perhaps the most influential of these early formulations were Max Nordau's two volumes with that title, published in 1892–1893, which made the concept famous. Nordau, who was himself from a Jewish family, built his case about cultural degeneracy on abnormal psychology rather than race, characterizing it as a product of the unnatural urban context of modern life, not of Judaism. He may well have intended his own argument as a defense against (or at least an alternative to) antisemitism in cultural critique.[81]

Certainly many did attempt to tie their judgments about the Judaism of art to some "reality," often enough imagined as racial. Hans Günther's *Rasse und Stil* (Race and Style) and Paul Schultze-Naumburg's best-selling *Kunst und Rasse* (Art and Race) taught readers how to distinguish the race mixtures of artists by looking at their works, works whose style was in turn meant to reveal the artist's internal racial worldview.[82] Conversely, the newest tools of art criticism could be put to the work of mapping pictorial style onto a nation, race, or culture. Heinrich Wölfflin (1864–1945) was a founding father of the formal analysis of art, the prize student and successor of Jacob Burckhardt. He believed his analytical techniques could reveal not only the artist's "Being" (*Dasein*) but also that of the people (*Volk*) for whom the work was made. In *Italy and the German Sense of Form* (1931), for example, he explained the differences he perceived in Italian and German realism in terms of differences in the two peoples. According to him the German spirit expects more resistance than the Italian, and therefore German expression prefers concrete particularities and fights harder for freedom from abstraction.[83]

These new sciences of art sought new foundations in vocabularies of race and nation. But for all their modernity, they remained dependent on the basic axioms of the aesthetics of transcendence we have been exploring. The twentieth-century debates among artists, critics, professors, philosophers, and politicians about the relative merits of abstraction, realism, Expressionism, and many other schools and -isms are inseparable from a long history of European thought characterized by the belief that some forms of representation offer more truth, transcendence, and freedom; others more alienation, falsehood, and slavery. That belief was widely shared by all involved in the Degenerate Art exhibition, not only the organizers but also the condemned. Like Emil Nolde, many German Expressionists understood themselves as attempting to free art from the alienation of representation. The same was true of the French Cubists, Dadaists, Expressionists, and other avant-gardists we encountered in the previous pages. And yet all could be classified by Goebbels—who himself had earlier celebrated Expressionism for wanting "to build a new world from within"—as alienating, degenerate, and Jewish. And all could find that description meaningful.[84]

We should attempt to catalog the many registers of culture that made such classifications convincing. And we should chart the vectors of corruption through which so many modern Europeans imagined that art, artist, and beholder could become infected. Judaism had many mediators—indeed mediation itself threatened all of its participants with Judaism. According to Philipp Stauff, El Greco and van Gogh had been Judaized through the art galleries and art critics who sold and celebrated their works. Writing in 1913 he claimed that the dealers of his day were all Jews, and that their taste making was corrupting the German spirit. Goebbels himself used a similar logic in 1936, when he banned the practice of art criticism (*Kunstkritik*) in Germany because of its alleged role in the Judaizing of German art. Henceforth only descriptions of works (*Kunstbericht*) should be published, so that the folk could decide without Jewish corruption what art they liked.[85]

We need to study these various logics in order to understand how the Judaism of art could prove so compelling in this particular time and place. I will, however, leave such study to others and bring mine to an end. I conclude with the Nazis not because they represent the end point or the climax of my brief history of art, but because they offer a modern and clear example of the power that an aesthetics of transcendence can discover in figures of Judaism. Judaism had menaced the Christian beholder ever since Paul and his successors translated the most basic problems of ancient critical thought into the terms of Christian and Jew. The Nazis attempted to project that danger onto new (and newly racial) figures of Judaism. If the goal of such projection was to contain the dangers of Judaism in order to mark the space of an ontologically true and good German art, their efforts failed as badly as those of all of their predecessors. The racialization of Christian aesthetic discourses heightened the risks of Judaizing rather than containing them, much as the turn toward genealogy and Inquisition had done in late medieval Spain.

Indeed insofar as the status of the artist, the art object, and the beholder were explicitly interpenetrated and interlegible within Christian aesthetics, Nazi projection only made the potential Judaism of art more dangerous. If the Jewishness of an artist produced art objects with a Jewish style, if art objects with Jewish styles could make Jews of their German beholders, or, conversely, if Jewish beholders and critics could turn German art makers into Jews: in short, if our aesthetic relation to objects in the world is so easily corruptible into Judaism, then the de-Judaization of art becomes that much more urgent.[86] And yet for all its urgency it remains impossible, since every aesthetic relation remains potentially Jewish. Within such a double bind, "to call someone a Jew" becomes, as Max Horkheimer and Theodor Adorno put it with this aspect of Nazi aesthetics very much in mind, "an excuse to work him over until he resembles the image."[87]

I hope to have convinced you that thinking about Judaism played a significant role in the development of Western art. At the very least this chapter is a reminder that art did not get over its Christian anxieties about Judaism as easily as we might think, and that the ways in which it has dealt with those anxieties have had important consequences not only for art but for living people as well. The reminder is important, because although today the word Jew is no longer a conscious part of our critical vocabulary, many of the ontological distinctions and yearnings for transcendence historically underwritten by the term remain basic to our thinking about art. Some postwar artists (such as Joseph Beuys) and critics (such as Yves Bonnefoy) have made the recuperation of these distinctions and the remystification of the art object the central program of their work. My sense is that, of late, this centrality has expanded. Presence, Grace, and even Eucharist and Incarnation are once again positive key words in contemporary aesthetics, often posed against a negative foil of literalism. Perhaps we cannot do without these concepts, so basic to Western ontologies and epistemologies. But neither should we forget that these yearnings and the concepts they generate retain the *potential* to summon the enemies through which they have so often defined themselves. They continue, in other words, to threaten art with Judaism.

CHAPTER TWO

Every Poet Is a Jew

> Ghetto of the chosen-ones! Wall and ditch.
> Expect no mercy!
> In this most Christian of all worlds,
> The poets are Yids!
> —"Poem of the End" (1924)

These words were addressed to the ghetto of Prague by the Russian (and not Jewish) poet Marina Tsvétayeva, then living in that city an exile from her native land. They are well known, not only because Tsvétayeva's reputation as a poet has grown ever greater since her suicide in 1941 but also because they were taken up by the yet more famous (and famously Jewish) poet Paul Celan as an epigraph for a poem in his 1963 collection, *Nobody's Rose* (*Die Niemandsrose*). The juxtaposition of Judaism and poetry in these lines fascinates. What might it mean for a poet to place herself, and all poetry in a Christian world, within the Jewish ghetto?[1]

There are many ways to approach this question. We could, for example, turn to context and biography for hints about what Tsvétayeva (or Celan) might have understood herself to mean. It is easy enough to interpret "Poem of the End" in terms of the alienation of its author's exile, or of the failed love affair that prompted its writing. And Celan (who was Jewish by the definitions of the Holocaust's engineers, and suffered for it) himself demanded that we understand his *Nobody's Rose* both as a meditation on Jewishness and exile and as a self-conscious engagement with a poetic tradition that he stretched from Dante, Shakespeare, and Hölderlin to Tsvétayeva and her Russian contemporary Osip Mandelstam (the dedicatee of Celan's volume). Alternatively we might imagine that some specific similarity between Jews and poets is being asserted, as Kierkegaard had done a century or so before: "It is a big question: in what sense are the Jews to be called the chosen people; they were not the happiest; rather they were a sacrifice demanded by the whole human race; as no other people they had to endure the pain of the law and of sin. They were the chosen people in the same sense that poets, etc. often are, i.e., they are the unhappiest."[2]

But we can also take Tsvétayeva's words as a more general statement: poetry is a Judaizing practice in a Christian world, one that makes "Yids" of its practitioners. Why and in what sense might this be so? And with what consequences for poetry and for poets, for Christians and for Jews? As in the previous chapter, these questions can lead us across vast swathes of time and place. I'll begin with a brief review of the dangers of poetry as imagined in classical and Christian culture, before focusing on a few examples of medieval and early modern poetry to show how poetics, like painting, explored the threat of Judaism within itself in order to expand the possibilities for its own practice. And finally I'll return to the nineteenth and twentieth centuries to demonstrate just how high the stakes remained in the eras we like to call modern.

Deceitful Muses

As with painting there is an ancient debate about poetry's relationship to truth. Does poetry lead its readers (or, more commonly in the ancient and medieval worlds, its hearers) toward truths, and if so, how? Already in the eighth century BCE, in the invocations with which the Greek ur-poet Homer opened his epics, we can see a poetic path being charted toward truth. *Andra moi ennepe mousa*, "Sing to me o muse": the poet presents himself as voice and vessel for the divine. But that path proves forked almost as soon as it is blazed. Hesiod, writing, like Homer, near the very beginnings of the Greek poetic tradition, opens his *Theogony* with a vision that brings a warning from those very muses:

> We know how to tell many false things that are like truths,
> and we know, whenever we want, how to sing out truths.
> So they said, the accurate speaking daughters of mighty Zeus,

and they gave me a branch of flourishing laurel for a scepter
after plucking it, an admirable one; then they inspired in me
divine voice, so that I could celebrate the things to come and
those past. . . . (24–34)

Hesiod's prologue provides poetry's own staging of its ambivalent relationship to truth. Many of the Greek philosophical treatments of that ambivalence that emerged in later centuries would be less charitable, particularly those committed to a hierarchical distinction between the life of the body and that of the soul, between the contingency and confusion of carnal perception and the clarity of the eternal truths achieved by spiritual cognition. Philosophers with such commitments tended to agree with Plato and Aristotle that poetry's first principle is the imitation of the forms of nature, and that its fundamental appeal is to the bodily senses. In this, poetry was thought to be much like painting except, as Aristotle explains in the *Poetics* (1447a), with rhythm, language, and harmony as the building blocks of its mimetic appeal, rather than painting's color and form.

Which of these—poetry or painting—was the higher form of representation, which potentially more virtuous and which more deceitful, was a subject of debate well into the twentieth century. I will not take sides but simply note that the terms of critique were often interchangeable. When Plato wanted to demonstrate that poetry could never perceive the higher reaches of truth, which were accessible only to the intellect, he did so in terms that condemned painting as well: "The place beyond heaven—none of our earthly poets has ever sung or will ever sing its praises enough! . . . What is in this place is without color and without shape and without solidity, a being that really is what it is, the subject of all true knowledge, visible only to the intelligence, the soul's steersman" (*Phaedrus* 247c). In the *Phaedrus* Socrates adds metempsychotic insult to ontological injury by assigning to poets a place in the hierarchy of souls just above that of the lowly farmer, whose job it is to extract bodily nourishment from the earth (248e).

But the poet's materialism, like the painter's but unlike the farmer's, is politically and morally dangerous, because its guise of beauty can (according to Plato) seduce hearers away from truth.[3] Hence Socrates concludes his discussion of poetry in the *Republic* with a warning that conflates poetry's threat to both person and polity in one potent metaphor: "At all events we are well aware that poetry being such as we have described is not to be regarded seriously as attaining to the truth; and he who listens to her, fearing for the safety of the city which is within him, should be on his guard against her seductions and make our words his law" (595A–608B). There is a great deal more to say about this particular passage, about the political analogy it establishes between the individual involved in an aesthetic experience and the government or soul of a city, and about Greek philosophical views of poetry more generally. But that commentary must be left to others, since we are in a hurry to get to Christianity.

Fortunately the distance is not great. Already in the earlier pages on painting we saw how steeped the early Christians were in Hellenistic philosophy. From their point of view the challenges of poetry were, if anything, more acute than those of painting. In addition to dangerously delighting the senses, the poetry celebrated in their day seemed inextricably bound to erotica or, worse, to false myths and false gods. Countless students have been exposed to one of the few Christian critiques of classical poetry that remain on our college curricula: Saint Augustine's self-critical recollection in his *Confessions* of having wept over Dido's fate while reading the Roman poet Virgil's *Aeneid* (*Confessions* 1.13). The emphasis there is on the foolishness of being moved to tears by the beauty and pathos of a poetry that is pagan, and therefore cannot bring one closer to the true God and eternal life (or worse, seduces one away from that eternal truth). Later and elsewhere he was more emphatic, repeatedly pointing out in *The City of God* that even the pagan philosophers condemned poetry, which they realized was inspired by Satan and his servants. Augustine mentions Plato, Seneca, and Varro (116 BCE–27 BCE), among others.

Of these perhaps the most interesting example is the last, not least because Augustine relied so heavily on Varro's accounts of Roman language, religion, and culture. According to Augustine a Roman such as Varro, the greatest scholar of that people's culture, found it easy enough to dismiss the truth value of the Romans' "poetic theology" (*poeticam theologian*), even when he did not dare to criticize their "political theology." By invoking these pagan authorities Augustine is presenting the Christian condemnation of poetry as lies (*mendacia*) and poisonous delight (*noxia delectatio*) as if it were entirely continuous with the classical philosophical critique.[4]

The problem is not restricted to pagan poetry, or even to purely poetic forms of linguistic arts. It is more generally a problem about the relation between beauty and truth in language itself, a relation that within early Christian ontology was often negative: a surface of beautiful words—in poetry as in rhetoric—often conceals falsehood, a whitewashed tomb full of dead men's bones, to paraphrase Jesus once more. Many early Christians developed the gospel's suspicions about masters of language and learning such as the Pharisees—"all their works they do to be seen by men"—into a critique of verbal beauty in general. As Cyprian explained to his friend Donatus in the middle of the third century, "When speech is about the Lord and God, its pure sincerity depends on facts, not on the power of eloquence in support of faith. Therefore accept not elegant words, but strong ones; not dressed in cultured rhetoric in order to win approval of the audience, but . . . simple words of un-cultivated truth" (*Ad Donat.* 2, CSEL 3.1.4).

Not only poetry but all forms of eloquence and verbal cleverness posed these risks. This is why the poet (and eventually bishop) Paulinus of Nola, writing circa 400, could condemn the sophistic powers of philosophers, the deceitful art of rhetoricians, and the figments of poets all in one breath.[5] At more or less the same time as Paulinus, albeit on a different continent, Augustine quotes the great (non-Christian) rhetorician Cicero to make the point in Book IV of *On Christian Doctrine*: "Eloquence without wisdom is frequently a positive injury, and is never a positive service." Beauty must be deployed only in the service of truth, "for of what use is a golden key, if it cannot open what we want it to open?" The problem is that over the course of human affairs "so much labor has been spent by men on beauty of expression" not in order to teach the good but, on the contrary, to teach the bad, "merely for the sake of being read with pleasure." Augustine concludes: "May

God avert from His Church what the prophet Jeremiah says of the synagogue of the Jews: 'A wonderful and horrible thing is committed in the land: the prophets prophesy falsely, and the priests applaud them with their hands; and my people love to have it so: and what will you do in the end thereof?'"[6]

Augustine is once again (recall his treatment of the golden calf in the previous chapter) using the Jews to represent a deadly aesthetics, an incorrect relation to representation, in this case to verbal beauty. Metaphorical and figurative language is particularly at risk. As Augustine says elsewhere in the same treatise, citing Paul's famous dictum from the second letter to the Corinthians:

> The ambiguities of metaphorical words . . . demand extraordinary care and diligence. What the apostle says pertains to this problem: "for written letters kill, but the Spirit gives life" (2 Cor 3:6). That is, when that which is said figuratively is taken as though it were literal, it is understood carnally. Nothing can more appropriately be called the death of the soul than that condition in which the thing that distinguishes man from beasts, which is the understanding, is subjected to the flesh in pursuit of the letter. [3.5(9)]

To read carnally, "to be unable to lift the eye of the mind above what is corporeal and created," was "a miserable slavery of the soul." This was in fact, as Augustine went on to say, the slavery of the Jews. But no Christian, at least none who utilized language, was immune to the potential slavery of reading carnally, with all its attendant risks of hermeneutic Judaization.

Augustine does not insist on verbal ugliness or plainness as an antidote to the danger, as some of his predecessors had. Not only does scripture itself abound in metaphors and figures, but rhetorical beauty in general is pedagogically too important to do without. In fact at times Augustine even proposes that God created the world with such beauty in mind: "God would never have created any, I do not say angel, but even man, whose future wickedness He foreknew, unless He had equally known to what uses in behalf of the good He could turn him, thus embellishing the course of the ages, as it were an exquisite poem set off with antitheses. For what are called antitheses are among the most elegant of the ornaments of speech . . ." (*City of God* 11.18).

Realizing that communication without imitation, figuration, or verbal eloquence is not humanly possible, the bishop of Hippo insists only on the Christian's strict orientation of beauty toward truth as communicated by scripture. But the difficulty is that preachers cannot teach *only* in the words of scripture, although many did strive to knit their sermons as much as possible out of biblical citations. And even if a preacher mouthed only scriptural words, he could not guarantee on his own that his invocation and interpretation of those words were in accord with divine truth: God alone can provide such a guarantee. The preacher should therefore pray, before each deployment of his eloquence, that he might be able "to lift up his thirsty soul to God, to drink in what he is about to pour forth, and to himself be filled with what he is about to distribute" (*On Christian Doctrine* 4.15[32]).

Perhaps it is not surprising that we find poets appealing to the same guarantor as did preachers. They too called upon the grace of God to inspire them and authorize their verse, as Juvencus did in the conclusion to his own biblical epic: "My mind had received such strength of faith and reverent fear and the grace of Christ shone on me so strongly that in my verse the glory of the holy law readily received the earthly adornments of language." We might call these invocations Christian versions of Homer's formula "Sing in me o muse." We should not be surprised if, as a solution to the dangers of verbal representation, such prayer was scarcely more definitive than its Homeric or Hesiodic antecedents.[7]

There was certainly positive space for poetry to be found in early Christian culture. Paul, for example, had exhorted the Colossians to sing psalms and hymns and spiritual songs (Col. 3:16). But what exactly were these spiritual songs? Did they include only those revealed by God to prophets such as David and Solomon (traditionally understood as authors of the Psalms and the Song of Songs), or also those authored by poets from their own ingenuity (*de proprio ingenio*) in ages after Christ's coming had ended the production of scripture? It was easy enough to treat the biblical poets as the divine counterparts to the demonically inspired pagans, as Jerome did when he cast David as the poetic antipode to the early Greeks Pindar and Simonides. It was, however, more difficult to justify contemporary composers without any clear title to prophecy. Poets nevertheless strove for such justification. As Paulinus puts it in the thirty-second and last song attributed to him,

> let it not displease that I compose this sort of song:
> David himself implored God with metered voice (*modulata voce*),
> after which example we, substituting small for great, will sing,
> announcing those things we must flee, and those we must
> cultivate.[8]

Through such efforts poets made room for new poetry, often in the shape of adaptations of the Psalms. Augustine himself, for example, wrote a collection of "Psalms against the Sect of the Donatists" so that (as he explained) the unlearned in his flock would have a weapon against these Christians whom Augustine and his church considered heretics. Lactantius had long before made the similar, albeit sociologically diametrically opposed, argument that rhetoric was necessary in order to convert the learned: "The truth . . . should also be illustrated and in some way asserted with clarity and beauty of discourse, so that both through its own force and adorned by the light of oratory, it might more powerfully flow into souls."[9] Sedulius justified his early fifth-century *Easter Song* in similar terms: "Rarely . . . has anyone shaped the gifts of divine power into song, and there are many who delight instead in the study of worldly pursuits due to its poetic decorations and the pleasures of songs. They read over whatever has rhetorical charm, but they pursue [scripture] more neglectfully since they do not love it at all. Any verses they have seen, however, sweetened with charm, they take up with such heartfelt enthusiasm, that by going over these things more often, they store them deep in their memory and repeat them."[10]

As with previously discussed arguments in favor of art, poetry could present itself as a powerful pedagogical tool, one particularly useful in the struggle against unbelief, error, and heresy. In fact according to Augustine, one criticism the Donatists had made of the Catholic Church was that it had *failed* to produce any nonbiblical poetry! Augustine's teacher Saint Ambrose had done precisely that in Milan, composing verses to provide his flock with a "defensive weapon" against another group of Christians cast by Catholics as heretics: the Arians.

But within a transcendent frame that stressed the Christian's obligation to turn away from "every deadly delight in passing things," such verses could just as easily be charged—as Ambrose himself tells us his verses in fact were—with "deceiving the populace" rather than leading it toward truth.[11] Sectarian disagreement provided a soteriological framework within which to argue about the status of a given poem—is it killing or salvific?—but it could not provide poetry itself with a firm ontological foundation. Thus although Augustine in his *Confessions* presents Ambrose's hymns as opening the gates for poetic psalmody in all the parishes of the Western Church and the wider world ("et per cetera orbis," as he writes in 9.7.15), the debate over such poetry did not end. The bishops gathered at the Council of Braga in 563 found it "pleasing that beside the psalms and the canonical scriptures of the New and Old Testament, no poetical compositions be recited (*psallatur*) in church." In 633 those at Toledo's Fourth Council, on the other hand, not only found space for extracanonical verse but vigorously enjoined it, menacing with excommunication anyone who rejected such hymns.[12]

In short Late Antique Christians found room for poetry, just as we have already seen that they found room for art. But although some viewed the powers of verbal beauty more optimistically than others, all agreed that its seductions were potentially dangerous.[13] Like art, poetry had to announce its own engagement with these dangers, as Paulinus of Nola did in one of his songs: "Though I use the poet's art, the song I sing will not be invented. I shall tell it with an historian's truthfulness and without the poet's deceit, because a servant of Christ should not utter lies."[14] Such explicit engagement did not, however, suffice to free poetry from the ontological stigma under which it labored. It was not enough for the poet to convert from profane subjects to Christian ones, as Augustine had urged his correspondent Licentius to do. Each step toward Christ could always be seen as requiring a further step away from poetry. Paulinus, for example, seems to have stopped writing his songs after becoming bishop. And when Sidonius Apollinaris took up his religious profession in the second half of the fifth century, he understood his choice "in the first place" as a renunciation of verse.[15]

Sensible Figures

If we jump forward a handful of centuries into the Middle Ages, we find the space available for poetry still fraught. Saint Thomas Aquinas (1225–1274) sketched that space in his *Summa Theologica*, revealingly placing the discussion in a section dedicated to questions about the "ceremonial precepts" of the "Old Law." Why are those fleshy ceremonies in the scripture, and how should a Christian relate to them? In clarifying this difficult question of Christianity's relationship to the ceremonies of Judaism—the same question that had animated Peter and Paul's debate discussed earlier—the "Angelic Doctor" turns to a cognitive analogy: "Just as human reason fails to grasp poetical expressions on account of their being lacking in truth, so does it fail to grasp Divine things perfectly, on account of the sublimity of the truth they contain: and therefore in both cases there is need of signs by means of sensible figures." In other words poetry has to depend upon aesthetic representations because of a lack of truth, whereas scripture does so because of an excess of the same: divine truth is so great as to be beyond human comprehension.

Saint Thomas had made a similar point at the very beginning of the *Summa*, when confronting the question of why holy writ makes use of metaphors: "It seems that Holy Scripture should not use metaphors. For that which is proper to the lowest science seems not to befit this science, which holds the highest place of all. But to proceed by the aid of various similitudes and figures is proper to poetry, the least of all the sciences. Therefore it is not fitting . . ." He responds to the objection by defending as natural necessity the use of sensible objects for conveying intellectual truths. All human knowledge (he says) must originate in the senses. But then he immediately draws a distinction between the two domains of poetry and prophecy: "Poetry makes metaphors to produce a representation" entirely for pleasure. "But sacred doctrine makes use of metaphors as both necessary and useful."

Saint Thomas was fully aware that the Christian cannot escape aesthetics. Even the salvific domains of scripture and liturgy depend upon the senses and the sensible. It is perhaps for this reason, and to heighten the contrast, that he insists on condemning poetry to a position even more distant from truth than Plato had done: "Poetic fictions have no purpose except to signify; and such signification does not go beyond the literal sense." Remember the Pauline dictum: "for written letters kill, but the Spirit gives life" (2 Cor. 3:6). For Aquinas, as for many other divines, poetry is restricted to the domain of the flesh and the letter—that is, to the deadly domain of "Judaism."[16]

Medieval poets could and did contest the judgment. There were many across the long Middle Ages who asserted poetry's relation to Christian truth. Sometimes, like their Late Antique predecessors, they did so by imitating or citing scriptural verse, or by limiting themselves to sacred subjects: the lives of saints, the deaths of martyrs. (These latter were a favored subject for epic poetry, with the saintly hero replacing, so to speak, the pagan one.) At other times they exulted in allegory, clambering heavenward along Neoplatonic ladders. Such was Bernard Silvestris's approach in his twelfth-century commentary on Virgil's *Aeneid*, in which, for example, Aeneas's abandonment of Dido represents the soul's turn from fleshy desires to intellectual truths. Poets might attempt to counter the common charge that their products were beautiful but not useful (which we have just seen made by Aquinas) by invoking the famous claim of the Roman poet Horace in his *Ars Poetica* that the best poetry instructs as well as delights:

> Poets aim either to benefit, or to amuse, or to utter words at once both pleasing and helpful to life. . . . Fictions meant to please should be close to the real . . . He has won every vote who has blended profit and pleasure, at once delighting and instructing the reader. That is the book to make money . . . this the one to cross the sea and extend to a distant day its author's fame.

Or they might even develop hybrid forms of prose and meter (*prosimetrum*) in order to produce work that, as Alexander Neckam (1157–1217) said of Martianus Capella's *Marriage of Philology and Mercury*, "confers utility in prose and delight in meter."[17]

Such defenses pale in comparison to the "theological poetics" developed by the great Italian vernacular poets in the thirteenth and fourteenth centuries, beginning with Dante (1265–1321) and continuing through Petrarch and Boccaccio.[18] These poets dared to articulate not only the Christian bona fides but even the salvific potential of poetry, even of verse in vulgar tongues rather than learned Latin, and of genres that dealt not only with saints and martyrs but also with the poet himself as a subject of the world in its plenitude. Dante's strategy in this regard was both precocious and exemplary. In a letter dedicating the Paradise section of his *Divine Comedy* to the nobleman Can Grande de la Scala (a letter I will here treat as authentic, although there is debate among scholars on that point) Dante touches upon many of the traditional defenses of poetry.[19] He invokes its powers of moral instruction, and he cites scripture to insist that God can be approached through all of his creation, not only through prophetic revelation: "Full of the glory of the Lord is his work" (Ecclus. 42.16). Citing Psalms 1:7, Dante suggests that "God's spirit is everywhere," even in poets and their poetry.

More provocatively he proposes that his poetry ought to be read *as if it were* prophecy. "For the elucidation, therefore, of what we have to say," he explains to Can Grande, "it must be understood that the meaning of this work is not of one kind only; rather the work may be described as polysemous, that is, having several meanings; for the first meaning is that which is conveyed by the letter, and the next is that which is conveyed by what the letter signifies." Dante is not simply speaking here about the difference between "sign" and "signified," as a modern philosopher of language might. He is instead embedding his poetry in a medieval Christian system of interpretation, built upon distinctions incipient in the letters of Paul and the gospel, a system that distinguishes between the literal and spiritual meanings of scripture. Indeed he turns explicitly to the language of biblical exegesis, explaining distinctions between its various senses:

> the former of which is called literal, while the latter is called allegorical, or mystical. And for the better illustration of this method of exposition we may apply it to the following verses: "When Israel went out of Egypt, the house of Jacob from a people of strange language; Judah was his sanctuary, and Israel his dominion" (Ps 113:1–2). For if we consider the letter alone, the thing signified to us is the going out of the children of Israel from Egypt in the time of Moses; if the allegory, our redemption through Christ is signified; if the anagogical, the passing of the sanctified soul from the bondage of the corruption of this world to the liberty of everlasting glory is signified. And although these mystical meanings are called by various names, they may one and all in a general sense be termed allegorical, inasmuch as they are different (*diversi*) from the literal or the historical; for the word "allegory" is so called from the Greek *alleon*, which in Latin is *alienum* (strange) or *diversum* (different).

Dante is expounding what theologians call "the fourfold senses of scripture" but applying them to his own work. How might these senses help interpreters of his *Divine Comedy*? About this he does not leave his reader in doubt:

> 8. . . . The subject, then, of the whole work, taken in the literal sense only, is the state of souls after death, pure and simple. For on and about that the argument of the whole work turns. If, however, the work be regarded from the allegorical point of view, the subject is man according as by his merits or demerits in the exercise of his free will he is deserving of reward or punishment by justice.[20]

The assertion here is a bold one, tending toward a hermeneutic equality between Dante's works and God's. The prophetic words of the *Biblia Vulgata* and those of the vernacular poet require the same kind of interpretation, and offer similar spiritual treasures to the dedicated readers who penetrate their secrets. Poetry and theology are one. It is difficult to imagine a more pointed response to Thomas Aquinas's stark condemnation, a generation before, of poetry to the Jewish realm of mere letter: "Poetic fictions have no purpose except to signify; and such signification does not go beyond the literal sense."

The Jew in the Castilian Poem

By presenting Dante and Aquinas as two poles I do not mean to imply that one or the other carried the day. On the contrary, both positions proved powerful, and there were others as well, each exerting its own peculiar force in the tense theological field of poetic representation. Vernacular poetry emerged into this field—and into the written record of many of the European languages—in the twelfth and thirteenth centuries, and here we begin to see its practitioners attempting to legitimate their practice within that field. One way they did so, like their contemporary colleagues in the visual arts, was by staging figures of Judaism within the poem itself.

Consider "The Miracles of Our Lady" ("Milagros de Nuestra Señora"), composed by Gonzalo de Berceo (ca. 1195–ca. 1265) just a few decades before Aquinas's quodlibetal critique. Compared to French or German, the Castilian vernacular poetic record emerged relatively late: these poems count among the earliest examples of Spanish verse by a known author. They constitute as well the appearance of a new genre of poetry in that language, a genre called *mester de clerecía* (clerical service, or clerical mastery), presumably because composed by clerics rather than lay troubadours. Distinctive in its form and meter—stanzas consisting of four Alexandrine lines (two heptasyllabic half lines separated by a caesura) united by a common consonantal rhyme—and in its didactic intent, its proclaimed goal was to produce a poetics without sin: "mester es sin pecado" (it is a mastery without sin), as one of Gonzalo's colleagues put it.[21]

And yet Gonzalo is only too well aware of poetry's dangers: so much so that he prefaces his collection with an extended allegory—a dream landscape of visions followed by their explications—on the nature of poetic inspiration. That allegory concludes with an explicit warning about how his poetry should be read:

16: Señores e amigos,   lo que dicho avemos
palavra es oscura,   esponerla queremos;
tolgamos la corteza,   al meollo entremos,
prendamos lo de dentro,   lo de fuera dessemos.

Lords and friends,   what we have said
Is an obscure word   we wish to expound.
Let's cut off the husk   and get to the marrow,
Take what's within,   what's outside discard.

The warning is a standard one in the Christian sciences of interpretation: do not stop (like the Pharisees) at the literal exterior of the word, but penetrate into its spiritual interior. But as Gonzalo's metaphor itself suggests, our apprehension of the spiritual cannot escape carnality, no matter how assiduously we apply this hermeneutics. We always depend on the "thingly," on the fleshy mediation of letters, signs, and symbols. In this particular verse, for example, the inner spiritual meaning of the nut is itself expressed in literal terms as meat and marrow: the metaphor remaps the spirit onto the flesh at the very moment it seeks to separate the two.

Some medieval Christian thinkers about language were willing to exploit the difficulty. This had been Albert of Montecassino's strategy a century before, in his beautiful definition of metaphor: "It is the function of metaphor to twist, so to speak, its mode of speech from its property; by twisting, to make some innovation; by innovating, to clothe, as it were, in nuptial garb; and by clothing, to sell, apparently at a decent price." Albert delights in flirting with what he hints is the essential fraudulence of every linguistic contract, every claim to equivalence. But Gonzalo's goal is very different. In order to defend his poetic practice, he tries to overcome the "fraudulence" of the symbolic economies his poetics depends on, rather than surrendering to it. He does so by deploying Jews as figures of false mediation, figures whose constant contrast with the Christian is meant to establish a strong difference between "Christian" and "Jewish" communication and exchange.[22]

Time after time Gonzalo juxtaposes Jews with Christians. In "The Debt Repaid" ("La deuda pagada," miracle 23), for example, he opposes

Jewish moneylender with Christian merchant in order to demonstrate the difference between "Jewish" and "Christian" attitudes toward money, profit, and the economic sphere of circulation. A Christian burgher of Constantinople, seeking to "rise to high price" ("sober en grant preçio," "el su preçio creçer"—that is, metaphorically, to increase in worth and esteem), gives away money to anyone who asks. Finally bankrupted by the profligacy of his gifts and unable to borrow from anyone else, he finds a Jew willing to lend with no other guarantor than a statue of Virgin and Child. The merchant invests the Jew's money on many ventures and makes great profit, but because of his sins he forgets the repayment date. When he suddenly remembers the obligation the day before it is due, he finds himself far abroad. Despairing, he puts the money into a container that he throws into the sea, while praying to his divine cosigners that the debt be repaid. The chest miraculously makes its way to Constantinople, where it is recovered, delivered to the Jew, and safely stored under his bed. Yet when the Christian returns to town, the devious Jew claims to have received nothing and that the debt is still outstanding. The merchant calls upon the images to testify on his behalf, and Jesus announces that all should look beneath the bed, where the money is found to the Jew's chagrin and conversion.

Through stories such as these Gonzalo seeks to emancipate the Christian from the Judaizing power of the flesh and its needs in this material world. The burgher may become rich by buying low and selling high, "according to the law of merchants," as the poet puts it (and note that *lei*, "law," is a word that also means religion in medieval Castilian), but despite this willing and profitable participation in a materialistic law he remains a Christian, his treasure in some sense stored in heaven. It is by heightening the contrast between the Christian's participation in the world and that of some wicked figure of Judaism that the poet seeks the wages of Christianity: the salvific relief of difference.

In the case of "The Debt Repaid" that difference is explored in terms of relation to symbolic mediators of value (money) and of the divine (devotional images). Other miracles in Gonzalo's collection explore other types of mediation, such as the miracle of Theophilus (miracle 24), in which the power brokers of Christian courts are contrasted with

Jews as power brokers of Satan and his polity.[23] All these figures of Judaism have a long history, and a long future (we will return to Theophilus and political mediation in the next chapter). But all of them, in a poet's hands, also do the work of poetry, for the constant contrast is meant to carve out a Christian zone of mediation in which communication and exchange, which is also to say poetics, can take shape protected from the threat of Judaizing that haunts aesthetics in a Pauline world.

The technique here is similar to what I loosely termed "projective identification" in the previous chapter: a negative potential is split off and projected away from the Christian and into a figure of Judaism. In Gonzalo's case the strategy is meant to produce poems that can lead the communicant, both poet and audience, toward eternal life. That claim and its attendant difficulties are performed in the prayer with which Gonzalo concludes his collection: "Madre, del tu Golzalvo seï remembrador / que de los tos miraclos fue enterpretador" (Mother, be mindful of your Gonzalo / of your miracles the interpreter) (911 ab).[24]

The prayer proposes a deal: the Virgin's memory and mercy in exchange for the poet's interpretation of her miracles. But this prayerful proposal cannot quell the perils of poetry, which entrap even the poem's last words. *Enterpretador*, "interpreter," never quite escapes its stigmatizing pseudoetymological roots in the Latin *inter+praestare* and *inter+pretium*, "interloaning," with their hints of mediation, usury, and fraud. (The etymological roots are no less stigmatizing for being obscure.)[25] Within a Pauline and Augustinian ontology in which every encounter with a sign, symbol, or thing has the potential to ensnare the soul in Judaizing, how can allegory or anti-Jewish projection ever guarantee a Christian poetics free from "Judaism"?

One way to confront this problem is by intensifying the projection. This was the strategy adopted by King Alfonso X of Castile and his group of poets, artists, and scribes who assembled, shortly after Gonzalo, their illuminated compendium of poetry and song, the *Cantigas de Santa María* (Songs of Holy Mary). Even more than Gonzalo's collection (from which they may well have borrowed), the hundreds of poems that appeared under the learned king's patronage are littered with Jews. In the previous chapter we saw how some of these songs marked the Jew as enemy of Christian images, and in the next we will meet the *Cantigas'* Jews as enemies of Christian politics. But perhaps the governing enmity in this massive compendium is the one that justifies the entire project: the enmity between Christian poetry and Judaism.

Alfonso's collection begins as Gonzalo's ended: with a prayer. The prologue explains that the composition of good poetry requires art and judgment, as well as divine aid. The princely poet promises to deploy his skills not in praise of "other ladies," as many troubadours do, but only of the Virgin Mary. In exchange he asks that, if his songs be pleasing to her, she reward him with "the reward she gives to those she loves." "He who has this assurance will gladly sing for her."

And yet this assurance seems difficult to come by. One symptom of the insecurity is that so many of the collection's early songs are focused on the dangers of Judaism. The opening pages of the *Cantigas* in all their various recensions are replete with anti-Jewish narratives. They begin (Cantiga 2) with a story about how the Virgin rewarded Alfonso's patron and inspiration, Saint Ildefonso of Toledo, for preaching against the Jews of Visigothic Spain, some six hundred years before Alfonso's reign. They continue (Cantiga 3) through the Theophilus story we've already encountered in Gonzalo de Berceo, and then linger (Cantiga 4) on an account of a Jewish father throwing his son into a burning oven because the boy had followed a school friend to church, where he had seen a vision of the Virgin and Child and been inspired to take communion.

The poetic stakes in these opening salvos against the Jews become more explicit if we contrast two of these early *cantigas*. Cantiga 8 (figure 2.1) invites the clerical critics of poetry into the anthology. It tells the story of a troubadour (whom it names as Pedro of Sieglar) who concluded his poem to a statue of the Virgin with a request: "Oh glorious one, if you are pleased by these songs of mine, give us a candle so that we may dine." Immediately a candle descends upon his fiddle, but a Benedictine monk (judging by the habit) snatches it out of his hand: "You are an enchanter and we shall not let you have it." The minstrel repeats the lay, and the miracle is repeated as well, but the monk again seizes the candle, threatening to accuse the poet of sorcery. A third time the miracle occurs, and this time the audience intervenes on the poet's

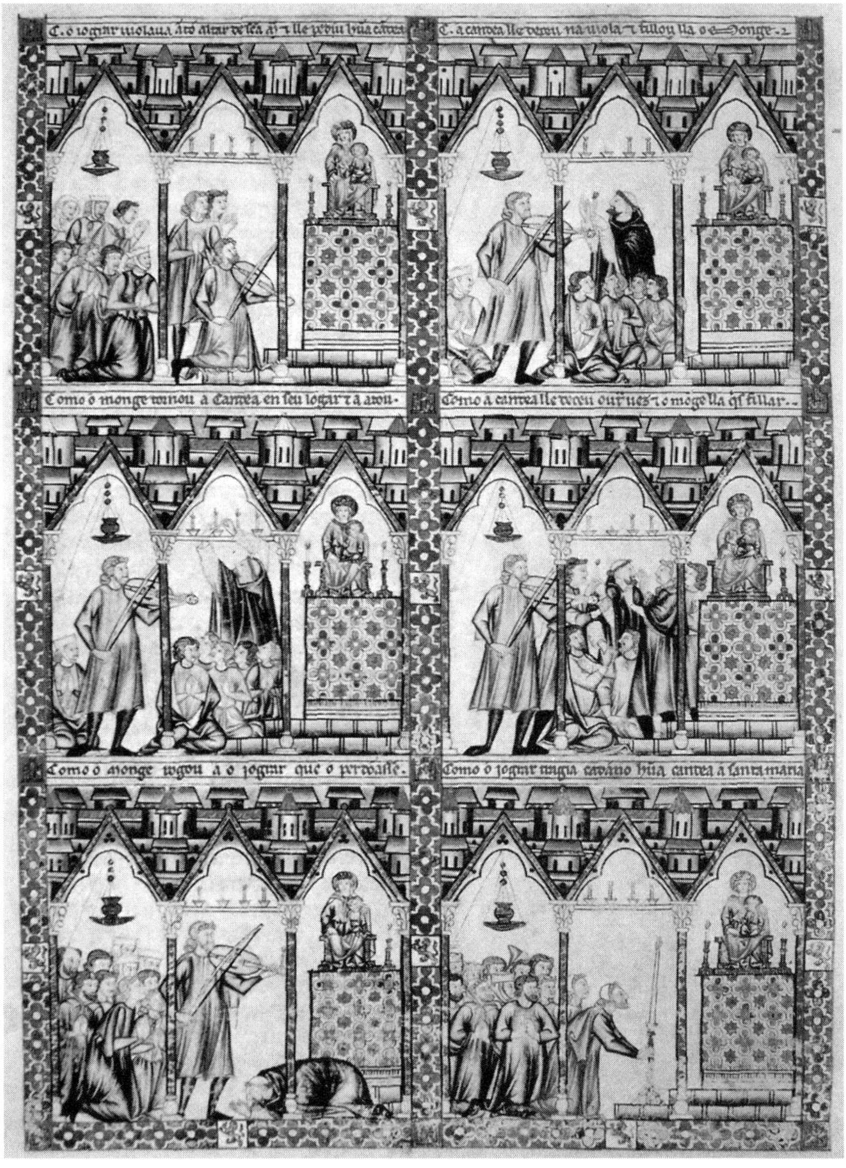

FIGURE 2.1

Cantigas de Santa María,

Cantiga 8, Escorial, MS. T.I.1, folio 15v.

PHOTO COURTESY OF EDILÁN-ARS LIBRIS.

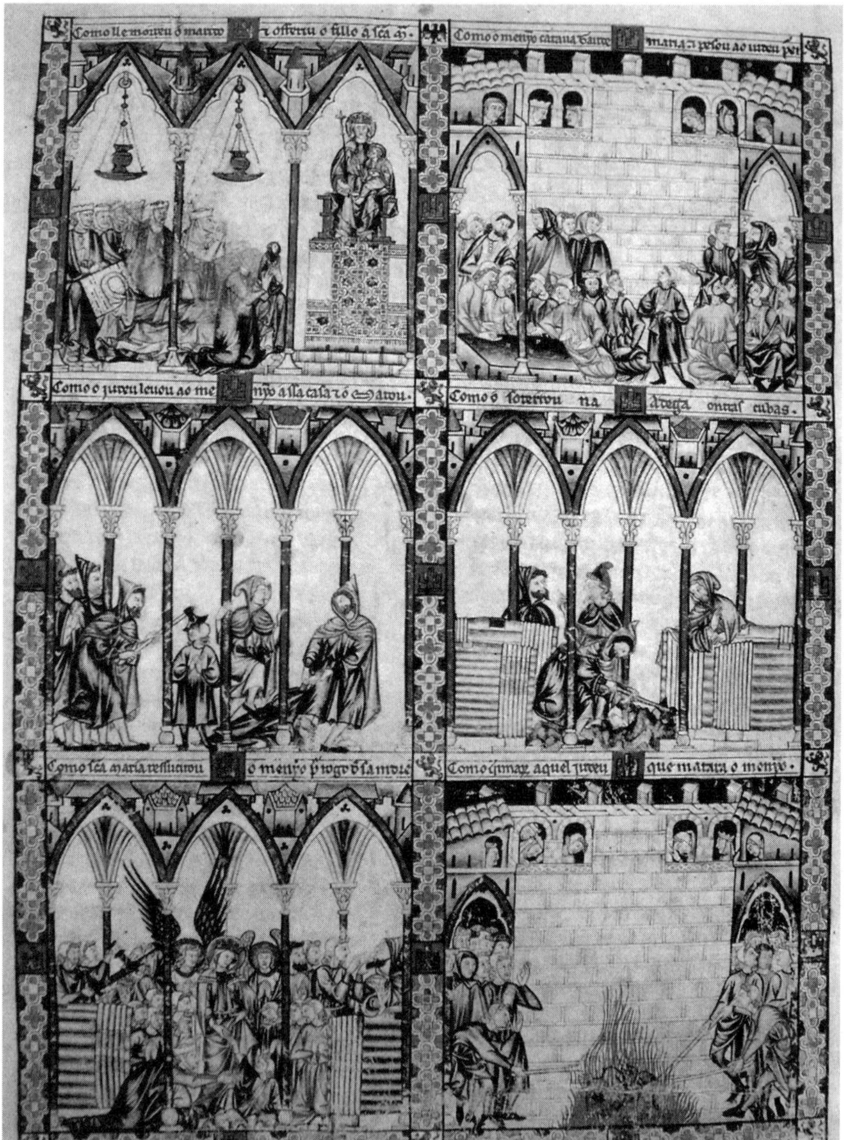

FIGURE 2.2

Cantigas de Santa María,

Cantiga 6, Escorial, MS. T.I.1, folio 13v.

PHOTO COURTESY OF EDILÁN-ARS LIBRIS.

behalf, at which point the monk prostrates himself, realizes his error, and converts, so to speak, to poetry.

Here poetry's ecclesiastical foes—think, for example, of the Dominican Thomas Aquinas—are engaged directly, represented as erring Christians. Cantiga 6 sketches a different approach (see figure 2.2). The song begins with a guarantee of truth: "Concerning this, the sacred writings, which neither lie nor err, tell us a great miracle performed in England by the Holy Virgin Mary, with whom the Jews have a great quarrel because Jesus Christ, who reproves them, was born of Her." The miracle concerns the son of a beggar widow: "The boy was wonderfully gifted and handsome and very quick at learning all he heard. Furthermore he sang so well, sweetly, and pleasantly, that he excelled everyone in his land and beyond."

The *cantiga* foregrounds the material wages of poetic mimesis, presenting the boy as a successful professional: "Mother, in all frankness, I advise you that from now on you cease to beg, for Holy Mary gives you all that you wish through me. Let Her provide, for She is very generous." All were pleased by his art and rewarded him, "except the Jew, who hated him for it," murdered him with an axe, and secretly buried the body. But the Virgin resurrects her young troubadour, making him sing from the grave so that all the town's Christians are drawn to the spot. They remove the boy from his grave, learn from him what had happened, and promptly kill all the town's Jews.

A double defense of poetry is being staged in this striking story. On the one hand the Jewish ritual murder of the child-poet is used to align the poet of the *Cantigas* with Christ, persecuted by the Jews. On the other the story aligns the critics of poetry with the Jews—who crucified Jesus because they blindly perceived only his carnality, and not his divinity—and fantasizes their extermination. It is difficult to imagine a more "projectively anti-Jewish" defense of poetry. And indeed Alfonso was not shy about his claims in favor of his own verse. Cantiga 70, for example, is a "song of praise of Saint Mary, about how she was greeted by the angel," as the first line announces. But the image is not of the Annunciation's Archangel Gabriel but of King Alfonso, presenting the Virgin with a scroll of his verses (see figure 2.3). It is difficult to miss, in

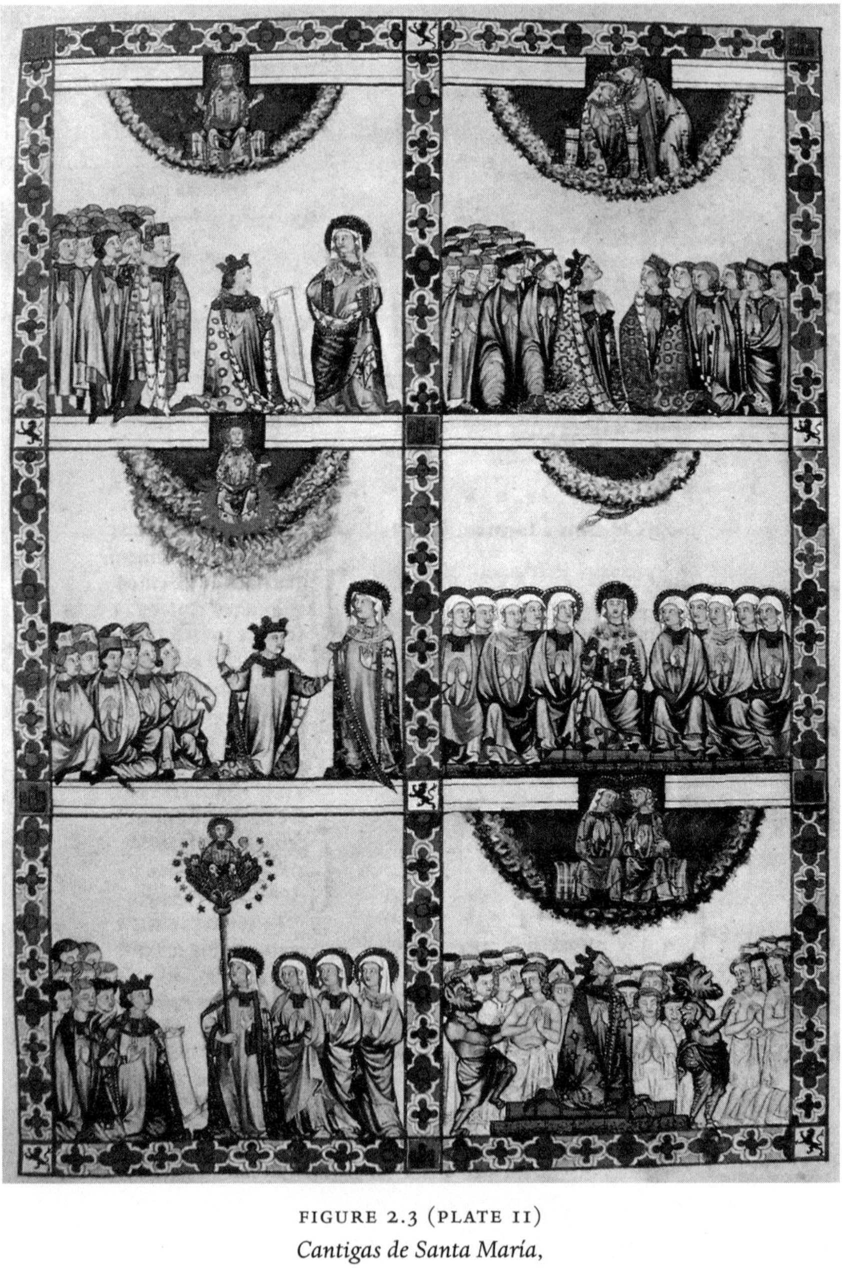

FIGURE 2.3 (PLATE II)
Cantigas de Santa María,
Cantiga 70, Escorial, MS. T.I.1, folio 118r.
PHOTO COURTESY OF EDILÁN-ARS LIBRIS.

this and the other illuminations to the song, the various and overdetermined claims to intimacy—sacred, erotic, poetic—being staged by the king and his scriveners.[26]

Alfonso was perhaps overly optimistic. As we have already seen in the case of painting, the technique of projection has no floor: an anti-Jewish defense of poetry, even one like Alfonso's that appeals to liturgical mimesis, can itself in turn be condemned as hypermimetic or excessively sensual, and thereby Judaized. Some poets (like some painters) realized this themselves and put the inescapable risk of Judaism to work. A prominent albeit anonymous example, from the same Castilian time and space as the *Cantigas*, is the Spanish version of the medieval Alexander the Great romances known as the *Libro de Alexandre* (Book of Alexander).

This poem too begins with a statement of its Christian bona fides:

> 2. Mester trayo fermoso, non es de joglería;
> mester es sin pecado, qua es de clerecía.
>
> A beautiful service I bring, not that of the jongleurs;
> it is a service without sin, for it is of the clerisy.

But unlike Gonzalo or Alfonso, the anonymous Alexander author seems to recognize that no amount of projection can purge representation, whether linguistic or pictorial, of its Judaism.

One of the places this awareness emerges is in the character of Apelles, a figure understood by many scholars as the poet's alter ego because of his explicit role as master of representation. Within the poem Apelles is in the first place a painter, as was in fact the Hellenistic historical personage Apelles of Kos (known to us and to the Middle Ages primarily through Pliny the Elder's much later report). In the *Libro de Alexandre* he decorates the hero's tents with historical and morally instructive murals. These paintings are ekphrastically presented within the poem as, on the one hand, providing a pictorial narration of history and, on the other, commenting on the temporal, spatial, and ethical limits of the empire Alexander aspires to. We might say that Apelles is a composite figure, playing multiple roles. He is first of all the historical figure of Apelles of Kos. But he is also described in the poem as if he were, like the poet himself, a Christian carrying out moral instruction: "A well-lettered cleric, / he had his entire ministry well decorated." Finally he is repeatedly identified in the poem—perhaps because of a confusion with the character of Apelles Hebreus in one of Horace's Satires—as "Apelles the Jew." Without any apology the Christian poet casts the master of mimesis within his own work as a Jew, and thereby seems to acknowledge the badge as his own.[27]

Just as extraordinary as the Jewishness of the painter in the *Libro* is that of the hero, Alexander himself. The danger is foregrounded at two moments in the hero's career: his childhood and his death. As a child, we are told, "he had such a sharp intellect and so subtle a heart" that a rumor spread that he was not the son of King Philip but of his tutor Nectanebo: "Because of his subtle intellect that mastered so much, / they said that he was similar to Master Nectanebo / and it was loudly bruited about that he was his son." In other European literary traditions Nectanebo is indeed presented as the father of Alexander, having used his magical arts to inseminate Alexander's mother, Olympia (readers looking for a graphic illustration of the scene may turn to Vincent of Beauvais's *Speculum historiale*, Bibliothèque Nationale de France, ms. fr. 50, 120v). Two dangers are being staged in these stanzas. The first is the obvious one of illegitimacy. But the second is a subtler one, of *subtlety* itself. The word, with its accompanying overtones of intellect and learning, was often enough associated with Judaism. The problem here is Alexander's thirst for knowledge, and his pride in the power of his own intelligence. Later in the book God, Mother Nature, and Satan will together condemn Alexander to death for this subtlety and its accompanying "*sobervia*" (pride). But here, at the book's beginning, Alexander attempts to solve the stigma of his intellect the way every hero should: he throws his tutor from the high tower on which they are stargazing in pursuit of astronomy, killing the subtle and learned "Jew" into which his studies threaten to convert him.[28]

Tutors are easier to kill than figures of Judaism. In the end it is the Judaism of the letter that kills Alexander, rather than the other way around. Although we moderns think of Alexander as dying from a drinking binge, in the medieval tradition he dies poisoned, in a devious but divinely authorized plan designed around the fact that no human dares try to kill him by the sword. (Jonathan Swift marks a turning point between traditions when, in his *Gulliver's Travels* of 1726, he has Gulliver ask the sorcerer Governor of Glubbdubdrib to summon the shade of Alexander in order to ascertain the mode of his death.) In the *Libro* he is poisoned not once but twice. The first dose comes in a chalice of wine. The second comes when Alexander, realizing he has just drunk poison, calls for an antidote, a feather or quill with which to make himself vomit:

> Metío el rey la peñola por amor de tornar. . . . [2617]

The line is untranslatable into English without tremendous loss. "The king inserted the quill, for love of . . ." *tornar*, which here means vomiting, turning, re-turning, converting, all in one. The vocabulary of love and conversion here is meant to remind us that not only a life but also a Christian ontology are at stake. Alas for Alexander the quill too has been dipped in poison, and this second dose proves fatal:

> No worse a fire could have entered his body,
> It poisoned all the veins it could reach,
> Instead of healing, it made them worse.[29]

In this feather we recognize the implement of the poet. And in its poison, the fear of every Christian writer: the fear that, no matter how much he tries to exorcise the "Judaism" that haunts his practice, his letters can still kill what they promise to vivify. This is in fact the moral with which the poem concludes its several thousand stanzas—that every impulse toward beauty can prove toxic to the Christian in this material world:

> The glory of this world, whoever wants to think rightly
> Must value no more than the flower in the field.
> For just when a man believes himself to be safest,
> It casts him down head-first, into the worst of places.[30]

Poetics of Conversion

Where Alexander's conversion failed, others succeeded. In the previous chapter we already encountered the thousands of refugees from Judaism whose entrance into Iberian Christian society began in 1391. We saw how that spiritual migration changed the ways in which Christians debated the "Jewishness" of Christian art, and the ways in which that art represented Jews. Spanish poetry, too, was transformed by the mass conversions, and we are fortunate to have a beautiful witness to the early stages of those transformations in a Castilian poetry collection called the *Cancionero de Baena*. Compiled by an otherwise obscure man called Juan Alfonso de Baena, the anthology contains some six hundred poems composed in the courts of four Castilian kings, beginning shortly before 1391 and concluding shortly after 1430, right when we see the first outbreaks of violence and discriminatory legislation against the converts or New Christians.

The collection is sometimes called the first "critical anthology" of Castilian poetry, because each poem is preceded by a short editorial introduction noting merits and demerits, and the whole is prefaced with a meditation on poetry's function and the nature of the poet's art.[31] But what is immediately striking for our purposes is that the *Cancionero*'s poets, nearly all Christian, are constantly defaming one another, and the accusation of Jewishness is prominent among their charges. They accuse one another of Jewish ancestry, of having too small a foreskin or too big a nose, of heterosexual and homosexual intercourse with Jews. The editor Juan Alfonso himself engaged heartily in this jousting. And indeed the collection includes many poems that insult him. His birthplace of Baena is impugned in one poem as a land where "much good eggplant" is grown, another mocks him for having "eyes of eggplant," yet another of eating *adefyna* (a Sephardic stew sometimes prepared for Sabbath), these all being dishes associated with Jews in Castilian culinary and literary culture. Other poets refer to his "bath in the water of holy baptism" or to his sexual encounters with Jews both male and female. The Mariscal Íñigo de Astuñiga, for example, claims that Baena is stuffed full of Jewish sperm.[32]

Modern scholars have deduced from such accusations that if a poet is attacked as Judaizing, or betrays any knowledge of Judaism, then he must be a New Christian. The result of such logic is the conviction that, as one critic put it already in 1871, the *Cancionero* is full of "half-converted Jews." [33]Yet in many cases where we have found further, non-poetic evidence about the poets, they turn out not to be converts or descendants of converts. They are in fact Old Christians.[34] The poets of the *Cancionero* accuse one another so often of Judaism not because they are Jews but because they are poets devising a novel defense of their practice against contemporary divines who were preaching the dangers of poetry.[35]

Of those there were plenty. Perhaps the most distinguished was Alonso de Cartagena, bishop of Burgos and a convert from Judaism, whose impact on fifteenth-century Castilian letters was so great that he was eulogized by a contemporary poet as the Plato of his day. Like a Christian Plato, he would undoubtedly have included the writings of all the *cancionero* poets among those who, as he wrote in the introduction to his translation of Cicero's *De Inventione*, "have no value because of the authority of the individual who produced them, nor have any moral or mythic reason, but only contain what the simple letter signifies."[36] Avila's Bishop Alfonso de Madrigal "el Tostado" was not a New Christian, but his condemnation of poetry was more categorical and more extensive (for he was famously prolific) than that of his converso colleague. Following Thomas Aquinas, el Tostado pointed out that it seemed "repugnant to the dignity and state of holy scripture to paint it with the colors of eloquence," for such color was only necessary to attract weak minds. Hence "the science of lesser value uses more colors of eloquence, as in poetry, which contains fables which are neither true, nor similar to truth, nor worthy in themselves of being heard, but so great is the ingenuity [*ingenio*] of the composition and the smoothness of the sweet words that even the most learned take pleasure in hearing them." Apparently the pious and learned bishop himself struggled with this pleasure, for he recounts successive visions in which he pledges his devotion to a gathered chorus of the muses. In the second vision (written ca. 1450) he confesses to the divine sisters that his soul has become disgusted by poetry, for he has found in it too many lies beautified by makeup. Urania, eldest of the muses, exhorts him to abandon the genre, appropriate only for children, and devote himself to more serious sciences.[37]

Against these clerical criticisms the poets of the *Cancionero* took up many of the weapons we have already encountered, among them theories of "poetic grace" such as Dante's.[38] Two lines of Latin verse scrawled across the top of the first manuscript folio take that position as the collection's starting point: "Unicuique gratia est data / Secundum Paulum relata"; "To each one is grace given / as is in Saint Paul scriven" (a paraphrase of Eph 4:7).[39] The proper use of poetic language, our poets claim, derives from the gift of divine inspiration, and through this inspiration the lay poet, if he is a *good* poet, gained access to spiritual truth.

What Baena and his colleagues need is a critical framework within which to argue about what makes a poem good. This is provided by the prologue to the *Cancionero*, the earliest poetic manifesto surviving in the Castilian language, which gives a long list of prerequisites for poetry. These are (1) the "infused grace of God," (2) knowledge of rules of meter and form, (3) subtle inventiveness, (4) exquisite discretion and judgment, (5) broad reading, (6) knowledge of all languages, (7) familiarity with court life, (8) "*fydalguía*" (nobility) and courtesy, and (9) always seeming to be a lover, loving whom one should, as one should, where one should.

The prerequisites of poetry are here presented as a list of the poet's personal attributes. Conversely, the degree to which a poet possesses these attributes can be diagnosed directly from the poetry he produces. With the poet's state of grace legible in the poetry itself, the poem became a literary marker of its author's place (at the moment of composition) on the continuum between letter and spirit, with the bad poet, the misuser of language, understood as (among other things, and only at the moment of poetic performance) a graceless Jew.

The pages of Baena's *Cancionero* are the lists in which the mettle of each poet and each poem is tested according to this complex standard. Juan Alfonso himself put this wittily in his challenge to the poet Ferrán Manuel de Lando: "Ferrán Manuel, for the public display / of your marvelous skill / in this great court of the King of Castile / Someone must give you a sting." It is out of provocation, according to Baena, that good poetry is born. But the substance of the provocation itself should not be taken to heart: "Ferrán Manuel, since to each / is given [poetic] grace doubled or simple, / don't let your face turn yellow / because my tongue splashes or stains you." Insult is only a picador's prod, meant to stimulate the revelation of a poet's virtues. Its "truth claim" is not to be taken seriously.[40] In this case Ferrán responds with insults, not about Baena's "Jewishness" but about his deficiencies as a lover. Ferrán claims he will have sex with Baena's girlfriend. The exchange escalates along these lines, ending with Baena's (poem 363) assertion that Ferrán's asshole is full of a shepherd's sperm. Confronted with this response, reports the *Cancionero*, Ferrán abandoned the field to Baena.[41]

Here the idiom of poetic criticism is primarily sexual. The idioms are more diverse in the contest that follows, between Baena and the most famous of the *Cancionero* poets, Alfonso Alvarez de Villasandino. Baena opens by challenging this "rotten old man, whose ribs are made of phlegm" to a contest of poetry. Villasandino, in turn, asserts that far from being the "fine troubador" he "pretends" to be, Baena is a "rustic mule" whose "villainy" is marked on his face and in his diet of wine and garlic. He is a "suzio cohino," a dirty Jew pig (the word plays with the proximity between Cohen and *cochino*), with the voice of a cormorant, not a poet. He knows nothing of "this science [of poetry]," and his words are worthless.[42]

This punning neologism "cohino" is redolent with meaning, poetic and ontological. Through the insult the target is charged with pharisaic deceit and false pretension to poetry ("enfinge"). But the charge is no more genealogical than any of the other assertions made in the course of this contest. Baena will respond by calling Villasandino "swine sputum," a drunk, an apostate gambler; Villasandino by calling Baena a bastard and a pig ("tuerto chazino," "gruniente cochino"). These claims drew their meaning and usefulness not from their target's biography but from the rules of the poetic contest in which they were deployed, in which provocation stimulated vulgar poetry, and that poetry revealed the competing poets' relative "state of grace."

This versified vulgarity is, in other words, the critical by-product of our poets' theology, a way of representing their rivals' lack of any one of their multiple prerequisites for poetry. Judaism, poetic incompetence, ignorance, rudeness, sexual deviance, even animality, are all the negative poles of poetic virtues: divine grace, good meter and form, learning, courtly love, and so on. Each of these virtues is closely related to its companions, and expressible almost interchangeably in their terms. The same is true of their attendant vices. The overlapping of these variables made possible a space of play in which claims to poetic or theological "çiençia" could be both made and criticized in a language of extreme carnality. Thus, for example, when Ferrán Manuel de Lando wrote a love poem placing his beloved among the heavenly spheres and treating her as a creature of the moon, Mars, and Venus, Alfonso de Moraña penned a response criticizing the astrological conceit as sinful and asserting that Ferrán would be loved (i.e., sodomized) only by Alfonso's Muslim slave.[43]

Within this system of thought Judaism was a governing insult that carried with it a host of theological, linguistic, and physical implications. The same could be said of other idioms of opprobrium in the *Cancionero*, such as the frequent charges of homosexuality and sodomy, meant to imply that a poet had "never served love."[44] Indeed these idioms were often combined, as when the Franciscan monk and theologian Diego de Valencia wrote a poem, whose rhyme scheme consisted almost entirely of Hebrew words, accusing Juan de Espanha of being a Jew with no testicles. Those critics who have focused on the poem's Hebrew vocabulary in order to argue (mistakenly) that Fray Diego was a convert from Judaism have missed the point.[45] The discourse of Judaism, like that of sexuality or animality, was a language of literary criticism, entirely separable from the genealogy and religious orthodoxy of its object.

The Jewishness of the *Cancionero*'s poetics is the product of a Christian theological linguistics that understood certain aspects of language (ranging from letter and literalism to rhetorical deceit and hypocrisy) in terms of Judaism and Judaizing. Our poets, stimulated by the sociology of a world in which mass conversions had brought Judaism and Christianity into a new proximity, rediscovered the poetic potential of Judaizing and put it to a new kind of work, delighting in the leap from the potential Jewishness of their rivals' language, to the potential Jewishness of their bodies, and exploiting the danger in the thrill ride of a Pauline poetics that threatened every Christian poet with Judaism. Such an approach was dangerous, inasmuch as it put the entire poetic community at risk, but the Judaism it threatened was a fleeting one, lasting only to the end of the poem.

Of course there were others putting Jewishness to different kinds of work and many who argued, with increasing stridency, that the language and the bodies of Christian converts from Judaism and their descendants were in fact essentially different from those of Old Christians, and would remain so forever. The institutions and practices produced by that view, such as the Inquisition and the Statutes of Purity of Blood, also transformed the possibilities for poetry, just as we saw they did for art. Through their efforts to remap Judaism onto the living flesh of converts and their descendants, these institutions and practices combined to make Jewishness too combustible a category for Christian poetics to embrace.

Within a few years of the completion of Baena's *Cancionero*, Castilian poetry turned away from its flirtations with Judaism as a metadiscourse for poetic criticism, and oriented its attention toward segregating the descendants of converts within its ranks. In his youth the convert poet Antón de Montoro had moved in poetic circles like those of Juan Alfonso de Baena, full of hope in the emancipatory power of poetry. By age seventy he claimed to have lost any such hope. In a poem addressed to Queen Isabel the Catholic in the 1470s he complained that, no matter how much he tried to worship and write about Christ and the Virgin, he could never escape "this trace of the convert," this name of "Old faggot Jew."[46]

But within our Pauline framework—"for written letters kill, but the Spirit gives life"—no amount of segregation could protect language from the Judaism of the letter. The attempt to make Judaism genetic had rather the opposite effect, of putting not only poets but all experts in language at heightened risk. This is surely what Rodrigo Manrique—himself the son of an Inquisitor General—meant in 1533 when he wrote to his exiled friend, the famous humanist Juan Luis Vives: "For now it is clear that no one can possess a smattering of letters without being suspect of heresy, error, and Judaism."[47]

The Jew in the English Poem

Once again I have spent too much time in Spain. My lingering there should not suggest that poetry's Jewish questions were particularly Spanish, although they did speak with a special accent there. The previous two sections focused on Castile because in that kingdom we could watch in particular detail the interplay of figures of thought with figures of flesh: the interaction of "Jews" produced from the innards of Christian poetics with actual Jews (or converts from Judaism and their descendants, which are not at all the same thing, it should be stressed!) living within a society. Still we must not forget that, as was also the case with art, the power of Judaizing as a tool of literary criticism did not require the presence of real Jews or of converts from Judaism and their descendants.

It is easy enough to see how poetic Judaism could be produced within a literary culture that had no living Jews within it, no figures of flesh, so to speak, but only of thought. England and English provide a good example, not least because Geoffrey Chaucer (1343–1400), writing when that country had not seen a real Jew for more than a century, turned to the same story of the murdered singing boy that had so attracted King Alfonso the Wise, albeit to make a rather different point. Recall the tale's outline from Cantiga 6: a boy who sings poems to the Virgin Mary is murdered by a Jew, but the corpse continues miraculously to sing, revealing the Jew's crime and God's glory. Alfonso had not invented the story. Like the story of Theophilus and other Marian miracles this one circulated across Europe in many different versions, genres, and languages, including even an Old Norse "Maria's Saga."[48]

In England itself there were multiple versions to be found in sermon collections and miscellanies of miracles. The mid-fourteenth-century Vernon Manuscript, for example, once contained a large number of Marian miracles, but all *except* the ones involving Jews were excised at a later date (probably during the Reformation).[49] The lucky survivors include several miracles we have already encountered in Castilian poetry collections dedicated to the Virgin: the Jewish boy thrown into an oven; Theophilus; the loan made by a Jew to a Christian on surety from the Virgin; as well as a number of others. Among them is the singing boy, accompanied by a fascinating pictorial narration of the murder and the miracle. But the most famous version of the story does not come from a collection of Marian miracles, and is unaccompanied by illumination: it is the one Chaucer penned as the Prioress's contribution to his *Canterbury Tales*.

The Prioress's tale is widely studied today, often with a view to understanding how Chaucer and his society thought about Jews and Judaism. Those questions are important, but we should not forget the obvious: *The Canterbury Tales* are not (or not only) a sociological or theological inquiry but rather an exploration of the act and the place of poetry. Their central topic is not the power of God or of the Virgin but rather the power of poetry to represent the world, a power that includes representing the poet as subject in the world.

The divine is certainly present, perhaps even omnipresent, in *The Canterbury Tales*, and there are miracle stories among them, most notably the Prioress's and the Second Nun's tales. But those miracle stories presumably do a different kind of work than they did in collections like the Vernon Manuscript or the *Cantigas de Santa María*, in which divine patronage provided the poet a first line of defense against the charge of worldliness.[50]

Consider the tale preceding the Prioress's in the section of Chaucer's poetic pilgrimage known to specialists as Fragment VII.[51] The "Shipman's Tale" presents a world full of ungodly loves: a merchant who would rather "plough" his money than have intercourse with his spouse; a duplicitous and horny monk; a wife who claims her marriage "debt" through quasi prostitution. Money, words, and sexual intercourse are deliberately intertwined in a comedy of adultery that nevertheless seems to end in confused but virtuous mercantile and marital concord: a concord that is itself presented as a metaphor for the poetic project of the *Tales* themselves:

> Ye han mo slakkere dettours than am I!
> For I wol paye yow wel and redily
> Fro day to day, and if so be I faille,

I am youre wyf; score it upon my taille
. . . .
And for I have bistowed it so weel
For youre honour, for Goddes sake, I seye,
As be nat wrooth, but lat us laughe and pleye.
. . . .
"Now wyf," he seyde, "and I foryeve it thee;
But, by thy lyf, ne be namoore so large.
Keep bet thy good, this yeve I thee in charge."
Thus endeth my tale, and God us sende
Taillynge ynough unto oure lyves ende. Amen[52]

Far from any fantasy of poetic salvation, tale, tail, and teller (which is to say money counter as well as narrator) are here consigned through sexual pun into perpetual embrace among the many confusions of the material world.[53]

Compared to this sexualized poetics, that of the Prioress which follows could not be more different. She begins her prologue with all the pious formulas we have already encountered in Christian poetry, first invoking the name of God and then professing her helplessness, and that of all humanity, to compose a poem adequate to the divine: "ther may no tonge expresse in no science." Before this task the Prioress stands, she says, "But as a child of twelf month oold, or lesse." She therefore asks the Virgin to guide "my song that I shal of yow seye" (lines 481*ff.*). The Prioress as poet presents herself as merely a vessel for the voice of Mary as muse.

The same is true of the tale's hero, the little singing boy. In the *Cantigas*, the boy had known full well how to deploy his skill, and even how to earn a living by it. The Middle English version of the Vernon Manuscript also highlights the child-poet's commercial success, having him each day bring home the poetic bacon, so to speak:

Þe Childes moder was wont to a-byde
Euery day til þe Non-tyde,
Þen was he wont to bringe heom mete,
Such as he mihte wiþ his song gete. (55–58)

Chaucer's child, on the other hand, is innocent of all exchange. He does not yet know how to read, and indeed he does not even know the meaning of the Latin words he chants from a Marian hymn ("Alma redemptoris"), since he has learned them by rote from an older schoolboy: "Noght wiste he what this Latyn was to seye, / For he so yong and tendre was of age." In the Prioress's version this innocence is invoked as the foundation for a miracle: "O grete God, that parfournest thy laude / By mouth of innocentz, lo, heere thy myght!" And with that invocation of the mouth of babes, the dead boy "with throte ykorven"—with slit throat—begins to sing.

Much has been made of the type of spirituality that the Prioress seems to advocate in her tale: one of routinized performance rather than understanding, ignorance and repetition rather than learning and artfulness. But we should not forget that there is also a hypermimetic poetics of innocence on offer, in extreme contrast and antidote to the Shipman's sensual pun and play. The Prioress presents herself as an example (like her child hero) of a Christian poet capable, through liturgical mimicry and anti-Jewish projection, of producing salvific, even miraculous, poetry.

This does not mean that Chaucer as author endorses the poetics his creature advocates. It would be surprising if a poet so insistent on representing his own presence within his work championed a poetics of quasi-liturgical repetition. What room would remain in such a poetics for the authorial "I" that surfaces already at the very beginning of the pilgrimage in the General Prologue: "In southwerk at the tabard as I lay"? (line 20) Far from endorsing the view of Christian poetry embodied in the Prioress, Chaucer does what we have already seen so many other poets do to poetics they do not condone: he condemns it as Jewish in order to make room for his own view of Christian poetry.

There are hints of this condemnation within the tale itself, but hints become howls outside the frame of her "composition," in the description of the Prioress that the poet/narrator provides in his General Prologue.[54] The lines (118–62) of the narrator's description alternate between explicitly aesthetic praise and implied moral critique. The poet's attraction to his subject's surfaces is obvious: her smile "ful symple and coy"; her singing of the divine service; her French spoken "ful faire and fetisly"; her table manners and her breast free of food stains; her courtliness; her outward displays of sympathy, conscience, and emotion; her face and body; even her jewelry—all these are lovingly described by the narrator. But each sensuous appreciation undercuts itself. She swears oaths despite her coy simplicity; her liturgy is "entuned in hir nose" (whether this is praise or blame is not clear, but it is certainly inappropriate as the focal point of liturgical attention); her French accent is bad; her courtliness is false ("countrefete cheere / of court"); not people but pets are the objects of her conscience and tender heart.[55] And if the narrator's attention to her figure and form is unseemly in its erotic aesthetics, she has herself invited that attention through the brooch she wears: a quote from the Roman poet Ovid, inscribed in gold: "Amor vincit Omnia" (love conquers all).

Some scholars have noted this oscillation between aesthetic praise and moral critique, and others have attempted to deny it. (Nineteenth-century scholars were fond of insisting, for example, that there is nothing inappropriate in the Prioress's jewelry, since love is a Christian virtue).[56] What is not noted is how thoroughly the oscillation Judaizes the Prioress. Her emphasis on appearances, on the outer form rather than the inner truth, aligns her entirely with hypocrites, rabbis, and Pharisees in the Christian imagination. Consider just these four lines of the General Prologue devoted to the care with which the Prioress wipes her lips at every meal:

> In curteisie was set ful muchel hir lest.
> Hir over-lippe wyped she so clene
> That in hir coppe ther was no ferthyng sene
> Of grece, whan she dronken hadde hir draughte. (132–35)

Perhaps we are not justified in hearing hints of a resonance between the "grece" (grease) that is nowhere to be found in the Prioress's cup and the Christian "grace" whose absence would be utterly damning. But who among the gospeled would fail to note the echo with Jesus' words of woe? "Blind Pharisee! Clean the inside of cup and dish first so that it and the outside are both clean" (Matt. 23:26).

The gap suggested both in the tale and the General Prologue between "appearance" and "reality," between true grace and grace of the flesh, between rote repetition and understanding, suggests that Chaucer's choice of the Jews as the villains of the Prioress's tale is meaningful. It is the Jews who represent, to Chaucer as to any medieval Christian audience, the dangers of excessive attachment to flesh, of an inability to understand the true meaning of their own texts, of slavishly repetitive devotion to an empty ceremonial practice. The Prioress's tale deploys every medieval strategy for casting the Jew as archenemy of Christian piety and poetry. But these anti-Jewish strategies are deployed in the service of a devotional attitude and a poetics that Chaucer himself depicts as overroutinized and carnal. There is therefore a good deal of irony in the story chosen for her: through the performance of her tale the Prioress approaches those she detests.

The example of Chaucer helps us see that the utility of Judaism for poetry is not strictly a Spanish but a pan-European phenomenon, and that it does not require living Jews in order to thrive. Perhaps more important, Chaucer's example reminds us that in poetry as in painting, the techniques of projection I've been describing have no floor. The "Prioress's Tale" deployed anti-Jewish projection in order to propose what we might call a conservative Christian poetics, one that limited the poet to the repetition of literal forms divinely endorsed through scripture, liturgy, or miracle. (We are not too far from the thought of Saint Thomas Aquinas.) The General Prologue deploys anti-Jewish projection in order to reject the Prioress's poetics as itself pharisaic, a Jewish adherence to appearance, rote ritual, and ceremony.

All this tells us very little about Chaucer's attitudes toward real Jews (who, to repeat, had all been expelled from England in the late thirteenth century). He may or may not believe that Jews murder Christian children, or persecute Christian poets. But it tells us a great deal about Judaism as a tool for the poet, and about poetry's Jewish problem. The Prioress's anti-Jewish defense of poetry (one closely related to Alfonso X's defense utilizing the same story) can itself in turn be condemned as hypermimetic and Jewish. Insofar as every Christian poetics (like every Christian piety) depends on letter and mimesis, the potential always exists for it to be criticized in terms of Judaism, a criticism that can expand the space available for the play of poetry in the world just as much as it can constrain it.

Alas, the space available for chapters is more difficult to expand. Had we but page enough and time, we could follow the work done by Judaism across the world of English letters as it was transformed by the discovery of new pieties (like Protestantism), new genres (such as theater), and new practices (such as commerce, law, politics). Such a voyage would help us understand why playwrights like Christopher Marlowe (1564–1593), William Shakespeare (1564–1616), and many others chose to explore the perils and opportunities of the new poetic and dramatic business in which they were engaged through powerful figures of Judaism such as Barrabas and Shylock, despite the centuries-long absence of real Jews from their societies. Such figures of Judaism were useful for the new theater precisely because it was through such figures that these precocious theatrical impresarios and their audiences had learned to think about theatricality itself: that is, about the inescapable need and the inescapable danger of figural representation in the material world. But since I have written about Shakespeare elsewhere, I will here say no more.[57]

The history of these explorations would also help explain why Judaism's literary utility seems to have expanded in English letters even as its reality receded into an ever more distant past. Thinking with Judaism was not—or not only—a way of thinking about Jews in early modern England. It was also a way of thinking about the relationship of the Christian subject to language, to the material world, to the rest of humanity, and to God. This utility only increased as debates about the nature of those relationships sharpened in an increasingly sectarian world divided between Catholics and Protestants of many stripes, a world in which even atheisms and materialisms were becoming broadly conceivable. In the light of such a history we can better understand why Judaism was such a key term in the discourses that England's poets developed for criticizing their own practices. The Protestant George Herbert put it well in 1633, some two decades before the readmission of "real" Jews to England, in a poem revealingly entitled "Self Condemnation":

> He that doth love, and love amisse,
> This worlds delights before true Christian joy,
> Hath made a Jewish choice.
> . . . He hath made a sorrie wedding
> Between his soul and gold . . .
> And is a Judas-Jew.

Such texts may deserve a place in histories of anti-Judaism. But they deserve one as well, too often overlooked, in the history of how poetry learned to think about itself.[58]

"Jewgreek is greekjew": In Search of Synthesis

Once we begin to think of Judaism not only as a religious identity but also as a quality of the Christian poet, we start finding it not only in English or Spanish but everywhere. Often the allusions seem isolated or unsystematic, as when the Italian poet (and friend of Titian) Pietro Aretino boasted in 1531 that he had called his rival Antonio Brocardo a Jew for disagreeing with Pietro Bembo's (1470–1547) rules for correct versification, after which Brocardo promptly died of rage. But even through such seemingly idiosyncratic outbursts we can see a "secular" (but nevertheless Christian) poetics emerging, understanding itself, and legitimating itself within Christian (even when professedly secular) theories of language and systems of critical thought that put all poetry at risk of "Judaism."[59]

There were many such systems of critical thought. From the early modern period, for example, we might focus on the Jansenist Catholic logicians and linguists of Port-Royal whom we met in the previous chapter, Antoine Arnauld and Pierre Nicole. Their *Logic, or the Art of Thought* of 1662, together with the earlier, accompanying *Grammar* of 1660, reshaped the intellectual landscape in significant ways, but it was quite "traditional" in the antipharisaic forms of its linguistic criticism. "The world values most things by the exterior alone, since we find scarcely any who penetrate to the interior and to the foundations of them." "All exterior things are but equivocal signs." "Accuracy of language, the use of figures, are to eloquence what color is to painting: its lowest and most material part." It would be easy enough to follow the development of these forms through the early history of cultural critique, for they were widely deployed by the most influential French writers on poetry, painting, theater, and even politics: figures such as Fénelon and Diderot, pioneers in what we today call "critical" writing about literature, theater, and art.[60]

François de Salignac de la Mothe-Fénelon, for example, was bishop of Cambrai and tutor to the eldest son of Louis XIV. He was no Jansenist, but he too advocated a self-negating style of representation, a striving after immediacy that would overcome the worldly alienation of the post-lapsarian soul and lead to a *pur amour*, a pure love of God "untainted by all self-concern." Representation that strives after truth must overcome self-love, self-interest, concupiscence, and all other false loves of the world. Fénelon's concerns extended to all forms of representation, including painting and poetry, and indeed he sometimes conflated the two, as here, where his favorite painters provide a positive role model for the writer: "One should write as the Raphaels, the Carracci, and the Poussins painted: not for the sake of seeking marvelous fancies and to have one's imagination admired through virtuosity with the brush, but for the sake of painting after nature." In order for any representation to serve the "salvation" of its audience rather than the "vainglory" of its author, in order for it to make its object present in the mind of the other, it must suppress all reference to the artfulness of its own mediation: "The poet disappears: we see only what he makes us see, and we hear only those he lends a voice to. That is the power of imitation and painting."[61]

Fénelon is but one of many conduits through which Christian ideas about love, grace, and the overcoming of the worldly entered into the aesthetic theories of the French Enlightenment. Delightful as it would be to trace the slow drip of transcendence into the critical thought of even the most radical members of that fraternity, we must leap into the modern. For that the philosopher Hegel can again serve, since his dialectical history of the unfolding of the human spirit proved so influential for the development of modern aesthetics. Perhaps because of the pervasiveness of that very influence we often forget how incarnational this dialectical history was, its evolving interrelation of spirit and matter explicitly patterned on the divine assumption of material form in the person of Jesus Christ.

As we learned in the previous chapter, Hegel understood art (and religion) as the historically evolving product of the human need to picture truth, the human dependence upon images and representations. This dependence on "pictorial thought" was for Hegel (as it had been for scholastics like Thomas Aquinas) a kind of unfreedom from which neither art nor religion could ever escape, but despite this imperfection, art (and religion) teaches the human what freedom looks like by giving it sensuous expression. In other words, art (like religion) depends upon sensuous expression to point us toward freedom, but within the governing aesthetics of transcendence, this same dependence limits the freedom that art and religion can produce. Only Hegel's own speculative philosophy can provide—through its pure conceptual clarity—true freedom, the culmination of the human spirit's understanding of itself.[62]

Hegel's history and taxonomy of the different kinds of art (and religion) were designed to show that these different types were age appropriate to different human societies at different stages in the unfolding of the spirit. Hegel's historicism here sounds a bit like Paul's divine pedagogy: "I fed you with milk and not solid food, for you were not yet able to take it" (1 Cor 3:2). And just as religion had evolved across the stages of human history (a process that for Hegel had more or less culminated in Lutheran Christianity), art too progressed, learning (often enough from religion) how to achieve a synthesis of the spiritual and material capable of producing a sensuous manifestation that, for all its sensuousness, nevertheless pointed beyond itself in order to stimulate consciousness of the spirit's freedom.

Within this taxonomy of arts, poetry was the "most perfect," "the absolute and true art of the spirit and its expression as spirit," "in its content . . . the richest and most unrestricted of the arts." By this Hegel meant, among other things, that whereas painting and sculpture appealed entirely to the eye, and music, at the other extreme, was entirely abstract, poetry had concrete content, but for the imagination rather than the eyes and ears. This meant that poetry could be at once the most particular and concrete of the arts and the most free and unrestricted: precisely the kind of Christological synthesis we should expect Hegel to praise.[63]

But note how this taxonomy of the arts intersects with Hegel's taxonomy of religions. Both Judaism and Islam were religions that lacked, according to Hegel, an incarnational synthesis of nature and spirit. In Hegel's Judaism the only free spiritual subject was the creator God, who transcends the created world of finitude and cannot become manifest within it (witness the Second Commandment). Everything finite, including and above all the human, exists in only a "negative" relation of absolute servitude to this God. Hence there can be neither art nor beauty nor love nor freedom in Judaism. And surely there can be no poetry, since a positive relation to the concrete is precisely what makes poetry the "most perfect art."[64]

The same was true for Islam, which was understood by Hegel and many others of his day as a type of Jewish disinterest in the created world, an enthusiastic subjection of the individual to a transcendent God: "This enthusiasm was a fanaticism, that is, an enthusiasm for something abstract—for an abstract thought which sustains a negative position toward the established order of things. It is the essence of fanaticism to bear only a desolating destructive relation to the concrete." If the goal of the art of poetry was to point to freedom through the concrete, then no one with a "destructive relation to the concrete" could be a poet. Hegel was aware that Islam had produced great poetry, poetry so great that it had inspired the verse of his own hero, the German poet Goethe (whose *West-Eastern Diwan* was published in 1819). He explained this as a fleeting historical accident. The initial fanaticism produced by Islam's complete submission to the One God had made it temporarily capable of exemplary martyrdoms, conquests, and flights of poetic fancy. But its rejection of the concrete world meant that nothing it achieved could be enduring. Its initial impetus spent, Islam became a religion of mere sensuality, driven back to the Asia and Africa from whence it had emerged, and surrendering its poetry into Goethe's more capable hands.[65]

Islam, for Hegel, was at least capable of producing poetry at some stage of its historical existence. The same could not be said for Judaism. Hegel pointed to the Psalms not to justify Christian poetry (as so many early Christians had done) but rather to cast "Jewish poetry" as an oxymoron. According to him the Psalms express the sublimity of God and give "the most brilliant" (*glänzendste*) expression to the fear of the sinner cowering before the sublime. But because there is no such thing as "spiritual freedom" in Judaism, there can be no such thing as true poetry in it either.[66]

We seem to have reached a position—there is no true Jewish poetry—very much the opposite of the one I set out to elucidate: "Every poet is a Yid." Do I need to reformulate Tsvétayeva's line to say that "in this most Christian of worlds, every *bad* poet is a Yid"? We can reconcile the seeming opposition and uphold the more general form of my claim if we notice that, in the Hegelian world, the category of "bad Jewish poets" is very large, indeed much larger than the literal category of "real Jewish poets." This is because Hegel's Judaism was as much a critical category as all the other Judaisms we've encountered: it could be applied to any poetry, not just that created by "real" Jews. When early nineteenth-century philosophers like Hegel or Schlegel called someone Jewish, they were often making a critical point, not ascribing a religious identity. In fact Hegel and his friends and followers were fond of referring to that other polestar of German philosophy, Immanuel Kant, as a "Moses," a "Pharisee," and a "Jew," not because of his religion (he wasn't Jewish) but because of the way in which, according to them, Kant's philosophy failed to overcome the alienation between subject and object, freedom and necessity.

In poetry as in philosophy, the targets of Judaizing criticism in Hegel's day were largely non-Jews, since there were still few confessed Jews writing poetry (or philosophy) in Western Europe. But the same is true in the following generations, which did indeed see many Jews or converts from Judaism emerge as important figures in European culture. The admiring student of Hegel's whom we met already in the previous chapter, Heinrich Heine, provides the best-known example. Himself a convert from Judaism, he was frequently attacked as a Jew writer. But he was quite capable of returning the criticism, and his use of it provides a vivid and influential example of how Judaism as a poetic criticism could be put to work far beyond the boundaries of Judaism as a people or community of faith.

"The beard does not make the Jew, nor the wig the Christian," Heine quipped in an essay he wrote about another well-known convert from Judaism, the writer, journalist, political activist, and critic Ludwig Börne. On the contrary, Heine went on to explain, categories like Jew versus Greek, or Nazarene and Pharisee versus Christian, designated ways of thinking about and relating to the world—asceticism versus worldliness, abstract versus concrete, faith versus reason, the sublime versus the beautiful, and so forth—rather than adherents of a particular religion. The struggle between the outlooks they represented was ongoing in every thinker and in every artist regardless of confession or nation, their synthesis the achievement of every true genius.

Determining the outcome of the struggle between the "Jewishness" or "Greekness" of a given thinker or artist, explaining how a "nation of shopkeepers" gives birth to a Shakespeare, how warring strands of worldviews give rise to new manifestations of the human spirit, these were for Heine and many of his contemporaries the basic tasks both of art making and cultural critique. When he attacked "the Jew Pustkuchen, the Jew Wolfgang Menzel, the Jew Hengstenberg," it was not because they were Jews (they were in fact Christians) but because he judged their writing to be a "pharisaic hue and cry" against the joyful worldliness of "Athens." Shakespeare, on the other hand, though by religion a Christian, was for Heine "simultaneously Jew and Greek" because he had achieved Heine's (and Hegel's) ideal, integrating "Jewish" spirituality with "Hellenic" worldliness and thereby elevating both to a "higher Whole."[67]

Heine's example shows us both how the category of "bad Jewish poets" could be vastly expanded to include many avowedly Christian writers and how "good" poets (like Shakespeare) could come to partake dialectically of "Judaism," albeit suitably synthesized with "Hellenism," its opposite in this system of thought. This form of Judaizing cultural criticism was widespread, not only in Germany but throughout Europe.

Matthew Arnold's (1822–1888) *Culture and Anarchy* was itself much influenced by Heine, and launched a broad critique of "pharisaism" in English literary and political culture. Heine's idea that European culture should strive for the dialectical overcoming of a set of oppositions understood in relation to Judaism became so common that, in the early twentieth century, Thomas Mann praised Heine's essay on Börne as the greatest work of German letters prior to Nietzsche, because its "psychology of the Nazarene type" (as Mann called it) provided such a powerful critical tool. James Joyce, on the other hand, writing at much the same time as Mann, was to my mind more reflective when he mocked this synthetic solution to the aesthetic alienations of the modern subject as a representative idiocy of the age: "Jewgreek is greekjew. Extremes meet. Death is the highest form of life. Bah!"[68]

Jews Becoming Poets, Poets Becoming Jews

Heine's Hegelian synthesis of Athens and Jerusalem is only one of the many forms taken by the aesthetics of transcendence in modernity. We might even want to consider it one of the more benign forms, since its "incarnational" founding paradigm can be used (as Heine did) to stress the need to incorporate (or synthesis with) its "enemies," rather than seeming to require their elimination, as a more Manichean aesthetics might. I present it here as just one example of a more general possibility. Within an aesthetics founded on a hierarchical distinction between letter and spirit—one in which the letter and its many analogues (law, flesh, matter, form, formalism, abstraction, sublimity, appearance . . .) are associated with Judaism—every poet can be made a Jew through one more turn of the dialectical screw. It is this potential that made Judaizing so useful for the many literary cultures of modernity, struggling for ways to understand and justify the value of their aesthetic forms and practices, at a time when more transcendent guarantors of meaning and value seemed to be giving way to the mammon of a literary marketplace mediated by publishers, agents, critics, and other brokers of taste.[69]

Among the many possible products of this potential was that of both condemning and justifying the poetry of "real" Jews, living and confessed. In 1911, for example, the German-Jewish literary critic Julius Bab published an essay entitled "The Participation of the Jews in Contemporary German Poetry." In it he argued that German Jews could not become poets or creators (*Schöpfer*) because they lacked the "innocence of the senses [*die Unschuld der Sinne*]" and "operate only through idea, reflection and comparison." This deficiency was produced by the Jewish historical experience: a long history of economic mediation had transformed them into "middlemen" or "intermediaries" (*Mittler*). Jews did have a literary function, but it was not one of creation. As publishers, agents, and literary critics they could facilitate the work of true German poets, just as Rachel Varnhagen's salon had facilitated the work of Goethe. What they could not do was write good poetry.[70]

The German-Jewish (later Palestinian) poet Ludwig Strauss responded to Bab in 1913, and his arguments illustrate both the degree to which Jewish poets had themselves internalized anti-Jewish aspects of the poetics we've been exploring and the flexibility of the dialectical critique generated by that poetics. Strauss does not challenge the underlying categories of critique. He accepts the opposition between sensual and spiritual, but inverts it. The German lyric tradition, he suggests, begins with the sensual and moves to the spiritual. Strauss argues that the Jewish poetic tradition, from the Psalms and Song of Songs to twentieth-century German-Jewish poets like Elsa Lasker-Schüler, does the reverse: "The German detects [*erfaßt*] the sensual form and senses [*ahnt*] the spirit in it." "The Jew," by contrast, "experiences [*erlebt*] the spirit and creates [*erschafft*] the sensual world from and in service of it." German poetry lingers first in concrete sensuality, while Jewish poetry is first characterized by spirit (*Geist*). But both proceed to the necessary synthesis.[71]

One of the more striking aspects of the debate between Bab and Strauss is that although one is arguing against and the other for the possibility of German Jewish poetry, both deploy the same (semi-Hegelian) poetics: a poetics predicated on hierarchical distinction between the sensual and the spiritual. That distinction applies equally to writer, word, and world. Each is to be judged by how it represents within itself the unbridgeable gap between human experience and eternity. And each is to be judged by how it brings forth within itself the overcoming of that distinction, much as the Incarnation overcame the radical distinction between God and creation.

I say *much as* because the aesthetic anxieties of late nineteenth- and early twentieth-century Europeans were different from those of their ancestors. We can already see, as we did in the case of art, that the difference does not reside so much in the categories available for thinking about the nature of human alienation in the world of representation, nor in the hierarchical ordering of those categories. A young Walter Benjamin, for example, could still speak without irony circa 1920 of beauty as Being hidden under the deceitful shell of appearance: an aesthetic ontology that by now should feel very familiar to us.[72] What changed was less the categories and hierarchies than the confidence in the possibility of their being overcome. Even among the intelligentsia some, like Martin Heidegger, continued to insist on transcendent guarantors of the human symbolic order, convinced that the grounds of human communication "have to be prepared even more fundamentally, a preparation which of course again requires the [divine] address and its protection [*Geheißes und seines Schutzes*]."[73] But many others were increasingly convinced, or increasingly terrified, that there were no such foundations to be found.

The emergence of that conviction marks the threshold of modernity, but the ways in which moderns dealt with its attendant terrors were not entirely new. One of those ways was, once more, by contrast with the Jew. Like Gonzalo and Chaucer, like Baena and his friends, like Shakespeare and George Herbert, many late nineteenth- and early twentieth-century poets and writers turned to the language of Judaizing in order to assert the virtues of their poetry (or prose, or art) and criticize those of others. There are notorious examples, such as Wyndham Lewis and Ezra Pound—whose journal *Blast* championed an antimimetic modernism they called Vorticism—both of whom would come to deploy that language frequently and in surprising ways. (Lewis, for example, dedicated reams of paper to the proposition that James Joyce was a Jewish writer.) In France the corrosive envy of a writer like Louis-Ferdinand Céline could produce the Judaism of more or less the entire literary establishment. And in Germany in 1922, a doctoral candidate in literature surveyed the attempts of the great nineteenth-century German Romantic dramatists to achieve what they considered to be a synthesis of sensuality and spirit, art and philosophy, and condemned their efforts as Judaism. They had achieved not a synthesis but rather the alienation of the German creative spirit from true art, and the enslavement of the German poet to Jewish "matter" and "form." The scholar was Joseph Goebbels, future Nazi minister for propaganda and enlightenment of the folk, whom we met in the previous chapter organizing the 1937 exhibition on Degenerate Art but whom we could just as well have approached through his earlier burning of "un-German" (because Jewish) books.[74]

I do not mean to equate these figures, and could just as well have named many others. The ones selected are simply well-known examples of a much more general calamity. As for Goebbels, the choice may seem melodramatic. But it reminds us that the critical categories of our aesthetics can have catastrophic consequences for their figures in the flesh. And here I do not mean only real Jews in the flesh (although certainly they suffered particular horrors). In the first half of the twentieth century, as in every previous period we have looked at, the aesthetic Judaism of the word, of the poem, of the work of literature or art, had the power to Judaize all readers and beholders. In the words of one of the greatest impresarios of this idea in modernity, Houston Stewart Chamberlain:

> One need not posess the authentic Hittite-nose in order to be a Jew; the word signifies above all a particular type of feeling and of thinking; a person may very quickly, without being an Israelite, become a Jew. Some need only to traffic actively with Jews, to read Jewish newspapers and get used to Jewish art, literature, and conception of life (*Lebensauffassung*). With the Apostle Paul, we must learn to perceive that "he is not a Jew who is one outwardly in the flesh, but he who is a Jew inwardly." (Rom. 2:28)[75]

There is a chillingly tragic irony in Chamberlain's citation of the apostle. For Paul in his Epistle to the Romans, inner (as opposed to outer) Jewishness had been the salvific goal of gentile followers of Jesus, and it was to that end that he had oriented his aesthetic theology. But over the course of centuries the application and adaptation of that same aesthetics had produced a very different world, one in which inward Judaism could be cast as a deadly threat to society, a threat that could spread through any "killing letter," any "Jewish" word, symbol, or work of art.

And what of today? Let us give Jacques Derrida the last word: "[The] experience of language is from the outset an experience of circumcision (cutting and belonging, originary entrance into the space of law, non-symmetrical alliance between the finite and the infinite). And so in quotation marks and with all the necessary rhetorical precautions, a 'Jewish experience.'" Derrida is not offering here to overcome the alienations inherent in language and representation. On the contrary, perhaps more than any other critic of our time, he is insisting that there is no escape. But like so many heirs of Saint Paul, he still maps the alienations and asymmetries of communication and exchange in the world onto the difference between Jew and Christian. Within such a *mappa mundi* every poet, indeed every user of language, remains potentially a Yid.[76]

CHAPTER THREE

Judaism as Political Concept

The Polity's Two Bodies

Representation: the modern English word applies to politics as comfortably as it does to art and literature. Like painting and poetry, politics too is ruled by mediation and mimesis. This aesthetic dependence has long been a source of discomfort for theorists of politics in a Christian world. For Jean-Jacques Rousseau, for example, it was precisely this dependence that could lead politics astray. Hence in his "Letter to D'Alembert" he counseled against admitting theater into the polity, fearing that the citizen would learn from the actor "the art of counterfeiting himself, of putting on another character than his own, of appearing different than he is . . . [a]nd of forgetting his own place by dint of taking another's."[1] Written in the midst of the English Civil War, Thomas Hobbes's condemnation of metaphors—which he characterized, perhaps with some irony, as sources of sedition (*Leviathan* 5.36)—was motivated by related anxieties about language more generally. Conversely, Machiavelli opened his *Prince* with an image of the politician as landscape painter in order to reverse the ontological emphasis, stressing the political importance of *seeming to be* rather than truly *being*. And all of these thinkers were wrestling, albeit in very different ways, with the legacy of Plato's *Politeia*—*The Republic*, as we call it in English—with its fundamental analogy between the body and soul of the individual on the one hand, and the body and soul of the polity on the other.

We've already encountered some of Plato's own analogies: "poetry being such as we have described is not to be regarded seriously as attaining to the truth; and he who listens to her, fearing for the safety of the city which is within him, should be on his guard against her seductions

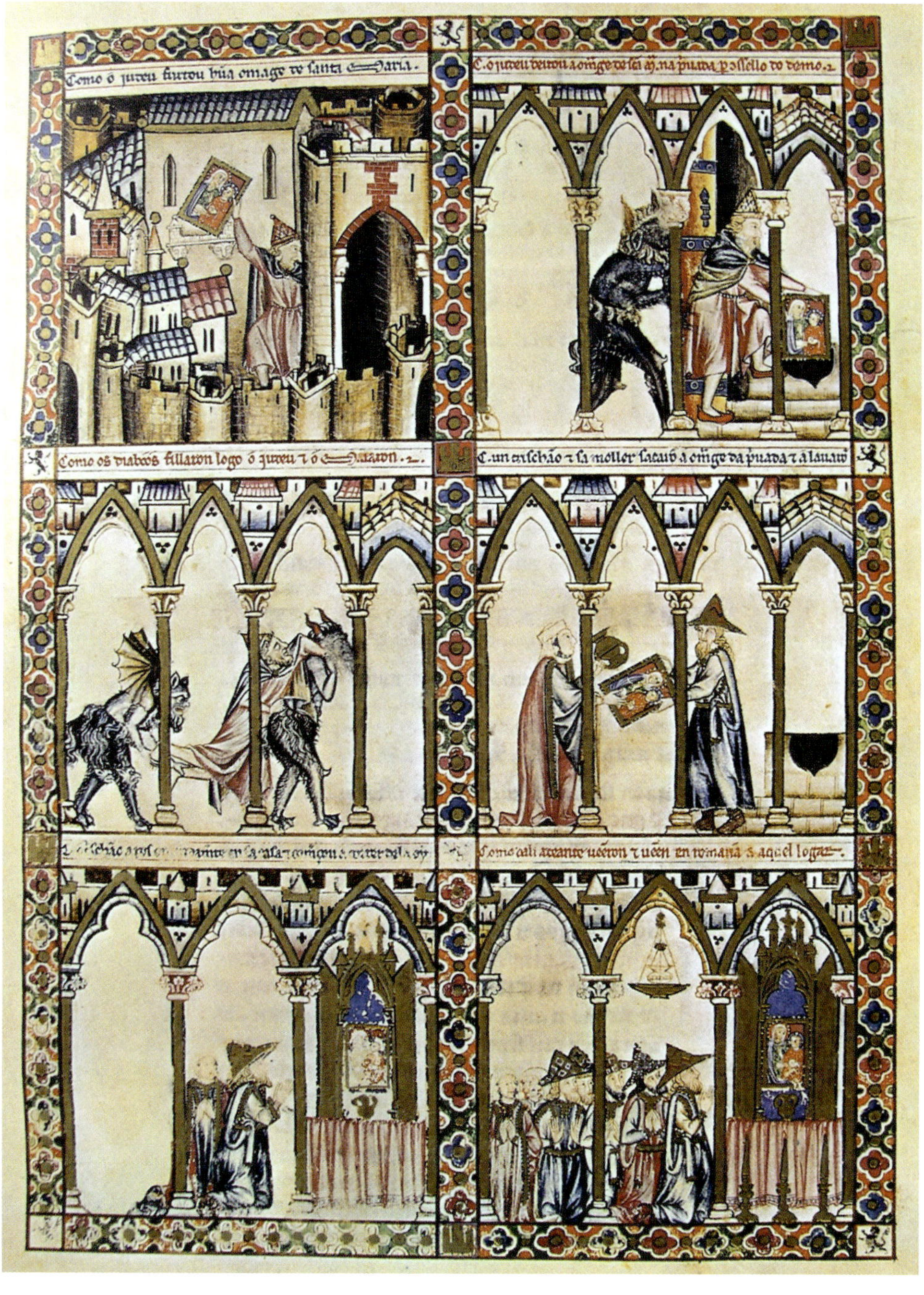

PLATE I

Cantigas de Santa María, Cantiga 34, Escorial, MS. T.I.1, folio 39r.

PHOTO COURTESY OF EDILÁN-ARS LIBRIS.

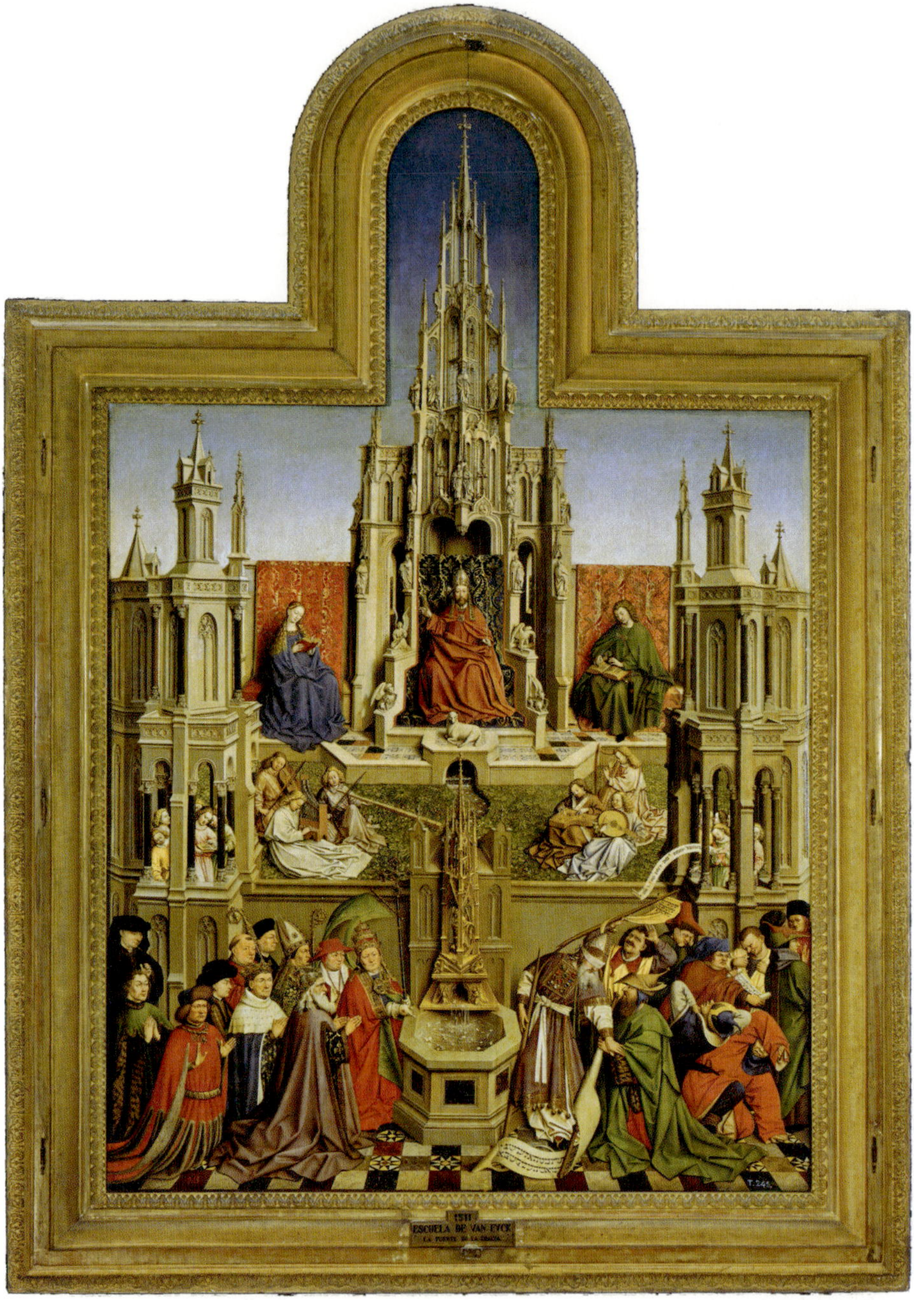

PLATE 2

Jan van Eyck, *The Fountain of Grace, or the Dispute between Church and Synagogue*, workshop of Jan van Eyck, Prado Museum, Madrid.

PHOTO COURTESY OF ALBUM/ART RESOURCE, NY.

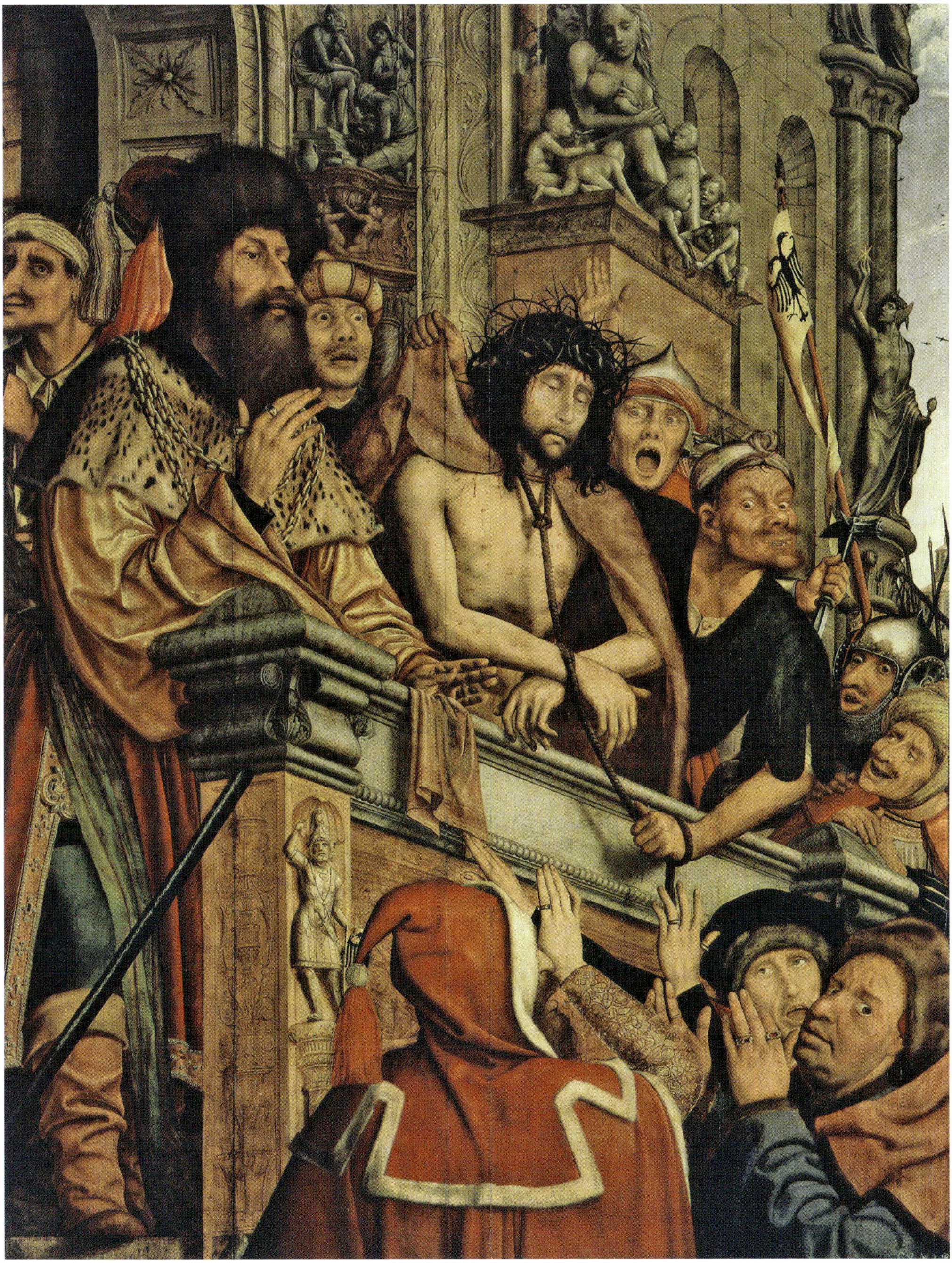

PLATE 3

Ecce Homo, Quentin Massys, Prado Museum, Madrid.

PHOTO COURTESY OF THE ART ARCHIVE AT ART RESOURCE, NY.

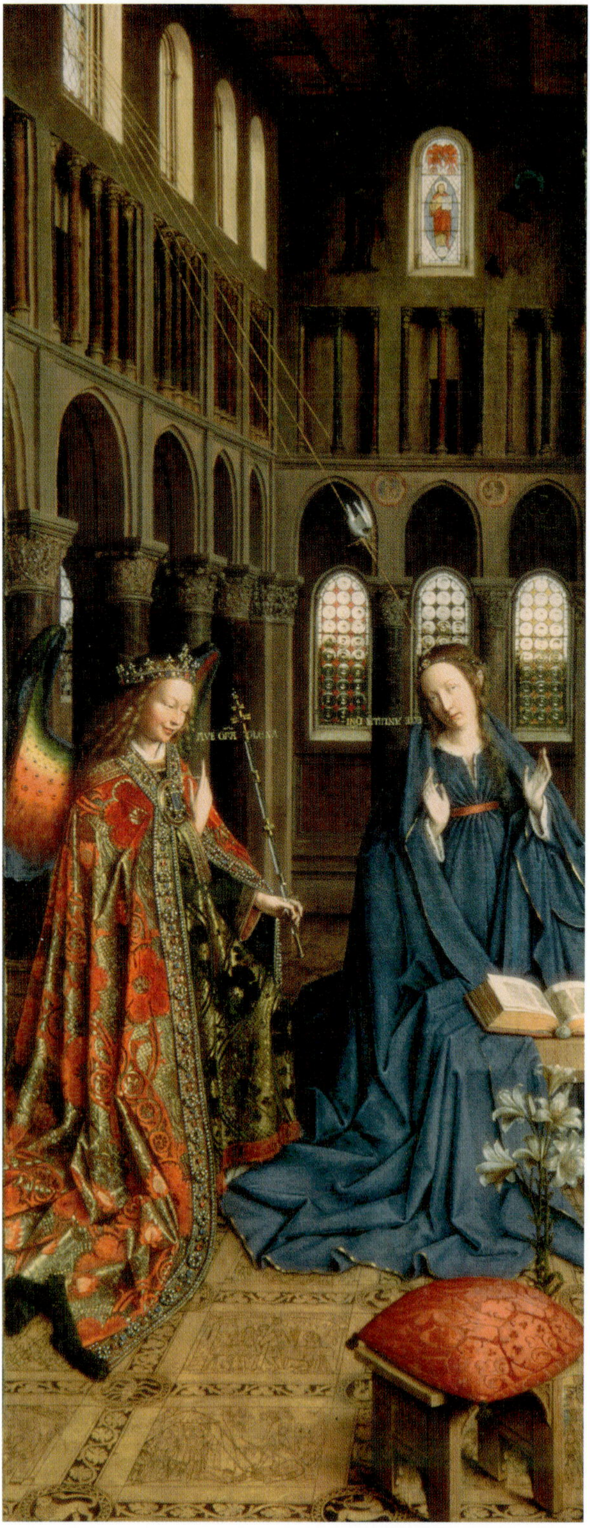

PLATE 4
Annunciation,
Jan van Eyck,
National Gallery,
Washington, D.C.
PHOTO COURTESY OF HIP/
ART RESOURCE, NY.

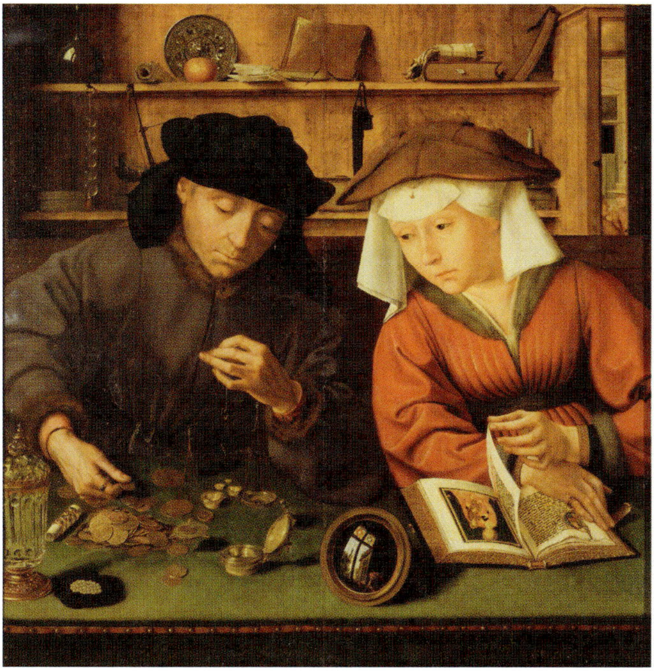

PLATE 5

The Moneychanger and His Wife, Quentin Massys, Louvre Museum, Paris.

PHOTO COURTESY OF SCALA / ART RESOURCE, NY.

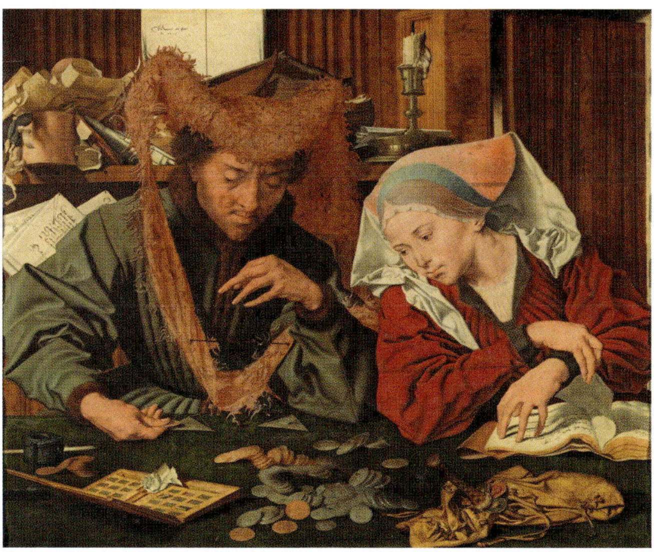

PLATE 6

The Moneylender and His Wife,

Marinus van Reymerswaele, Prado Museum, Madrid.

PHOTO COURTESY OF MUSEO NACIONAL DEL PRADO / ART RESOURCE, NY.

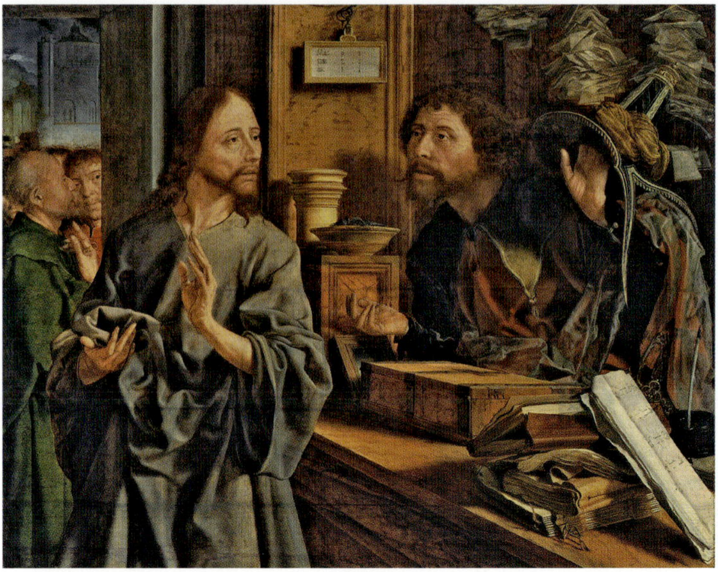

PLATE 7

The Calling of St. Matthew, Marinus van Reymerswaele, Thyssen-Bornemisza Museum, Madrid.

PHOTO COURTESY OF HIP/ART RESOURCE, NY.

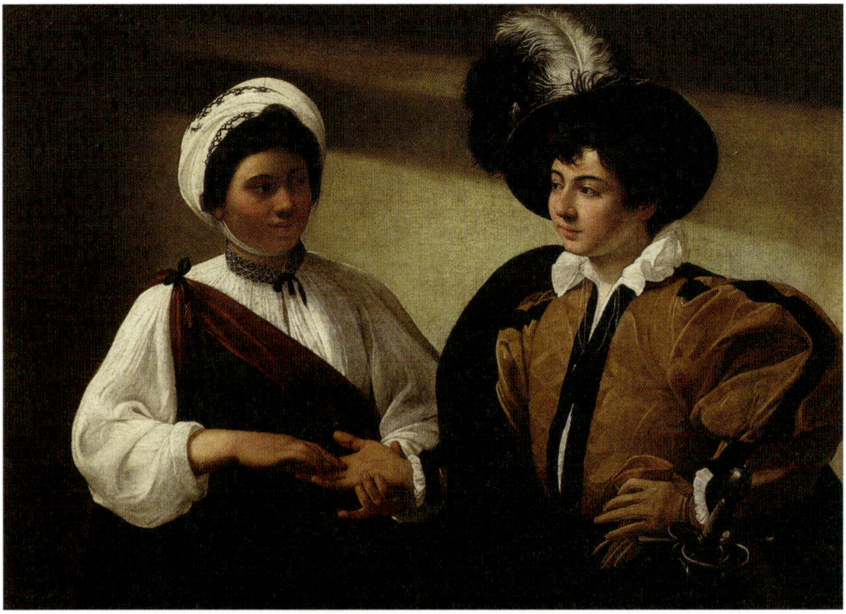

PLATE 8

The Gypsy Fortune Teller, Michelangelo Merisi (Caravaggio), Louvre Museum, Paris.

PHOTO CREDIT GIANNA DAGLI ORTI/THE ART ARCHIVE AT ART RESOURCE, NY.

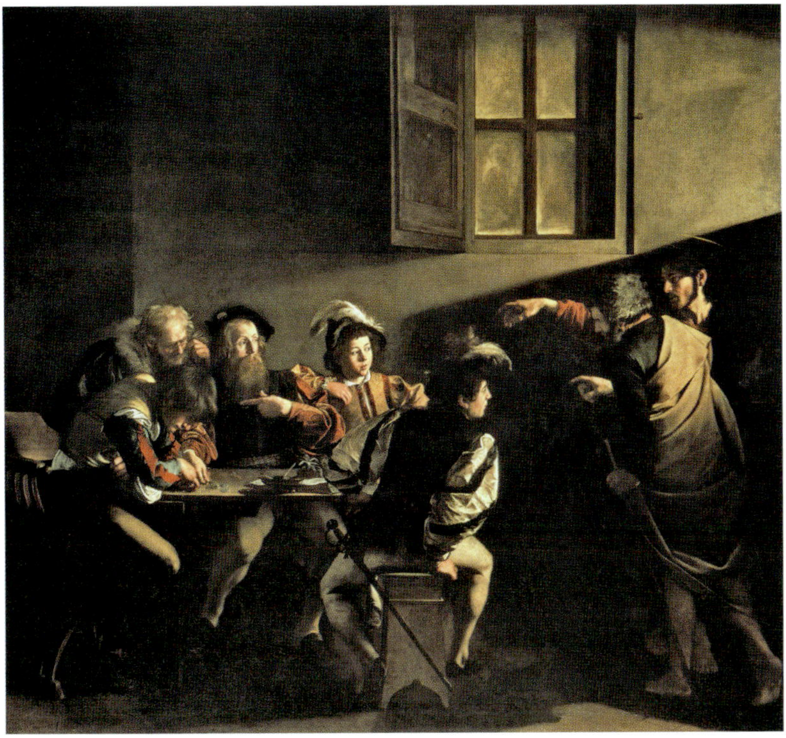

PLATE 9

The Calling of St. Matthew,

Michelangelo Merisi (Caravaggio), San Luigi dei Francesi, Rome.

PHOTO COURTESY OF SCALA/ART RESOURCE, NY.

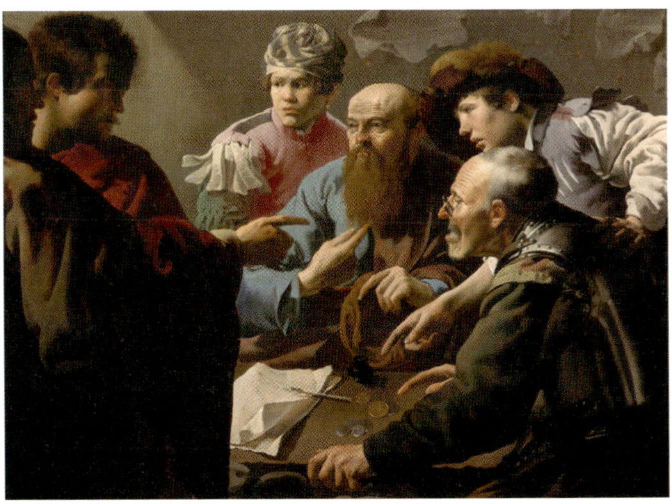

PLATE 10

The Calling of St. Matthew, Hendrick ter Brugghen, Centraal Museum, Utrecht.

PHOTO COURTESY OF CMU/ERNST MORITZ.

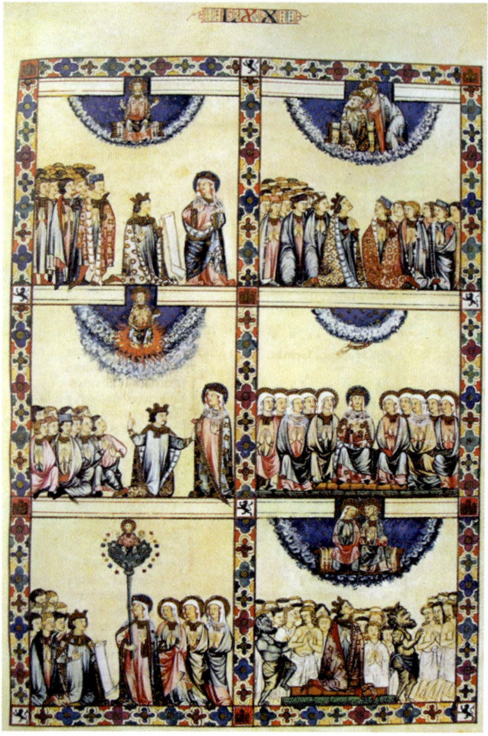

PLATE 11
Cantigas de Santa María, Cantiga 70, Escorial, MS. T.I.1, folio 118r.
PHOTO COURTESY OF EDILÁN-ARS LIBRIS.

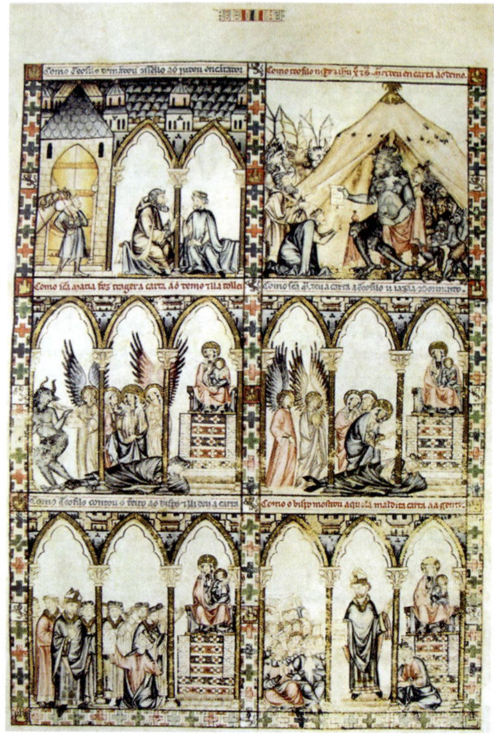

PLATE 12
Cantigas de Santa María, Cantiga 209, Florence, MS. B.R. 20, folio 119v.
PHOTO COURTESY OF EDILÁN-ARS LIBRIS.

and make our words his law" (595A–608B). It might seem odd that in this critique of poetry the polity is being used to represent the individual's soul, rather than the other way around. But Plato had earlier (441C) asserted that "the structure of the city corresponds to the structure of the soul." Now he is merely treating this identity as symmetric.

Analogies like this one, based on the relationship between body and soul, occupy a central place in Plato's political writing, and hence in the history of political philosophy in the West. Just as there is health in the body, Plato argues, there is a health of the soul. And just as there is a health of the individual soul, there is a health of the polity, for the relationship between individual and city, he states over and over again in *The Republic*, should be understood as that between body and soul. His treatment of tyrants and tyranny in Book IX provides a good example. In a tyrannical regime both the soul of the city and the soul of the tyrant are enslaved. The tyrant himself (whom, apropos Rousseau's worries about politics as theater, Plato represents as wearing an actor's mask in public [577B]) is perhaps the least free of all, for he is enslaved to his passions and appetites.

For our topic the implications of this analogy are obvious: it orients politics away from the body and toward the soul (*psychē*), that is, away from the changeable and the corruptible and toward the eternal, transcendent, and true. (Later Platonists such as Plotinus would draw a more extreme conclusion: there is no such thing as a politics of the eternal. Man must abandon politics as he approaches the divine.[2]) With respect to this orientation, at least, Aristotle's politics will amplify Plato's. For just as, according to Aristotle's *Politics*, each man is "born with regard to life, but existing essentially with regard to the good life," so the state is born "to secure a bare subsistence; but the ultimate object of the state is the good life."[3]

The relationship of soul to body provides Aristotle with a powerful political analogy even more explicit than Plato's: "although in bad or corrupted natures the body will often appear to rule over the soul, because they are in an evil and unnatural condition. . . . It is clear that the rule of the soul over the body . . . is natural and expedient."[4] It is the task of rulers to direct the politics of their polities away from the demands of the body toward those of the immortal soul. As Aristotle put it elsewhere: "we must not follow those who advise us, being men, to think of human things, and being mortal, of mortal things, but must, so far as we can, make ourselves immortal." A rule that reverses these priorities, placing worldly gain ahead of a common and immaterial good, Aristotle defined as tyranny. Tyranny is the perverted preference for self-interest over the commonwealth, for the mortal over the immortal, for the body over the soul. In this sense we can call tyranny an aesthetic error. Good government aims at transcendence.[5]

What does any of this have to do with Judaism and Judaizing? My argument is that within the Christian political discourses of Western Europe and their secularized heirs, Judaism became a political concept through which to make sense of the relationship between the body and the soul of the polity. More accurately put: of the relationship between the *two bodies of the polity*, the physical body and the spiritual body. For in human (as opposed to angelic) politics, as in human (as opposed to angelic) language and art, there is no escape from the particular and the material. Transcendence can be pointed toward, even fantasized, but it can never be fully realized in this world. An earthly politics oriented toward transcendence can never quite escape the claims of body, law, and letter. It remains always subject to the charge of falling short of its ideals. Judaism and Judaizing are, I am proposing, the key critical terms through which Christian Europe and its secular heirs have struggled to achieve their political ideals. And here as in the previous chapters I don't mean Judaism as a historical or lived religion, but Judaism as a figure of Christian thought, a figure produced by the efforts of generations of thinkers to interpret the world, a figure projected into that world and constitutive of it.

A Brief Excursus on Political Theology

Bibliophiles will have already recognized my vocabulary's resonance with some well-known twentieth-century titles on political theory and history. My *two bodies of the polity*, for example, brings to mind Ernst Kantorowicz's *The King's Two Bodies* of 1957, in which that erudite migrant from Hitler's Germany to the Berkeley Hills took up the question of how medieval and early modern Europeans thought of the distinction between the perishable body of the king and the eternal body of the sovereign. That book itself bore an enigmatic subtitle, *A Study in Medieval Political Theology*, which was almost certainly an allusion to the German antiliberal (and later Nazi) theorist Carl Schmitt's even more famous book published with the title *Political Theology* in 1922. (I say enigmatic because Kantorowicz did not credit the borrowing.)[6] The title of my chapter, too, is meant to resonate with one of Schmitt's, in this case his *The Concept of the Political* of 1932.[7] But unlike Kantorowicz I will not be cryptic about my claim, which is that key European conceptions of the political—including Carl Schmitt's and Kantorowicz's—emerged through thinking about Judaism.

"Political theology" is one of these conceptions of the political that emerged through Christian projections of Jewish enemies. Like so many other concepts, its meanings are multiple and unstable across time, but I will use the phrase only in a very general sense common to Schmitt and Kantorowicz as well as to many other thinkers: the grounding of human political action in a commandment of obedience to a transcendent sovereign authority often (but not always or necessarily) imagined as God.[8] Political theology has become a very fashionable concept in the early twenty-first century, and I will conclude with this modishness. But first, and precisely because of its contemporary vitality, I hope to convince you that the representation of Jewish enmity has been historically important to the theorization of Christian political theology; and second, that this importance is not primarily the product of some essential aspect of lived (not to say "real") Judaism but is rather produced by the key terms and practices of Christian thought.

When it comes to Carl Schmitt's own concept of the political and of political theology, the centrality of Jewish enmity is not difficult to demonstrate. The "essential insight," Schmitt explained in 1936, in a lecture entitled "The Battle of German Legal Studies against the Jewish Spirit" ("Die Deutsche Rechtswissenschaft im Kampf gegen den jüdischen Geist"), is that "with every new period of history [there occurs] a change in the general behavior of the Jews, and a *change of masks* possessed of demonic enigmaticness also occurs, so quickly that we grasp it only with the most careful attention."[9] Behind the shifting masks lies an essential and unchanging Jewish hostility that explains the meaning of Christian history, a meaning revealed—as Schmitt put it long after the Second World War and the Holocaust might have made clear even to him some of the disastrous consequences of his thought—by reflection on "what it meant politically-historically that the Jews cried out before the crucifixion of the Savior: 'We have no king but Caesar' (John 19:15)." Allegiance to the satanic princes of this world, a murderous enmity toward God's sovereignty, the exile of miracle and the subjection of the world to "lawful regularity": these were for Schmitt the basic attributes of the "Jewish spirit" and remained so over the long course of his career.[10]

It is true that Schmitt's writings need to be understood in the context of early twentieth-century Weimar thought and society. But it is also true that these writings drew on and were nourished by a long tradition of using figures of Judaism to think about Christian politics and law, a tradition that was powerful even in societies with no real Jews living in them. Without a history of that tradition—that is, without the long history of Jewishness as a concept in Christian politics—we cannot understand the habits of thought that shaped Schmitt's politics, nor the figures of Judaism that these habits were capable of producing in a given place or time, including Schmitt's and perhaps also our own.

It is obviously impossible to recapitulate that history in a chapter of this or any other length. Here I propose only to take a brief look at some early Christian sources, in order to make plausible my claim that the production of Judaism as a figure of the political is encoded in Christian hermeneutics. Then I will leap to some medieval examples from England, France, and Spain, in order to illustrate how different figures of Judaism were produced by and put to work in foundational moments of basic ideas about monarchy and sovereignty, before concluding with a few words about the implications of my approach for political thought and the history of ideas more generally.

Early Christianity: "That King Has Become a Jew"

The Christian version of the problem begins with the Apostle Paul. You will remember from the introduction that one of the crucial questions generated by Paul's mission to the gentiles concerned the relationship of non-Jewish followers of Jesus to Jewish law. Did gentile converts need to observe commandments such as circumcision and dietary laws? Circumcision, Paul argued, was a bodily sign whose spiritual meaning was "faith." Gentile followers of Christ were already circumcised in this spiritual sense and did not need the body of the sign. In his letter to the Galatians, Paul had sharpened the distinction between body and soul, desires of the flesh and desires of the spirit. Paul presented the danger confronting the Galatians as one of mistaken aesthetic priorities: a preference for the bodily meaning of scripture over its spiritual one, and for the bodily sign of circumcision over its spiritual significance. He coined a verb to describe this misplaced priority: to Judaize (Gal. 2:14).[11] And he repeatedly stressed the mortal dangers that attended the wrong choice. As he so memorably put it, albeit in a different epistle and context: "for written letters kill, but the Spirit gives life" (2 Cor. 3:6).

Paul's concern may look to us more hermeneutic than political, or more about religious than civil practice, but we should remember that such a distinction was not easy to make in a society such as Paul's, in which God and government walked hand in hand. Recall for a moment that passage in Galatians in which he reinterprets Abraham's biography in order to expound his reading practice:

> Abraham had two sons, one by the slave girl and one by the freewoman. The son of the slave girl came to be born in the way of human nature; but the son of the freewoman came to be born through a promise. There is an allegory here: these women stand for the two covenants. The one given on Mount Sinai—that is Hagar—. . . represents Jerusalem in its present state, for she is in slavery together with her children. But the Jerusalem above is free, and that is the one that is our mother. . . . But what is it that scripture says? *Drive away that slave girl and her son; the slave*

> *girl's son is not to share the inheritance with the son of the freewoman.* (Gal. 4:22–31)

In the introduction I described this as an interpretive revolution achieved by allegory, in which the spiritual and the bodily voices of the text are arrayed against one another. But notice that it is potentially a political revolution as well. Hagar and Ishmael, flesh and slavery, are associated with the law given on Mount Sinai and "the present Jerusalem." Sarah and Isaac, spirit and freedom, are a new covenant and a heavenly city. The Mosaic law and the Jewish people and polity that possess it ("the present Jerusalem") are not the heirs of God's promise to Abraham but are condemned as "of the flesh," sentenced to slavery and exile. This terrestrial Jerusalem is to be cast out, replaced by the spiritual Jerusalem, set free by faith in Jesus.[12]

I say potentially because Paul himself may not have intended the political possibilities of his epistle. Whatever Paul's intent, we know that some readers of Galatians immediately interpreted him to be teaching that the political world and its rules were irrelevant, or worse, evil, and that spiritual freedom released the believer from the bonds of all earthly laws. We know this because Paul felt obliged to correct these antinomian readers a few years later, in the Epistle to the Romans, where he first touched openly upon the political dimensions of the problem. Believers were not free to flout the laws of the world, he insisted: "Everyone is to obey the governing authorities . . ." (Rom. 13:1).[13] And yet the same letter that subjected souls to earthly governors proclaimed that to set the mind on the flesh is death, that "those who live by their natural inclinations can never be pleasing to God," and even associated this condition of being in the flesh with Judaism and Judaizing (Rom. 8:6–8).

To put Paul's political problem in aesthetic terms: how can we stress the value of the spiritual world as infinitely above that of the phenomenal and material one through which it was perceived without at the same time representing the world and its necessities as irrelevant or, worse, evil? There is a potential tension in this balancing act between law and flesh on the one hand and spirit on the other. Paul attempted to contain that tension in a complex vocabulary of flesh and body (*sarx*, *sōma*), soul and spirit (*psychē*, *pneuma*). At 1 Corinthians 15:44 he can even speak of a "soul body" (*sōma psychikon*). The vocabulary is obscure, and that very obscurity would prove extraordinarily productive for early Christians working out their views of the proper relationship between body and soul.[14]

Perhaps explicitly political questions were of limited interest to Paul himself, given his sense that the end of the world was near and that the new creation was at hand: "the time has become limited . . . This world as we know it is passing away" (1 Cor. 7:29–30). But as the apocalyptic revolution was repeatedly postponed, later generations of Christians found themselves having to think more and more about earthly princes. Were these princes (all of them pagan, and some of them persecutory) agents of God or of the devil? At times the gospel authors attempted to draw relatively unprejudicial distinctions between celestial and terrestrial jursidictions, such as Matthew's "pay Caesar what belongs to Caesar—and God what belongs to God" (22:21). Even Matthew, however, found the distinction difficult to maintain in the face of a more transcendent political ideal: "Your kingdom come, your will be done, on earth as in heaven" (6:10). The Gospel of John went further, and imagined sharp conflict between the power of the divine word and the "prince of this world" that would only be resolved with the defeat and disappearance of the latter (12:31, 14:30, 15:18).

We have already seen Carl Schmitt deploying in his own writings John's tight association between the Jews and Satan, Caesar, and other "princes of this world." But of course early Christian exegetes had developed this and many other positions long before Schmitt took up his pen.[15] All of these exegetes shared a tendency to think of earthly politics in carnal terms. Some, like the anonymous (roughly third-century) Pseudo-Cyprian, agreed that the Jews, in executing Jesus, had provided the most terrible example of a perverted preference for Caesar's kingdom over God's. (In this we might say that they prefigured Schmitt.)[16] And many, indeed most I am familiar with, mapped their distinctions onto dualities of flesh and spirit, old dispensation and new: distinctions that pointed their political theories and theologies toward the Jew.

In the early third century, for example, Origen of Alexandria (ca. 185–254) founded a school of biblical interpretation that also produced a political theory. The politics was founded upon the same distinctions as the hermeneutics. Building on Paul, Origen divided mankind into three classes: the hylics (from *hylē*, matter), or materialists, who were pagans and Jews; the psychics (from *psychē*, soul), who corresponded to the average Christian; and the pneumatics (from *pneuma*, spirit), who included only the most spiritual and ascetic of Christians.[17] According to Origen the claims of earthly politics were only on the body, and only those who were of the body had to answer to them: Jews, pagans, and average Christians, but not pneumatics, not those who dwelt truly in the spirit. Hence, he explained, Peter's line in Acts 3:6: "I have neither silver nor gold." The apostles have no money because they are pneumatics, of the spirit. They have no business in the world and no need to "pay Caesar."[18]

In Origen's politics, to quote one of its most illuminating historians, "the state is related to the Church, very much as in his exegesis the letter is related to the spirit," a position that strongly associates the state and its politics with "Jewish" literalism and materialism. The same general claim could be made of many other theologians, both Latin and Greek, who came after him. One consequence of this analogy is the tendency, even among those theologians most sympathetic to the possibility of a Christian politics, to discuss political error in the same terms used to assess hermeneutical error: Judaism and Judaizing.[19]

The most revealing example of such slippage comes from more than a century later, after the conversion of the Roman emperors to Christianity had sharply raised the stakes involved in questions about the relationship between the powers of princes and those of priests. In 388 a crowd of monks burned down a Jewish synagogue and a Valentinian (heretical Christian) church in the town of Callinicum, on the Euphrates River in the Eastern Roman Empire. The military Count of the East ordered their punishment and instructed the local bishop, who had incited the attacks, to pay for the reconstruction of the synagogue. The future saint Ambrose, bishop of Milan and a leading churchman of his age, opposed these orders in a letter and a sermon addressed to the Emperor Theodosius. In the first five paragraphs of his letter Ambrose sketches the outlines of a model of sovereignty with which Christian political history would become familiar. The monarch, he explains, has the power to compel obedience "in state causes," the priest has the obligation to state the will of "one whom it is even more perilous to displease," the eternal King of Kings" (*cf.* Matt. 10:19–20).[20]

Ambrose then explains that the synagogue "began to be burnt by the judgment of God." The bishop and his monks were but the instruments of God's justice. Should the emperor punish them, he will have placed his earthly imperial law over the justice of God, and the Jews will have "triumphed over the people of Christ."

It is as if Ambrose had read the opening lines of Schmitt's *Political Theology*: "Sovereign is he who decides the exception." The emperor and his count presumably understood themselves as acting to defend the Roman legal order from the monks' claims to place both themselves and their victims outside the law. Ambrose is contending that it is God and not the emperor who is sovereign, that the monks acted according to a higher law, and that the insistence on upholding earthly law is Judaizing. He pointedly reminds the emperor of his predecessor's unhappy fate: "Maximus . . . hearing that a synagogue had been burnt in Rome, had sent an edict to Rome, as if he were the upholder of public order. Wherefore the Christian people said, No good is in store for him. That king has become a Jew. . . ." The threat rests in implication: a ruler who upholds earthly law over the divine deserves deposition as a Jew.

Ambrose did succeed in obtaining the revocation of the count's order, but his victory was anything but decisive. For the project he had set himself—the assertion of the supremacy of heavenly over earthly law through the exclusion of the Jews—proved just as problematic (and productive) as its hermeneutic analogue: the attempt to purge Christian letters of Jewish literalism. If earthly politics is tied to a heavenly ideal, as Ambrose advocated, then the inescapable earthly necessities of that politics—necessities like law, public order, contracts, courts—would continue to generate the Judaism of governors, no matter how much they persecuted, or even eliminated, any real Jews who might happen to inhabit their realms.

Augustine and the Politics of Exile

Ambrose's most famous student, Saint Augustine, perceived the danger, just as he also perceived the perils of relying too heavily on allegorical and spiritual interpretation in dealing with the Old Testament. His solution to the hermeneutic problem was to defend the literal (rather than just the allegorical) truth of the biblical text by transforming the Jews into guarantors (but not interpreters!) of that truth. The Jews were, he said, "slaves" of the Christian, illiterate servants carrying the books that declared the truth of Christ.[21]

Commenting on a line from Psalm 59—"Slay them not, but scatter them in your might, lest your people forget your Law"—Augustine reminded his readers that, according to Paul in Romans 9:22, God had poured his message into two vessels, one of mercy, the other of wrath, the former made visible through the latter. These vessels of wrath were God's enemies the Jews, destroyed spiritually but preserved in the flesh ("dead men"), "perfected unto perdition" so that His sovereignty might be known. Exiled yet ubiquitous, conquered but still a distinct nation, enemies of God who nevertheless adhere to His laws, the Jews serve as the best evidence for the nature of Christ's sovereignty over the world, and as a lesson for heretics everywhere. Hence the psalmist had sung, "slay them not."[22] The Jews were murderers, but they should be punished as that other murderer, Cain, had been: "[God] says; 'but whosoever shall kill Cain, vengeance shall be taken on him sevenfold.' That is . . . not by bodily death shall the ungodly race of carnal Jews perish. . . . So to the end of . . . time the continued preservation of the Jews will be a proof to believing Christians of the subjection merited by those who . . . put the Lord to death. . . . [Hence] no emperor or monarch who finds under his government the people with this mark [of Cain] kills them, that is to say, makes them cease to be Jews. . . ."[23]

Along with the hermeneutic function of these living dead, there was a political one: the Jews' spiritless and undying misery of flesh attested to the truth of the Christian claim that the Hebrew prophets had proclaimed Christ's coming kingship. But Christ's kingship was one thing, and man's another. Here too Augustine put Cain and the Jews to work, using them, in *The City of God*, to argue against the possibility of a political theology, much as we have already seen him take on poetic theology. All earthly politics, he writes, takes place under the curse of Cain—who was the first politician, the founder of the first city. Like Cain, the founder of every polity is of necessity "a fratricide." (Augustine gives the example of Romulus, the founder of Rome.) Like Cain and the Jews, who sinned by subjecting their reasoning soul to the desires of the flesh —"that part which the philosophers call vicious, and which ought not to lead the mind, but which the mind ought to rule and restrain by reason"—every earthly city "has its good in this world, and rejoices in [the material world] with such joy as such things can afford," so that it will at the end of time be "committed to the extreme penalty." The anthropology is Platonic, but more pessimistically than Plato (or Aristotle), Augustine explicitly assigns all earthly politics to the sphere of the appetites. There is no earthly politics of the spirit, only a politics of flesh. Secular power, designated as pure carnality, stands under the curse of Cain, side by side with Judaism. Political theology, according to the elderly Augustine, is a lie.[24]

In 1935 Erik Peterson invoked Augustine in order to argue, contra Schmitt, that there can be no truly Catholic political theology. Certainly the elderly Augustine was skeptical about the possibility, and his skepticism (e.g., in *The City of God*) contributed to bringing phrases like "civil theology" and "political theology" into disrepute for centuries. Still, from a historicist point of view Peterson's argument is odd, since we know that countless readers across the Christian centuries interpreted Augustine very differently, as maintaining the possibility and even the necessity of a spiritual politics.[25] My own point is simply that, whether Christian exegetes were optimistic about this possibility (like Ambrose) or skeptical (like the elderly Augustine), their arguments all tended to Judaize earthly politics. The struggle to control this potential charge of Judaism will turn out to be one of the most persistent and explosive themes of Christian politics, from the Middle Ages to modernity.

The King's Jewish Body

It was in the Middle Ages, beginning around the twelfth century, that Jewish questions became central to Christian politics in Western Europe. Those questions were asked with a specific vocabulary. In the words of a law code (known as the "Laws of Edward the Confessor") from the reign of the Anglo-Norman king Henry I (d. 1135): "for those Jews, and all that they possess, belong to the king . . . as if they were his private property (*proprium*)." Half a century later, in 1176, lawyers working for King Alfonso II of Aragon spoke in slightly different terms: "the Jews are the *servi* of the king, and are always subject to the royal fisc." This special vocabulary spread quickly, and by the end of the twelfth century it was pan-European.[26]

There is controversy over how we should understand the word *servus* (slave? serf? servant?) as it applies to the Jews. Let me just note two things. First, the word is overdetermined. Its theological history alone stretches from Paul's "enslavement" of Sarah's earthly progeny in Galatians, through Augustine's characterization of the Jews as exegetical "slaves" of the Christians, to the justifications penned by medieval popes for the protection of Jews in Christendom (such as Innocent III's *Etsi Iudaeos* of 1205). And second, although modern scholars may quibble, kings and their lawyers knew quite well what they wanted the word to mean. Listen to King John of England in 1201: the Jews and their property are "like our own private thing" (*res nostre proprie*), "like our chattel property." In his *Commentaries on the Laws and Customs of England* the thirteenth-century jurist Henry Bracton explains the consequences of this status to his medieval colleagues: "The Jew can truly not have any property of his own, for whatever he acquires is not acquired by him but by the king, for the Jew *does not live for himself but for another*, and thus the other acquires, and not the Jew himself."[27]

These English laws provide stark examples of the Jews as "our private things" (*res nostre proprie*), that is, as representations of utter subjection to the prince's fiscal interests. In order to understand the full power of this representation, we need to compare it to its opposite. The same

Henry Bracton, in words cited by Ernst Kantorowicz in his *The King's Two Bodies*, associated the *res fisci*, the royal "fiscal thing," to the spiritual and eternal body of the polity: "A thing fiscal is a thing quasi sacred, which cannot be given away or sold or transferred upon another person by the Prince . . . ; those things make the Crown what it is, and they regard to common utility such as peace and justice."[28] I am suggesting that in the space between these two antipodes—that is, in the space between carnal Judaism as *res privata* and the *res publica* (public thing, or republic) understood as Christian and eternal—we can build an entire political theology.

Kantorowicz mentioned Jews and Judaism only four times in his book of almost six hundred pages. But his study of *The King's Two Bodies*—that is, of the idea that the king was both a mere mortal, a body natural, and an immortal body politic, even a hypostatization of divine justice—is an example of just such a political theology. The difference between mortal and eternal, private and public, tyrant and legitimate monarch, could be, and often was, articulated in the Middle Ages by being mapped onto the difference between Jew and Christian. And although one would not know it from Kantorowicz's work, it is between these two poles, trembling like a cheap compass needle, that medieval monarchs pursued their politics.

A cartoon contemporary with Bracton and drawn on an English tax receipt roll of 1233 makes the point visually in what may well be the earliest known medieval caricature of Jews.

The drawing, presumably by a clerk of the exchequer of the Jews whose taxes are registered in the roll, represents a city under siege by a demonic army. In the foreground we have two Jews in profile, united by a demon tweaking each by the nose. Towering over the city is a crowned three-faced figure—a traditional representation of the Antichrist—wearing the distinctive trefoil crown of the then reigning King Henry III but bearing the name of Isaac of Norwich, one of the most powerful Jewish moneylenders of the day.[29]

The cartoonist is here representing the Christian city (the "fortalitium fidei," as later polemicists would have it) besieged and conquered by the

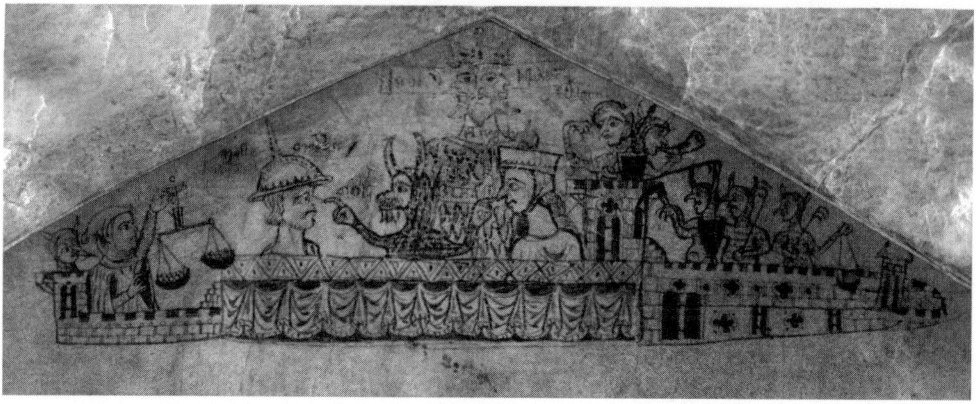

FIGURE 3.1
Exchequer Receipt Roll, 1233, London,
National Archives, Public Records Office, E 401/1565.
PHOTO COURTESY OF NATIONAL ARCHIVES, LONDON.

Antichrist and his ministers, demons and Jews. There is, of course, a context for the representation. For a little over a century, and culminating in Henry's reign, the English crown channeled the economic activity of England's tiny Jewish community toward lending at interest to Christians, and then expropriated the lion's share of the proceeds from the Jews in the form of loans, taxes, and extraordinary seizures. The tax roll that serves as material support for our drawing is itself evidence for this practice, a practice so controversial that it became a focal point of two great baronial revolts, first against King John and then against Henry III.[30]

But beyond the "reality" of Jewish economic activity in Angevin England, there are at least two points to be made. The first is that the criticism of Jewish economics was aimed not only at the Jews but also at the king. Through such criticism the king was himself Judaized. In the cartoon this is achieved by mapping his crown onto a Jewish figure of the Antichrist. The chronicler Matthew Paris (ca. 1200–1259) took a more direct route and circumcised the king. Recounting Henry's reaction, in 1255, to the news that his Jews have no money left to give him, the chronicler has the king "woefully" exclaim: "I'm divided all around! I am a mutilated king and a shortened one, even cut in half! . . . I need money . . . no matter how I get it!"[31]

The second point is that this medieval Judaizing of princes and their administrative practices was not simply a strategic response to royal uses of real Jews. Rather it draws on a long tradition of representing the satanic aspects of worldly power as Jewish, a discourse that itself responds to a basic question of Christian politics we already encountered among earlier Christians: how to differentiate a Christian rule, oriented toward the spirit and eternity, from a politics oriented toward the world, temporal and carnal. Our medieval sources show us how this discourse was being applied in new and creative ways to evolving practices of princely power.

Among these evolving practices were the many attempts of princes to profit from the increasing monetization of society and the growing market in money. Usurers, Peter the Chanter explained in twelfth-century Paris, "are both the coffers and leeches of princes, because all things they shall have sucked up, they vomit into the fisc."[32] These usurers need not be Jewish: indeed they most often were not. But regardless of their faith their practice could be mapped onto Judaism, and it often was. Thus in one of the famous moralized bibles—lavishly illuminated manuscripts produced in French clerical circles to translate biblical passages into moral lessons intelligible to medieval princes—from circa 1225, we read of flattering courtiers (*losengiers*) who "counsel kings and princes to do ill with their power" (see figure 3.2). The roundel illuminating the commentary portrays a moneyman with his counting board and various figures whispering into the king's ear, none of them characterized as Jews. But its companion roundel depicts their Jewish counterparts in the court of the Antichrist, making the analogy clear.

Another moralized bible (ÖNB Ms. 1179, fol. 65c) from the same time and region skips analogy and complains directly that "lying Jews and usurers [or: Jewish usurers] tell princes and prelates that they are better than they are." In subsequent illuminations Jews and princes march together toward Hell.

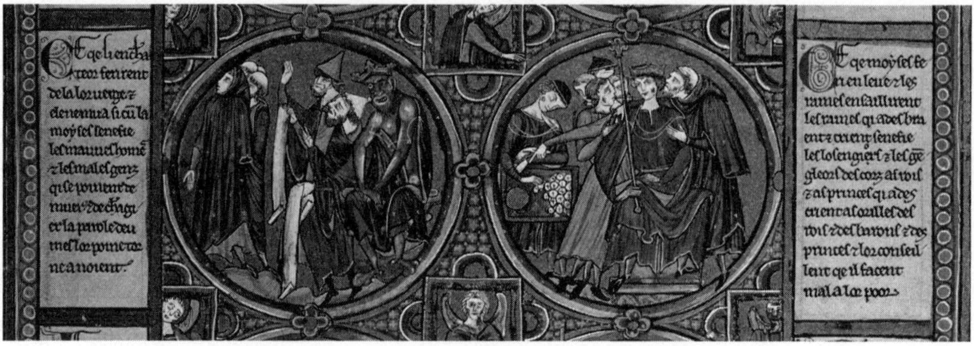

FIGURE 3.2
Bible moralisée, Österreichische Nationalbibliothek, MS. 2554, folio 19b.
PHOTO COURTESY OF THE ÖSTERREICHISCHE NATIONALBIBLIOTHEK.

In these examples it is not only financial administration that is being Judaized but also many other practices of governance, such as the taking of counsel, the delegation of authority, and the assertion of administrative power and legal jurisdiction. The same occurs in many other medieval moral discourses, such as the miracle story of Theophilus that spread across Europe in the mid-twelfth and early thirteenth centuries. Theophilus (in Gonzalo de Berceo's early thirteenth-century Castilian version) was the intimate councilor and minister—*privado*, in Castilian —of a bishop, so trusted that the bishop placed the entire administration of the see in his hands. When the bishop died, Theophilus was offered the miter but turned it down out of humility. Yet as his influence waned under the next bishop, he regretted the decision and turned for help to a very different *privado*, a Jewish minister of Satan who brokered the sale of his soul to the devil in exchange for renewed administrative power. Theophilus eventually repented and prayed to the Virgin Mary, who interceded for him in the heavenly court and convinced her Son to recover the contract from Hell.

There are two options represented in this morality tale: a Christian court, in which power is mediated through virtuous Christian ministers with eternal salvation the goal; and a satanic one with Jewish ministers, thirsting for earthly power and condemned to damnation. In this exemplum it is the episcopal courtier who must choose between two models

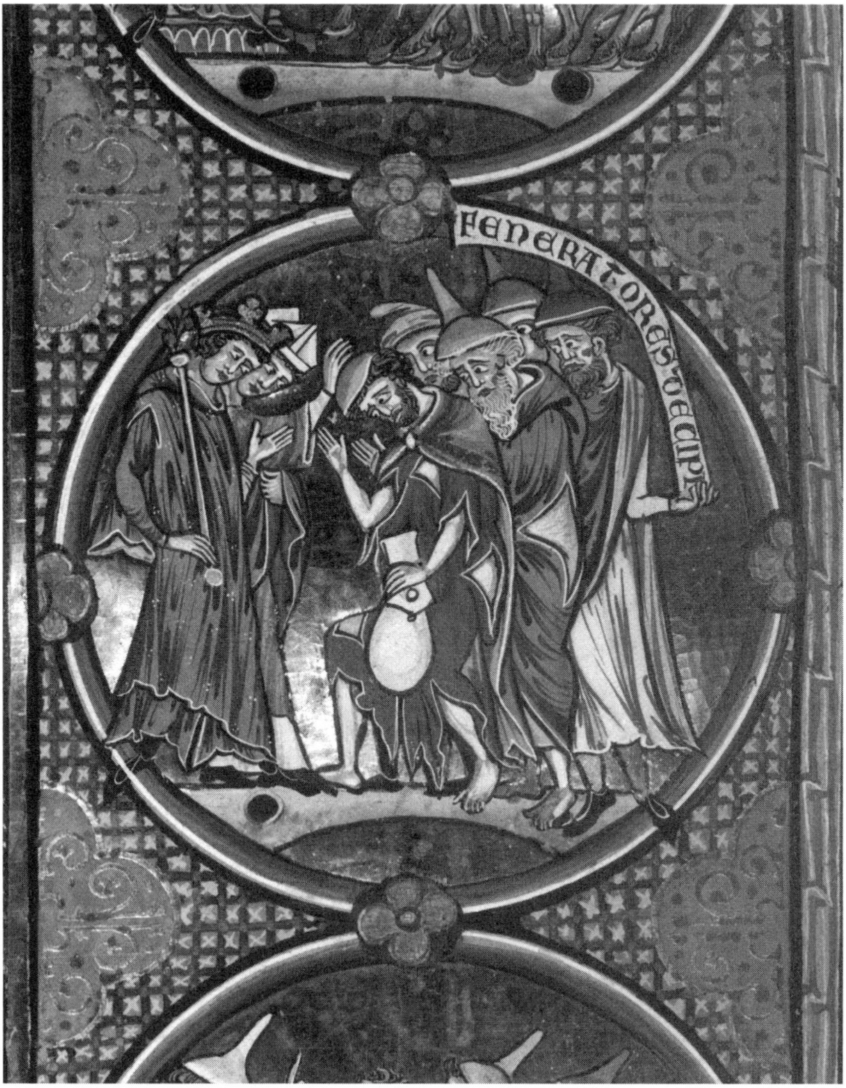

FIGURE 3.3.

Bible moralisée, Österreichische Nationalbibliothek, MS. 1179, folio 65c.

PHOTO COURTESY OF THE ÖSTERREICHISCHE NATIONALBIBLIOTHEK.

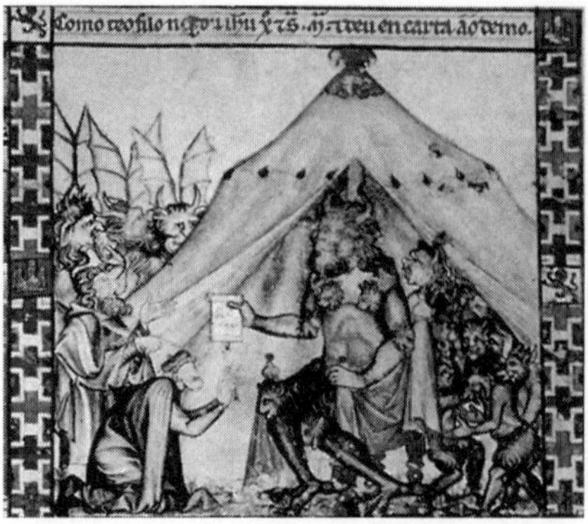

FIGURE 3.4
Detail of Theophilus, *Cantigas de Santa María*, Cantiga 3, Escorial, MS. T.I.1, folio 3r.
PHOTO COURTESY OF EDILÁN-ARS LIBRIS.

of power, that of the Jew as intercessor in Satan's court and that of the Virgin in the heavenly realm. Nevertheless the potential analogy with princely power remains encoded in the story, as we can see in a late thirteenth-century version recounted in the collection *Cantigas de Santa María* (Songs of Holy Mary) undertaken by King Alfonso X of Castile. The collection's third *cantiga* is dedicated to Theophilus (now called, in Castilian, Teófilo), and in its illumination (figure 3.4) we see Satan enthroned with all the trappings of monarchy, with the Jew acting as minister, presenting his client's plea to the demonic king.[33] In the Christian ontology of governance illuminated here, Judaism serves as a figure for the susceptibility of political mediation to the deadly attractions of worldly power and the sovereignty of the flesh.

Spain Again: Jewish Thought Becomes Jewish Flesh

The example is especially interesting, because King Alfonso X was himself deeply enmeshed in the Jewishness of politics. In more or less the same period as these illuminations were being prepared, Alfonso was confronted by multiple rebellions of clerics and aristocrats who accused him of being a lover of Jews. In 1279, for example, many of the bishops of his realm gathered to characterize him in formal complaint as, in the words of Peter Linehan, "a barely Christian tyrant manipulated by Jewish counselors, intent upon subjecting churchmen to an intolerable yoke of persecution and servitude."[34] The *Cantigas* should itself be understood as an example of how Christian kings attempted to defend themselves against these charges of Jewish carnality. From its dedication —to the memory of Alfonso's namesake Ildefonso, the seventh-century bishop of Toledo famous for his treatise defending the virginity of Mary against Jews and heretics—and throughout its hundreds of poems, the collection strives to represent Alfonso as a champion of a Christian polity of the spirit, and an enemy of the sovereignty of the flesh that Judaism represents. Consider, for example, Cantiga 209, entitled "He Who Denies God and His Blessings Commits a Great Error and Is Grievously Wrong." In this song, written by the king himself, he tells how when he was ill and seemed about to die in 1270, he refused the advice of his doctors and turned to the Virgin instead: "I shall tell you what happened to me while I lay in Vitoria, so ill that all believed I should die there and did not expect me to recover. . . . The doctors ordered hot cloths placed on me but I refused them and ordered, instead, that Her Book [that is, a manuscript of the *Cantigas* itself] be brought to me. They placed it on me, and at once I lay in peace. The pain subsided completely, I felt very well and cried no more. I gave thanks to Her for it, because I know full well She was dismayed at my afflictions."[35]

The illumination to this poem in the Florence manuscript of the *Cantigas*, left incomplete at the king's death, represents the king's choice as one between the sciences of the flesh and of the spirit. And unlike the poem itself, the illumination represents the choice as a rejection of Judaism. Thus on the verso of folio 119 (figure 3.5) the artists assign to the instructing physician in the first panel the type of hat used to characterize Jews throughout the manuscript. The king refuses the Jew's advice, and the Jew disappears from the scene while the Virgin's book is brought forth, with the Jew returning only to witness the miraculous cure.[36]

It is easy to overlook the Christian political claim staged in the illumination, in which King Alfonso's refusal of Jewish medicine addressed only to the flesh represents his preference for the spiritual body over the carnal one. In this sense the miraculous healing power of the king's collection of songs is itself represented as a defense of his body politic against the charge of Judaism. The point is even more explicit in Cantiga

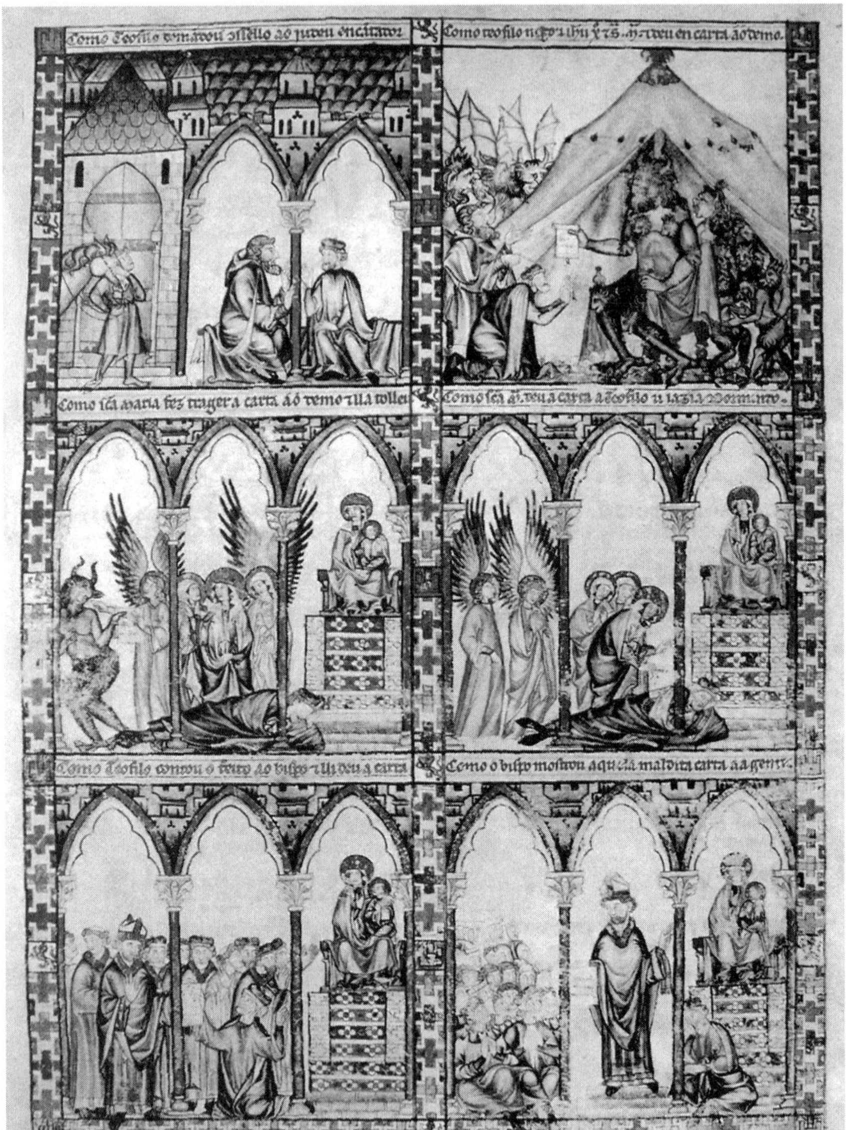

FIGURE 3.5 (PLATE 12)
Cantigas de Santa María, Cantiga 209,
Florence, MS. B.R. 20, folio 119v.
PHOTO COURTESY OF EDILÁN-ARS LIBRIS.

235. Alfonso is now in fact upon his deathbed, in the agony of his final illness, and the *cantiga* presents him as Jesus persecuted unto death by the enmity of his own Jewish people. Just as God's enemies the Jews were punished with eternal misery, so would Alfonso's suffer, for they were also enemies of "the Son of God," who would consign them all to eternal fire. On the other hand (the song continues) Alfonso, like Jesus, was resurrected by the Virgin into eternal life "on the happy day of Easter." She cradled him in her arms just as she had cradled her Son, "who was nailed on the cross . . . and Who . . . bestows his mercy and grace amidst the perils of the world."

In Alfonso's versified and illuminated world the king is not only Christian but a figure of Christ, while his persecutors and critics—that is, his own rebellious Christian subjects—are placed among the murderous Jews. Outside the folios of the manuscript, however, it was otherwise. Alfonso died deposed by his son, defeated, among other things, by the charge of Judaism he had tried so hard to protect himself from.

It is not for me to say whether Alfonso was a tyrant and Jew-lover, or beloved of Christ. But he was certainly a firm advocate for the power of the monarchy and its ministers, and one who sought, like all his successors, to implement and expand that power. It is precisely that claim to power that was met by its rivals with charges of Judaism. There is in fact no Spanish king, from Alfonso forward, who was not accused at some point or other of being a Jew-lover, of favoring "Jewish" councilors and *privados*, or even—as with Ferdinand and Isabel—of being descended from Jews. And again, as in the case of painting or poetry, these political charges were not the product of the "real Judaism" of their objects, but of a system of thought that made "Judaism" a meaningful critical term in the political sciences of the age.

It is perhaps easiest to perceive the power of this critical term in the century or so that followed the first mass conversions of Jews to Christianity in 1391. In the previous chapters we saw how these conversions changed how Christians thought about the Jewishness of painting and poetry. They transformed politics as well, giving—and this may seem like a paradox—accusations of "political Judaism" even greater power than they had before. As an example of this power consider the rebellion that broke out against the policies of Isabel the Catholic's father, King John II of Castile, and his *privado* or prime minister, Álvaro de Luna, in 1449.

The revolt was centered in the city of Toledo, but it was supported by many—including the king's son and heir, Prince Henry—who saw their share of government spoils affected by the centralizing taxation and fiscal strategies of Álvaro and his administrators (all of them, by the way, Christians, some of them New Christians). The rebels were quite explicit in their complaints about taxes and administrative practices, but it was the "Jewishness" of the government that provided the ideological heart for their justifications.

Let's look at just one of those justifications to highlight once again the complexities of the interrelationship between what we might call "real" or "sociological" Judaism (the Jewishness that threatens those who look like or act like the roles assigned to living Jews within a society) and "ontological," "epistemological," or "aesthetic" Judaism (the Jewishness that, in Christian thought, threatens every embodied human being, dependent as we are on letter, flesh, law, and the created things of this world). The text in question is a treatise penned in the last days of the revolt. The city of Toledo is already surrounded by royalist troops, surrender is imminent, and the rebellion's ideologues are seeking to justify their revolt in general, and in particular one action they have taken: the proclamation of a decree of purity of blood forbidding anyone who is converted from Judaism or descended from converts from holding public office. We need not read beyond the opening sentences of the treatise in question, which is cast as a final appeal to a Christian sovereign:

> [I address this letter] to the Holy Father . . . and to the high and powerful king or prince or administrator to whom, according to God, law, reason and right there belongs the administration and governance of the realms . . . of Castile and Leon, and to all other . . . administrators in the spiritual and temporal [affairs] of the universal orb, in the Church militant, which is the congregation and university of faithful Christians, [that is, those] truly believing

> in the birth, passion and resurrection [etc.] . . . [but I do not address it to those administrators who are] the unbelieving and the doubtful in the faith, who are outside of us and in confederation [*ayuntamiento*] with the synagogue, which is to say a congregation of beasts, for since such bind themselves like livestock to the letter, they have always given and still give false meaning to divine and human scripture. [In short, I address this letter to those] attesting to the truth and saying: "the letter kills, the spirit vivifies" [2 Cor. 3:6].[37]

This treatise is often treated as the first argument for biological or racial Judaism in European history. But we should notice that it begins with a literacy test. "Administrators" who read like Jews, literally after the flesh, have joined the synagogue and lost the human right to participate in the *res publica*. We know exactly what governors and administrators the authors have in mind, and none of them were "real Jews": the royal favorite Álvaro de Luna, the king, Juan II, who supported him, and even the pope, if he ended up rejecting Toledo's appeal and overturning the Statutes of Purity of Blood. And what if all princes turn out to read according to the letter, enslaving their people with a killing "Jewish" politics? In that case, the treatise concludes, the city should place itself directly under the governance of the Holy Spirit: the only Christian "politician" at no risk of Jewishness.

We've read only the first sentences of the rebels' general claim that converts from Judaism and their descendants carry material greed, tyrannical governance, and poor reading practices in their blood. That claim later animated both the establishment of the Inquisition and the institutionalization of purity of blood tests for all public office and privilege (including immigration to the Americas) in Spain and its future empire. Today we might—following Foucault and some of his heirs—want to call this claim *biopolitical*. But the few sentences we have read of it are enough to suggest that this biopolitics is deeply rooted in a hermeneutics and an ontology—in this case, in the Hellenistic and Pauline discrimination between the body and the soul, both of the reader and of the text.

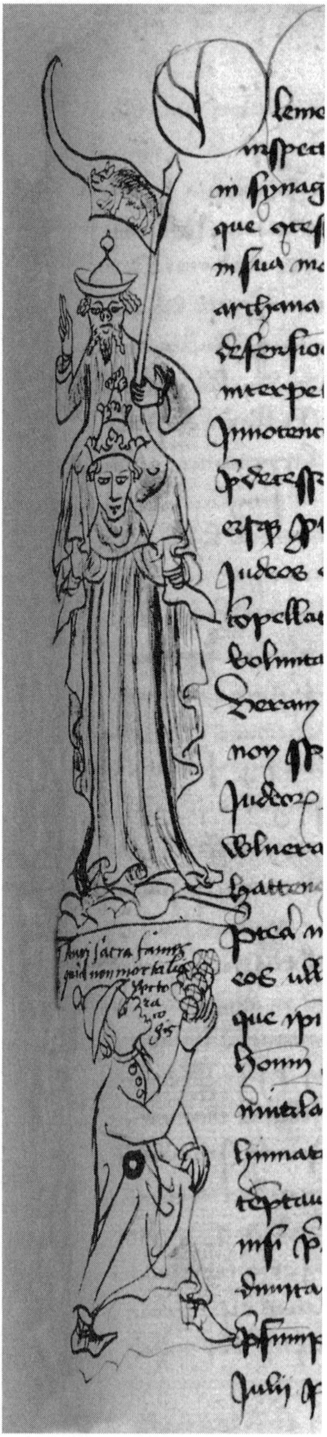

FIGURE 3.6
Cartoon of Pope with Jew, Kopialbuch 3, folio 269, Institut für Stadtgeschichte, Frankfurt.
PHOTO COURTESY OF THE INSTITUT FÜR STADTGESCHICHTE, FRANKFURT AM MAIN.

Once More Political Theology and the King's Two Bodies

The late medieval Iberian case is a particular and particularly interesting one, in part because—like the early Christian community of Paul, Peter, and their immediate successors—it involved significant populations of Christians converted from "real" Judaism. But for all its particularity it is also an example of a general phenomenon. In a Christian world oriented toward transcendence *all* politics faced a similar "two body problem." Every political community, and every political actor, is suspended between flesh and spirit, between the treasures of this world and those of the next. Insofar as every incarnate politics takes place in this world, no politics, no matter how "incarnational," can ever entirely free itself from the stigma that accompanies the claims of flesh and everything associated with those claims—such as letter, law, and Judaism—in Christian theology. Every choice of the flesh over the spirit has the potential to Judaize the Christian, and therefore every Christian politician can be represented as a "Jew," every politics can be mapped onto "Judaism." Even the pope is not immune, as we can see in a cartoon drawn in 1450, ironically enough in the margins of a copy of a papal bull prohibiting violence against Jews (*Sicut Judaeis*, first issued in the twelfth century) sent to the city of Frankfurt by Pope Clement VI in 1349, just after (doubly ironic!) that city's massacre of its Jewish inhabitants.

The revolutionary power of such mappings was enormous. Think only, to continue with papal examples, of the role they played in Martin Luther's revolt against Rome. Throughout his preaching and writings Luther worked constantly to associate the papal court—the "Devil's Synagogue" (*teufels Synagoga*), as he sometimes put it—with Judaism. And here again, as in some of our previous examples, the power of this mapping generates a new graphic imagery with which to express itself. In 1545, for example, Luther's great artistic collaborator Lucas Cranach produced a print of a bearded and hook-nosed Pope Paul III riding a sow while holding a handful of steaming feces ("Drecetta," as the accompanying Latin poem puts it, punning on "Decreta," decretals). Few among

Luther's audience would have missed the analogy that this "Papensau" was meant to establish with the Jews on their iconic "Judensau."[38]

The power of such analogies was not limited to the reformers. From the papist point of view, it was the Lutherans, with their literalism and their biblicism, who were the Judaizers. When Johann Eck wrote in 1540 that the Lutherans were "fathers of Jews," or an Augsburg Catholic preached in 1551, reacting to Edward VI's embrace of the Protestant cause, that "the King of England, his council and kingdom had all become Jews," their audiences would not have been puzzled. They understood that the danger of Judaism was a general one, stalking not only sovereigns and popes in their halls of power but rather haunting every individual and every possibility of relation in a Christian world.[39]

The "political theology" I am trying to describe through these examples is akin to that of Kantorowicz, in that the work done by the "king's two bodies" is central to it. But mine is much more general than his, and much less optimistic. More general because my argument is not simply about the king's "two bodies" but about all bodies politic. It is the very generality of this two-body problem that made "anti-Jewish" projection so useful for so many political theologies, both medieval and (as we shall shortly and briefly see) modern. But the generality of this projection should not make us optimistic about its efficacy. Unlike Kantorowicz, I want to stress that, within a material world inescapably dependent on systems stigmatized as Jewish within Christian thought—systems such as law, symbolic communication, material and economic exchange—the danger of political Judaism is inescapable. The king's bodies, indeed all political bodies, can always be accused of deadly Jewish fleshiness, no matter how loudly they protest their sacrality or immortality.

Kantorowicz does not seem to want to explicitly note this ambivalence, but both the ambivalence and the figures of Judaism that animate it are evident in many of his materials. For example, chapter 2 of *The King's Two Bodies* is dedicated to a reading of Shakespeare's *Richard II*, and points out that both the playwright and his medieval sources associate that king's murder by Bolingbroke and his followers with that of Jesus by Pilate and the Jews (much as the *Cantigas* tried to represent Alfonso's defeat and death as another crucifixion). In this sense Kantorowicz is right to point to the play as evidence for a Christological conception of sovereignty. But he does not mention that Richard's critics also Judaize the king in their complaints (again, theologically similar to those made against Alfonso X) about his administrative practices. In the unforgettable words that Shakespeare assigns to John of Gaunt, Richard's kingdom has been "bound in with shame, / With inky blots and rotten parchment bonds." This complaint of enslavement by letter, law, and contract is full of Judaizing force. But neither Shakespeare nor John of Gaunt stops there. Enter King Richard, and John speaks, like Ambrose a millennium before but pregnant with different meaning, a certain kind of truth to majesty:

> Why, cousin, wert thou regent of the world,
> It were a shame to let this land by lease;
> But for thy world enjoying but this land,
> Is it not more than shame to shame it so?
> Landlord of England art thou now, not king:
> Thy state of law is bondslave to the law; And thou—

A cruder dramatist might have furnished the speech with an Ambrosian conclusion: "art from a sovereign turned to tyrant Jew." Shakespeare leaves us hanging, but his silence is not innocent. In *The Merchant of Venice* he will address precisely these and many other questions raised by contract, law, commerce, and politics in Christian society—a society, it bears repeating, that had not housed a living community of "real Jews" for more than three hundred years—through much more explicit figures of Judaism. If Shylock and other such figures proved so good to think with in Shakespeare's England, it is because there, as throughout so much of the history of Christian thought, Judaism stood not only for a religion and its adherents but also and more generally for a mistaken attitude toward the material world of signs and things.[40]

Can Dialectics Succeed where Incarnation Failed?

Karl Marx and Friedrich Engels, in the very first paragraph of their first collaboration (*The Holy Family, or Critique of Critical Criticism* of 1844), singled out one by now familiar phrase for condemnation: "for written letters kill, but the Spirit gives life" (2 Cor 3:6). "Real humanism has no more dangerous enemy," they wrote, than this "spiritualism." They did not think this enemy obsolete. On the contrary, their "critique of critical criticism" was that the "philosophy" of their teachers and rivals—including and especially Hegel and a group of his followers to whom Marx initially belonged called the "Young Hegelians"—"is nothing else but religion rendered into thoughts and thinkingly expounded, and that it has therefore likewise to be condemned as another form . . . of the estrangement of man."[41]

Marx and Engels were right to point to the Christological foundations of Hegel's dialectic and to sense the potential for estrangement within them.[42] Hegel's own attempt to imagine the dialectical unfolding of history in terms of the Christian overcoming of an opposition between law and love had stumbled on the impossibility, in this imperfect world, of that overcoming. Do criminals, for example, not need to be punished by positive law? In the *Phenomenology*, Hegel tried to argue that the criminal wills his own punishment as a free self-authorizing subject, but even he seems to have found the argument unconvincing. Similarly in his *Philosophy of Right*, Hegel strove mightily to move property rights and contractual market exchange into the realm of love and recognition. He did so, in part, by deploying figures of Judaism as representations of an unfree, "slavish" relation to possessions and exchange. The difficulty is that in our embodied world, no "dialectical synthesis" can completely overcome the opposition between "law" and "freedom" and produce a fully self-legislating subject. But if the plenitude of freedom can never be reached, if the remainder of "Jewish" law cannot be reduced, then the unintended result of Hegel's patterning the history of philosophy upon the history of salvation turns out to be that every political and philosophical step, no matter how "progressive," remains Judaizable, just as every theological step had proven to be in Christian theology.[43]

Marx and Engels correctly perceived that Hegel's dialectic reinscribed rather than overcame the political dangers of Judaism, but they wrongly imagined that they themselves had escaped those dangers. In fact in another essay Marx wrote against the young Hegelians that same year—known today as "On the Jewish Question"—he offered a vision not so different from Saint Augustine's as we might think:

> The members of the political state are religious through the dualism between the individual and the species-life, between the life of civil society and the political life; religious in that they hold the political life of the state, something outside their true individuality, to be their true life; religious insofar as religion is here the spirit of civil society, the expression of the separation and distancing of man from man . . . man as he has been corrupted by the entire organization of our society, as he is lost to himself, alienated, and handed over to the rule of inhuman circumstances and elements—in short, man who is not yet a *true* species-being.

This too is a vision of two cities, two bodies politic. In one civic life is built on egoistic foundations of private property and mediated by money and market, alienating man from man. The other is a "truly" political city, oriented toward man's social and "species-being," his love of neighbor. Marx has a name for the "antisocial element" at the basis of civil society and the corrupted city: it is money, "the God of the Jews." In such a society the symbolic mediation of money Judaizes all users, so that "the Jew is perpetually created by civil society from its own entrails." Marx speaks not of the letter but of the coin, not of the spirit but of "true species-being." But his name for the political overcoming of the alienations of symbolic representation is the same as that used by much of the Christian tradition: "the *emancipation of society from Judaism*." And the result of his solution is also not so different from theirs: the creation of figures of Judaism from society's own entrails.[44]

Marx is exemplary precisely because he was precociously aware that certain forms of communication and exchange were somehow structurally Jewish within Christian culture. His own eager Judaization of the entire sphere of monetary circulation is therefore a powerful reminder of how difficult it is to avoid the dangerous enmity between a politics oriented toward transcendence (or in Marx's case "species-being") and whatever it is we might want to mean by "real humanism."

The danger of that enmity seems to me to be growing today, as we swim in currents of critical thought that pull with increasing force toward transcendence. Since the late 1980s "political theology" has come into ever greater fashion (it is in part thanks to that wave that Kantorowicz's own work has enjoyed such a renaissance). It is once more commonplace to assert that political order cannot found itself on values that it itself guarantees: that politics must point beyond itself. In the words of the Italian philosopher Roberto Esposito, "In order to save itself, life needs to step out from itself and constitute a transcendental point from which it receives order and shelter." Not only in political theory but in the humanities more broadly, there is a renewed willingness to take seriously the view that our participation in representation, both political and hermeneutic, requires transcendence, presence, grace.

Sometimes these invocations are explicitly modeled on incarnational or eucharistic theologies. But often enough, as in the cases of Hegel, Marx, and many others, the turn toward transcendence does not look much like an appeal to a god or a religion. There are many secularized ways of articulating the claim. Think, for example, of the Lacanian conviction, quite popular in many circles of critical theory today, that communicative life (or in Eric Santner's formulation, "the signifiers subjects are compelled to contract or take on as 'members' of a symbolic order to represent them to other signifiers") requires subjection to a "master signifier."[45]

It is not a coincidence that many of these moves toward transcendence generate figures of Judaism with frightening ease. Consider only Slavoj Žižek's description of "an interesting struggle which has been going on recently (not only) among Lacanians (not only) in France. This struggle concerns the status of the 'One' as the name of a political subjectivity. . . ."

> The question is: is the name of the One the result of a contingent political struggle, or is it somehow rooted in a more substantial particular identity? The position of "Jewish Maoists" is that "Jews" is such a name which stands for that which resists today's global trend to overcome all limitations, inclusive of the very finitude of the human condition, in radical capitalist "deterritorialization" and

> "fluidification" (the trend which reaches its apotheoisis in the gnostic-digital dream of transforming humans themselves into virtual software that can reload itself from one hardware to another). The name "Jews" thus stands for the most basic *fidelity* to what one is. . . . Jews here are the exception: in the liberal multiculturalist perspective, all groups can assert their identity—except Jews, whose very self-assertion equals Zionist racism. In contrast to this approach, Badiou and others insist on the fidelity to the One which emerges and is constituted through the very political struggle of/for naming, and, as such, cannot be grounded in any particular determinate content (such as ethnic or religious roots). From this point of view, fidelity to the name "Jews" is the obverse (the silent recognition) of the defeat of authentic emancipatory struggles.

We do not need to delve deep into the specifics of Lacanian vocabulary in order to realize that in this struggle both sides cast the Jews in their Pauline position of particularism. Both positions are equally fantastic, and both oscillate wildly between Judaism as an ethnicity, religion, or even nation claimed by real people and Judaism as a name, concept, or figure of thought: an oscillation that is perhaps confused, perhaps strategic, but whose implications are in any case too easily occluded by the use of scare quotes. Let us continue for a moment with Žižek's focus on Badiou's position, in which "Judaism" is quickly associated with enmity toward freedom and emancipatory revolution:

> No wonder that those who demand fidelity to the name "Jews" are also those who warn us against the "totalitarian" dangers of any radical emancipatory movement. Their politics consist in accepting the fundamental finitude and limitation of our situation, and the Jewish Law is the ultimate mark of this finitude, which is why for them all attempts to overcome Law and tend towards all-embracing Love (from Christianity through the French Jacobins to Stalinism) must end up in totalitarian terror. To put it succinctly, the only true solution to the "Jewish question" is the "final solution" (their annihilation), because Jews *qua objet a* are the ultimate

> obstacle to the "final solution" of History itself, to the overcoming of divisions in all-encompassing unity and flexibility.

What can I say about these words, which in any case cannot be debated, since they axiomatically condemn to death as Jewish all arguments such as mine? I cannot even say with certainty if they speak for Žižek, since he presents them as a description of the positions of others. He does not, however, hesitate to manifest his own allegiances: "This book is unashamedly committed to the 'Messianic' standpoint of the struggle for universal emancipation."[46]

There is, to my mind, a depressing déjà vu to this return to transcendence: depressing not because it looks toward the past for answers to the pressing questions of the present—this seems to me a wholly appropriate, even necessary, approach to many of the questions that confront us—but because it is so selective in the past it looks to and the conclusions it draws. This is not, after all, the first time the dangers of certain theological conceptions of the political have been pointed out. Leaving aside the prophetic Weimar souls who named those dangers before they became fact, there are also those who later synthesized them into something like an intellectual history. Martin Buber's first speech in Germany after the war ("The Validity and Limitations of the Political Principle," given at his reception of Hamburg's Goethe Prize in 1953) was dedicated to suggesting that Schmitt's concept of the political collaborated with a Hegelian tendency to grant history an ontological autonomy. According to Buber that tendency, which he felt reached its deepest expression in Heidegger, had helped produce the horrors of midcentury by making history and its political manifestations inherently self-validating.[47]

Without taking a position on Buber's knowledge of history or academic philosophy (Heidegger criticized him on the latter score to Hannah Arendt) I simply want to stress that, as far as Buber was concerned, the attempt to tie language, politics, and other forms of representation to any manifest reading of transcendence was dangerously misguided. That conviction was the major ground of his postwar engagements with Heidegger. Both thinkers were similar insofar as both sought to overcome—if Meike Siegfried is correct in her recent *Abkehr vom*

Subjekt—a modern conception of the cognitive subject.[48] But according to Buber that overcoming should not be obtained by looking away from the human or toward the divine. "The human truth of which I speak," he explained in what we may take to be his final response to Heidegger (in "The Word That Is Spoken," delivered in Munich in 1960), "the truth vouchsafed to men, is no *pneuma* that pours itself out from above on a band of men now become super-personal (*überpersonhaft*): it opens itself only in one's existence as a person."[49]

We know more or less how Heidegger would have responded, in part because we have the letter he had written to his wife a few years earlier, after reading another essay of Buber's: "The question remains whether this 'either-or' is sufficient at all or whether both the one and the other have to be prepared even more fundamentally, a preparation which of course again requires the [divine] address and its protection [*Geheißes und seines Schutzes*]."[50] Again, we need not take a position in order to concede that something about the shape these debates had taken in the 1920s, '30s, and '40s motivated a thinker like Martin Buber to dedicate much of his later years to fighting against their manifestations, not only in the rarified sphere of the theology and philosophy of language but also very much in the sphere of politics and its theologies. For myself, I confess that my sympathy here lies with Buber, for I very much admire the ways in which he pursued his yearning for the transcendent truths of the divine without fantasizing that those truths could ever become clearly legible in the confusions of this world. As he put it in 1946: "Even those communities which call the spirit their master and salvation their Promised Land, the 'religious' communities, are community only if they serve their lord and master in the midst of simple, unexalted, unselected reality, a reality not so much chosen by them as sent to them just as it is; they are community only if they prepare the way to the Promised Land through the thickets of this pathless hour."[51]

"This Pathless Hour"

In the preceding pages I have offered a thumbnail sketch of the history of Jewishness as political concept. At the very least I hope the sketch will remind us that commitments to a politics of transcendence have a historical potential to produce Jewish figures of enmity. I realize that my historical approach can never be robust, insofar as each specific commitment can proclaim its innocence from the past, and demand its own historical context and its own critique. There is no answer sufficient to that demand. I could, for example, attempt to demonstrate that the Lacanian, Hegelian, and Heideggerian formulations so many of these contemporary thinkers deploy themselves depend on the Christianized cognitive distinctions (letter and spirit, Jew and Christian, law and freedom) that I've been tracing throughout this paper, and therefore reproduce many of the stigmatizations that mark the history of those distinctions.

But that would be just another historical example, one more in an endless accumulation of possible examples that need not compel conviction. For those in the thrall of messianic hope, past failures are not sufficient guarantee of future ones. On the contrary, to the believer they may even serve as evidence of messianic truth. To quote once more from the same work of Žižek's: "as Badiou himself might put it in his unique Platonic way, true ideas are eternal, they are indestructible, they always return every time they are proclaimed dead." Žižek seems even to accept that the mere repetition of these eternal truths is enough to reveal the thought of their "Jewish" critics "in all its misery as what it really is, a worthless sophistic exercise, a pseudo-theorization of the lowest opportunist survivalist fears and instincts, a way of thinking which is not only reactionary but also profoundly *reactive* in Nietzsche's sense of the term."[52] Against such confidence perhaps all one can do is quote back Nietzsche's warning against accepting too easily even our most cherished axioms: "We have arranged for ourselves a world in which we are able to live with the postulation of bodies, lines, surfaces, causes and effects, motion and rest, form and content: without these articles of faith nobody could now endure to live! But that does not yet mean they are something proved and demonstrated."[53]

Rather than pile examples higher, let me summarize and generalize my claim. Christianity did not invent the political distinction between the physical and the metaphysical—between a mortal body politic of flesh and an immortal one of spirit—but it did, for reasons I have tried to describe, invent the mapping of that politics onto the cognitive categories of "Jew" and "Christian." My claim is that this mapping became so central to the history of political thought that key critical concepts of political thought came to encode it, so that those concepts, when applied in political critique, themselves generated new figures of Judaism, so to speak, from their own entrails.

The "long history" of the political that I've offered you here is one—admittedly insufficient—way of trying to support that claim. I recognize, of course, that sweeping histories of ideas (especially highly abbreviated ones such as this) violate the current conviction that, as Michel Foucault famously put it, "history is for cutting," a conviction particularly strong today among historians of political thought. Rather than attempt a theoretical defense of my approach, I can here offer only the metaphor of a mask. I don't mean the mask Carl Schmitt placed on the Jews, but the mask as deployed by the philosopher from whom Foucault derived his dictum, Nietzsche once again. Foucault was right that Nietzsche ridiculed certain fantasies of identity between present and past, but he forgot that Nietzsche also insisted on elements of formal continuity in historical memory: "All great things must first wear terrifying and monstrous masks in order to inscribe themselves on the hearts of humanity."[54]

These masks, the forms in which ideas presented themselves, were not for Nietzsche incidental to their future. On the contrary, great ideas impress themselves upon generations of human memory in part by concealing their ongoing and constant transformation behind the abiding terror of their masks. My claim, at its simplest, is that the great and difficult invention we call transcendence first wore the mask of death and then of Judaism. It was by splitting all that is human into dying body and immortal soul that philosophy tried to make its claims to truth eternal. And it was by mapping this split onto letter and spirit, Jew and Christian, that the followers of Jesus came to make theirs. Judaism became a terrifying mask: a pedagogical fear, perhaps, but one that has given enduring and sometimes horrifying form to key concepts and questions of painting, poetry, politics, and so many other practices of cognition, communication, and exchange in Western culture and its heirs.[55]

The power of transcendence as an ideal cannot be denied. Nor need it be. I am not advocating the death of God, the murder of another Messiah, the embrace of "mere life," nor surrender to "the lowest opportunist survivalist fears and instincts." I do believe—with Buber and perhaps with the elderly Saint Augustine in some but not all the pages of his *City of God*—that one can yearn for the Promised Land without insisting that it be found on earth. But even if you do not believe as I do, you will after this trinity of chapters perhaps be willing to concede that the distinction between the physical and the metaphysical, and the dialectics that distinction enables, has been thoroughly mapped across a long history of thought onto the cognitive categories of "Jew" and "Christian." It is for this reason that our critical concepts themselves have tended to reproduce these distinctions, and have had the potential to generate such ferocious figures of Judaism. I think this potential is as present in contemporary critical thought as it was in those moments of the past I've tried to describe. It is against that monstrous potential that I tilt these pages, not against transcendence itself. We can try to orient our thought toward transcendence. But if we wish to think critically, we need always to interrogate our certainties about what transcendence looks like, which is also to say about what shape its enemies take in our imagination. Anything else is dogma, the *mainmorte* of a long history of aesthetic theologies masquerading as critical philosophy, "religion rendered into thoughts and thinkingly expounded," as Marx and Engels put it, and "therefore likewise to be condemned as another form . . . of the estrangement of man."[56] No matter how intently we repeat them, such estrangements cannot emancipate us in this world or any other. They will lead us not to freedom, but to the return of our most familiar nightmares.

NOTES

List of Abbreviations

CCCM *Corpus Christianorum Continuatio mediaevalis*
CCSL *Corpus Christianorum: Series Latina*
CSEL *Corpus Scriptorum Ecclesiasticorum Latinorum*
MGH SS *Monumenta Germaniae Historica: Scriptores*
PL *Jean-Pierre Migne, ed., Patrologiae cursus completus. Series Latina*
WA *Dr. Martin Luthers Werke*, 127 volumes (Weimar: 1883–2009), known as the *Weimarer Ausgabe*

Introduction: Troubling Transcendence

1. See in general Hans Joas, "The Axial Age Debate in Religious Discourse," in *The Axial Age and Its Consequences*, ed. Robert N. Bellah and Hans Joas (Cambridge: Harvard University Press, 2012), 9–29. See also Benjamin I. Schwartz, "The Age of Transcendence," *Daedalus* (Spring 1975): 1–7; Shmuel Eisenstadt, "The Axial Age in World History," in *The Cultural Values of Europe*, ed. Hans Joas and Klaus Wiegandt (Liverpool: Liverpool University Press, 2008), 22–42. The "age of criticism" is Arnaldo Momigliano's felicitious term, from his *Alien Wisdom: The Limits of Hellenization* (Cambridge: Cambridge University Press, 1975), 8–9.

2. Karl Jaspers, *A Way to Wisdom: An Introduction to Philosophy* (New Haven: Yale University Press, 1951), 98.

3. Søren Kierkegaard, *Concluding Unscientific Postscript to "Philosophical Fragments,"* ed. and trans. Howard V. Hong and Edna H. Hong, vol. 1 (Princeton: Princeton University Press, 1992), 37–38.

4. See, for example, Aristotle's account of vision and the sensing soul in *De Anima*, beginning at 417a, together with the clarifying pages of Michael Davis, *The Soul of the Greeks* (Chicago: University of Chicago Press, 2011), 31–34.

5. "Kultur ist was ein Jud' vom anderen abschreibt": Reichsrat deputy Bielohlawek, quoted in Friedrich Heer, *Land in Strom der Zeit* (Vienna: Herold, 1958).

6. Philo, *On Abraham* 147, in *On Abraham; On Joseph; On Moses*, Loeb Classical Library 289 (Cambridge: Harvard University Press, 1935), 75; "soul characteristics" is F. H. Colson's rendering of *tropous psychēs*.

7. On Philo's neologisms see J. Leopold, "Philo's Vocabulary and Word Choice," in *Two Treatises of Philo of Alexandria: A Commentary on "De gigantibus" and "Quod Deus sit immutabilis,"* ed. D. Winston and J. Dillon (Chico: Scholars Press, 1983); D. T. Runia, *Philo of Alexandria and the "Timaeus" of Plato* (Leiden: Brill, 1986), 399–402; D. T. Runia, "'Verba Philonica,' 'Agalmatophorein' and the Authenticity of 'De Resurrectione' attributed to Athenagoras," *Vigiliae Christianae* 46 (1992): 313–27.

8. Philo, *On the Migration of Abraham* 92–93, in *On the Confusion of Tongues; On the Migration of Abraham; Who Is the Heir of Divine Things?; On Mating with the Preliminary Studies*, Loeb Classical Library 261 (Cambridge: Harvard University Press, 1932), 185. On Philo's (and later Origen's) middle- and Neoplatonic use of the analogy of body and soul for text and meaning see David Dawson, "Plato's Soul and the Body of the Text in Philo and Origen," in *Interpretation and Allegory: Antiquity to the Modern Period*, ed. Jon Whitman (Leiden: Brill, 2000), 89–107. See also A. J. M. Wedderburn, *Baptism and Resurrection: Studies in Pauline Theology against its Graeco-Roman Background* (Tübingen: Mohr, 1987), 127.

9. Paul invokes the blinding of the Jews' eyes in Rom. 11:10, citing Psalm 68:23–24. Augustine will take up Paul's point, for example, in *De civitate Dei* 18.46: "But the rest are blinded, of whom it was predicted, 'Let their eyes be darkened lest they see.'" It should be stressed that in describing Paul's Jewish "vessels of wrath" as "exemplary artifacts," I do not mean to imply that Paul intended the exemplarity that later Christian thinkers—most famously Saint Augustine—developed from them.

10. 1 Cor. 1:20–23; quoting Isa. 29:14. For a commentary see J. A. Fitzmyer, *First Corinthians*, Anchor-Yale Bible Commentaries (New Haven: Yale University Press, 2008).

11. Paul's chain here reaches back to Gal. 2:6. Antinomies were widespread in scripture and in popular oratory, as well as in Greek philosophical thought, rhetorical practice, and Greek traditions about the cosmos being constructed out of "pairs of opposites." See G. E. R. Lloyd, *Polarity and Analogy: Two Types of Argumentation in Early Greek Thought* (London: Bristol Classical Press, 1992); and, specifically on Paul, Norbert Schneider, *Die rhetorische Eigenart der paulinischen Antithese* (Tübingen: Mohr, 1970), 30*ff*. On the important ways in which, in Galatians, these traditions pressure Paul's presentation toward polarity, see J. Louis Martyn, "Apocalyptic Antinomies in Paul's Letter to the Galatians," *New Testament Studies* 31 (1985): 410–24. The cosmological use of polarity (for example, in apocalyptic dualism) is of course not only Greek and also has important antecedents in the Hebrew Bible, e.g., Isa. 45:7, or in the (for Jews noncanonical) Wisdom of Ben Sirah, 33:15: "all the works of the most high / are in pairs, / one the opposite of the other." Augustine will cite this latter passage in his *De civitate Dei*, Book 11, ch. 18.

12. Judaize: the Greek term (*ioudaïzein*, tr. into Latin as *iudaizare*) appears already in the Septuagint (e.g., in Esther 8:17), where it is not, however, negative. Paul's use of it is in the long run transformative. On the verb's history see Michele Murray, *Playing a Jewish Game: Gentile Christian Judaizing in the First and Second Centuries CE* (Ontario: Wilfred Laurier University Press, 2004), especially 3–4; Róbert Dán, "Judaizare—the Career of a Term," in *Antitrinitarianism in the Second Half of the 16th Century*, eds. R. Dán and A. Pirnát (Budapest and Leiden: Akadémiai Kiadó and Brill, 1982), 25–34; Gilbert Dagron, "Judäiser," in *Travaux et Mémoires* 11 (1991): 359–80.

13. The second part of this sentence is more controversial than the first, but it reflects much recent scholarship on Paul. For a summary of that scholarship see John G. Gager, *Reinventing Paul* (Oxford: Oxford University Press, 2000).

14. Carl Schmitt, *Politische Theologie: Vier Kapitel zur Lehre von der Souveränität* (Munich: Dunckner and Humblot, 1922); *Der Begriff des Politischen* (Berlin: Duncker and Humblot, 1932).

1. Painting between Christianity and Judaism

1. God, too, sometimes requires visual reminders of his covenant in order to know how to behave, as in Exodus 12:13: "The blood will be a sign for you on the houses where you are. When I see the blood I shall pass over you." For a brief survey of Israelite thought about loves that lead away from God, see my "The Politics of Love and Its Enemies," *Critical Inquiry* 33 (2007): 573–605.

2. Aristotle, *De Anima*, III.7.431[a] (*cf.* Plato, *Philebus* 39B–40E); John Locke, *An Essay concerning Human Understanding* (1689), Book II, chap. 11, sec. 17.

3. The canonical work on these consequences is Erwin Panofsky, *Idea: A Concept in Art Theory* (New York: Harper & Row, 1968).

4. On Plato's development of incorporeality and immateriality, compare R. Renehan, "On the Greek Origins of the Concepts Incorporeality and Immateriality," *Greek, Roman, and Byzantine Studies* 21 (1980): 105–38, with Heinrich Gomperz, "Asōmatos," *Hermes* 67 (1932): 155–67. I am here following Renehan's account. On intelligibles as incorporeal see, e.g., *Sophist* 246B. On the division between lesser and greater mysteries, *Symposium* 209E–210A (which scholars as illustrious as Cornford, Jaeger, and Guthrie have taken as marking the border between Socrates' interests in a philosophy of life in this world and Plato's in a philosophy of life in another).

5. Which some voices in the Platonic corpus take to mean cognition *tout court*, as when Critias remarks: "All statements made by any of us are of course bound to be an affair of imagery and picturing" (107A).

6. See, among a vast bibliography, Catherine Osborne, "The Repudiation of Representation in Plato's *Republic* and Its Repercussions," *Proceedings of the Cambridge Philological Society* 33 (1987): 53–73; John Hyman, *The Imitation of Nature* (Oxford: Blackwell, 1989); and more generally Stephen Halliwell, *The Aesthetics of Mimesis: Ancient Texts and Modern Problems* (Princeton: Princeton University Press, 2002).

7. All these points will find their echoes in the Christian tradition. Compare, for example, Saint Augustine's fourth-century discussion—in dialogue form—of the falsity of tragedy, painting, and sculpture (*Soliloquies* II.10 [18]); or the eighth-century complaints of the Caroline books about the representational promiscuity of artists (*Caroli Magni Capitulare de Imaginibus*, I.2).

8. Sublime: see Immanuel Kant, *Critique of the Power of Judgment*, §29, 5:274: "Perhaps there is no more sublime passage in the Jewish Book of the Law than the commandment: Thou shalt not make unto thyself any graven image. . . ." The sculptures and objects that decorate the Tabernacle provided a common focal point of Christian debate about devotional images from Late Antiquity throughout the Middle Ages: Herbert Kessler, "Shaded with Dust: Jewish Eyes on Christian Art," in *Judaism and Christian Art: Aesthetic Anxieties from the Catacombs to Colonialism*, ed.

David Nirenberg and Herbert L. Kessler (Philadelphia: University of Pennsylvania Press, 2011), 87.

9. Jerome, Letter 52, chap. 10. Jerome's Judaizing strategy here is much like the one he used against Saint Augustine in Letter 75, IV.13. Epiphanius of Salamis, *Testament*, ed. G. Ostrogorsky, *Studien zur Geschichte des byzantinischen Bilderstreites* (Breslau: M. and H. Marcus, 1929), 67, fragment 2. On Epiphanius's iconoclasm see most recently Olga Solovieva, "Epiphanius of Salamis and His Invention of Iconoclasm in the Fourth Century AD," *Fides et Historia* 42.1 (2010): 21–46; and "Epiphanius of Salamis between Church and State: New Perspectives on the Iconoclastic Fragments," *Zeitschrift für Antikes Christentum / Journal of Ancient Christianity* 16.2 (2012): 344–67.

10. John of Damascus, *Three Treatises on the Divine Images*, trans. Andrew Louth (Crestwood: St. Vladimir's Seminary Press, 2003), 24.

11. M. V. Anastos provides one of many versions of the arguments in "The Argument for Iconoclasm as Presented by the Iconoclastic Council of 754," *Late Classical and Medieval Studies in Honor of A. M. Friend, Jr.* (Princeton: Princeton University Press, 1955), 177*ff*. For the vast bibliography see Leslie Brubaker and John F. Haldon, *Byzantium in the Iconoclast Era (c. 680–850): The Sources, an Annotated Survey* (Burlington: Ashgate, 2001); and for a narrative of the conflict, Leslie Brubaker, John Haldon, and Robert Ousterhout, *Byzantium in the Iconoclast Era (ca. 680–850): A History* (Cambridge: Cambridge University Press, 2008).

12. The "tall tale" is cited here from the Seventh Ecumenical Council, 787 (Mansi, XIII, 197B–200B, with partial translation in Cyril Mango, *Art of the Byzantine Empire* [Toronto: University of Toronto Press, 1986], 150–51). For the many sources attesting to the generalized Byzantine attribution of the invention of iconoclasm to the Jews, see A. A. Vasiliev, "The Iconoclastic Edict of the Caliph Yazid II, AD 721," *Dumbarton Oaks Papers* 9/10 (1956): 23–47.

13. Kathleen Corrigan, *Visual Polemics in the Ninth-Century Byzantine Psalters* (Cambridge: Cambridge University Press, 1992), 31–32. The Khludov Psalter image (fol. 67r, Ps 68:22) is reproduced on p. 255. The psalter is quoting the eighth-century "Adversus Constantinum Caballinum," PG 95, 333A–336B.

14. The bibliography is vast, but many of the relevant sources, with much bibliography, are summarized in Brubaker and Haldon, *Byzantium in the Iconoclast Era*, 268–72. See also P. Speck, *Ich bin's nicht, Kaiser Konstantin ist es gewesen: Die Legenden vom Enfluss des Teufels, des Juden, und des Moslem auf den Ikonoklasmus* (Bonn: Poikila Byzantina, 1990). For a recent attempt to think through the uses of anti-Jewish polemic in Byzantium see Vincent Déroche,"Form and Function of anti-Jewish Polemics: Polymorphy, Polysémy," in *Jews in Byzantium: Dialectics of Minority and Majority Cultures*, ed. R. Bonfil, O. Irshai, G. Stroumsa, and R. Talgam (Leiden: Brill, 2012), 535–48.

15. Peter R. L. Brown, "Images as a Substitute for Writing," in *East and West: Modes of Communication*, ed. Euangelos K. Chrysos and Ian Wood (Leiden: Brill, 1999), 15–34, here 19. For the letter see Gregory the Great, *Registrum epistolarum*, ed. Dag Norberg (CCSL 140–140A) (Turnhaut: Brepols, 1982), 874; *The Letters of Gregory*

the Great, vol. 3, trans. John R. C. Martyn (Toronto: Pontifical Institute for Medieval Studies, 2004), 744–46. On the debate over the "Jewish" context see Vincent Déroche, "La polemique anti-judaïque au VIe et au VIIe siècle: un memento inédit, les *Kephalaia*," *Travaux et Mémoires* 11 (1991): 275–311. Kessler, "Shaded with Dust," 77. There were Jews in Marseille, as we know from Gregory of Tours, *History of the Franks*, trans. Lewis Thorpe (Harmondsworth: Penguin, 1974), Book 5, chapter 11, 267, who reports that when the bishop of Claremont forced the conversion of his city's Jews circa 580, "those who refused to accept baptism . . . made their way to Marseille."

16. Gregory of Tours, *Glory of the Martyrs*, trans. Raymond van Dam (Liverpool: Liverpool University Press, 1988), 40. See Leopold Kretzenbacher, *Das verletzte Kultbild: Voraussetzungen, Zeitschichten und Aussagewandel eines abendländischen Legendentypus* (Munich: Verlag der Bayerischen Akademie der Wissenschaften, 1977), 66–70. On the Patriarchs' letter see Heinz Gauer, *Texte zum byzantinishcen Bilderstreit: Der Synodalbrief der drei Patriarchen des Ostens von 836 und seine Verwandlung in sieben Jahrhunderten* (Frankfurt am Main: Peter Lang, 1994), 69–70. Jean-Marie Sansterre comments upon both episodes in "L'image blessée, l'image souffrante: quelques récits de miracles entre Orient et Occident (VIe–XIIe siècle)," in *Les images dans les sociétés médiévales: Pour une histoire comparée* (Brussels and Rome: Academia Belgica, 1999), 113–30, here 115–16.

17. The loudest Carolingian echo of the Byzantine controversy may be found in the *Opus Caroli regis contra Synodum*, ed. Ann Freeman and Paul Meyvaert (Hannover: Hahnsche Buchhandlung, 1998). Conrad Rudolph summarizes the Western critique of images in "La resistenza all'arte nel Occidente," in *Arti e storia nel Medioevo*, vol. 3 (Turin: Einaudi, 2004), 49–84.

18. On the cult of the True Cross in the West see A. Frolow, *La relique de la vraie croix: recherches sur le développement d'un culte* (Paris: Institut français d'études Byzantines, 1961). Frolow documents (pp. 111, 131) a sharp rise in references to relics of the True Cross beginning in the early eleventh century. On freestanding sculptures north of the Alps see Beate Fricke, *Ecce fides: Die Statue von Conques, Götzendienst und Bildkultur im Westen* (Munich: Fink, 2007). On Henry versus Wecelin see Sara Lipton, *Dark Mirror: The Medieval Origins of Anti-Jewish Iconography* (New York: Henry Holt, 2014), 40. Though the book appeared after these pages were written, her work has long guided me through these topics.

19. "Earliest Western medieval": we have already encountered many earlier Eastern examples, to which add Sergius the Stylite, *The Disputation of Sergius the Stylite against a Jew*, ed. A. P. Hayman, *Corpus Scriptorum Christianorum Orientalium* 338, *Scriptores Syri* 152 (Louvain: Secretariat du CorpusSCO, 1973), p. 41, cited in Brown, "Images," 24.

20. The exchange was transmitted by Alpert of Metz, *De Diversitate Temporum*, Lib. II, caps. 22–24 in MGH SS IV, ed. G. Pertz (Hannover: Impensis Bibliopolii Avlici Hahniani, 1841), 720–23; translated and analyzed in Anna Abulafia, "An Eleventh-Century Exchange of Letters between a Christian and a Jew," *Journal of*

Medieval History 7 (1981): 153–174. On the (common) distinction between eyes of the body and eyes of the soul in Late Antiquity and the Middle Ages, see the various works of Herbert L. Kessler, including his "Corporeal Texts, Spiritual Paintings, and the Mind's Eye," in *Reading Images and Texts: Medieval Images and Texts as Forms of Communication. Papers from the Third Utrecht Symposium on Medieval Literacy*, ed. M. Hageman and M. Mostert (Utrecht: Turnhout Brepols Publishers, 2000), 9–27; and *Spiritual Seeing: Picturing God's Invisibility in Medieval Art* (Philadelphia: University of Pennsylvania Press, 2000).

21. The miracle emerged in a sermon at the Iconophile Seventh Council of Nicaea in 787. Although translated into Latin in the ninth century, it began to circulate in Western Europe only in the eleventh, as part of the *Passio imaginis* office. See Michele Bacci, "The Berardenga Antependium and the *Passio Ymaginis* Office," *Journal of the Warburg and Courtauld Institutes* 61 (1998): 1–16. For an extended review of the office's influence on Western European and especially Iberian art, together with monographic treatment of an early fifteenth-century retable of the *Passio imaginis* today at San Salvador de Felanitx, Mallorca, see Carlos Espí Forcén, *Recrucificando a Cristo: Los judíos de la Passio Imaginis en la isla de Mallorca* (Mallorca: Objeto Perdido, 2009).

22. Adémar of Chabannes, *Chronicon* 3.52, ed. P. Bourgain, CCCM 129 (Turnhout: Brepols, 1999), 166–71.

23. An important example I will not analyze here is that of Rupert of Deutz (d. 1129?), who adopted this staging in his pro-image "Anulus sive dialogus inter Christianum et Iudaeum," ed. Rhabanus Haacke, in Maria Lodovica Arduini, *Ruperto di Deutz e la controversia tra cristiani ed ebrei nel secolo XII* (Rome: Istituto storico italiano per il Medio Evo, 1979), 232–35. See also, from Rupert's circle, the account of the conversion of the Jew Herman-Judah and his difficulties with images, on which Jean-Claude Schmitt's various works are central: "La question des images dans les débats entre juifs et chrétiens au XIIe siècle," in *Spannungen und Widersprüche: Gedenkenschrift für Frantisek Graus* (Sigmaringen: J. Thorbecke, 1992), pp. 245–54; "Les dimensions multiples du voir: Les rêves et l'image dans l'autobiographie de conversion d'Hermann le Juif au XIIe siècle," in *La visione e lo sguardo nel Medio Evo* 2, special issue of *Micrologus* 6 (1998): 1–27; and *La conversion de Hermann le Juif* (Paris: Seuil, 2007). See more generally Dagron, "Judäiser."

24. For a contemporary defense of church decoration see Suger of St. Denis, "De Administratione," 27, in *Abbot Suger on the Abbey Church of St. Denis and Its Art Treasures*, ed. and trans. Erwin Panofsky, 2nd ed. by Gerda Panofsky-Soergel (Princeton: Princeton University Press, 1979), together with the commentary of Conrad Rudolph, *Artistic Change at St.-Denis: Abbot Suger's Program and the Early Twelfth-Century Controversy over Art* (Princeton: Princeton University Press, 1990).

25. For Bernard's critique of images see Conrad Rudolph, *The 'Things of Greater Importance': Bernard of Clairvaux's Apologia and the Medieval Attitude toward Art* (Philadelphia: University of Pennsylvania Press, 1990), esp. Apologia 28, "De picturis et sculpturis, auro et argento in monasteriis": "et mihi repraesentant quodammodo

antiquum ritum Iudaeorum," p. 278; idols, dung, avarice, and usury, p. 280. On those who consider churches synagogues see Bernard's Letter 241:1. See also Jean-Claude Schmitt, "Les idoles chrétiennes," in *L'idolâtrie (Rencontres de l'École du Louvre)* (Paris: La Documentation Française, 1990), 107–18.

26. Bernard's Apologia 1 introduces "pharisaic boasting" (*pharisaica iactantia*) as the critical theme of the entire text, not only the critique of art. The *Apologia* is designed, as Conrad Rudolph suggests, to insulate his own order from the charge, while applying it to the Benedictines (or occasionally to excesses within his own order, as in Apologia 12).

27. This is a variant of a common distich: "It is neither God nor man, which you discern in the present figure, / But God and man, which the sacred image represents." On the distich see most recently Herbert L. Kessler, *Neither God nor Man: Words, Images, and the Medieval Anxiety about Art* (Freiburg: Rombach Verlag, 2007), discussing San Marco at 80–86.

28. In addition to the works of Herbert Kessler already cited see now Sara Lipton, *Dark Mirror*. See also Jeffrey F. Hamburger, "Body vs. Book: The Trope of Visibility in Images of Christian-Jewish Polemic," in *Kultbild 1: Ästhetik des Unsichtbaren: Bildtheorie und Bildgebrauch in der Vormoderne*, ed. D. Ganz and T. Lentes (Berlin: Reimer, 2004), 112–45; "The Medieval Work of Art: Wherein the 'Work'? Wherein the 'Art'?," in *The Mind's Eye: Art and Theological Argument in the Middle Ages*, ed. J. Hamburger and A-M. Bouché (Princeton: Princeton University Press, 2006), 374–412.

29. See, for example, Paulino Rodríguez Barral, *La imagen del judío en la España medieval: El conflicto entre cristianismo y judaísmo en las artes visuals góticas* (Barcelona: Universitat Autonoma de Barcelona, 2008), 58–82; Pamela A. Patton, *Art of Estrangement: Redefining Jews in Reconquest Spain* (University Park: Pennsylvania State University Press, 2012).

30. The allusions here are to two titles by Hans Belting: *Likeness and Presence: A History of the Image before the Era of Art*, trans. E. Jephcott (Chicago: University of Chicago Press, 1994); Hans Belting and Christiane Kruse, *Die Erfindung des Gemäldes: das erste Jahrhundert der niederländischen Malerei* (Munich: Hirmer Verlag, 1994).

31. On this painting see most recently Felipe Pereda, "'Eyes That They Should Not See, and Ears That They Should Not Hear': Literal Sense and Spiritual Vision in the *Fountain of Life*," in *Fiction sacrée: Spiritualité et esthétique durant le premier âge moderne*, ed. Ralph Dekoninck, Agnès Guiderdoni, and Emilie Granjon (Leuven: Peeters, 2013), 113–56.

32. Isidore of Seville, *Etymologiarum sive originum libri xx*, Lib. XIX.xvi, "De pictura." For a general study of the changes in aesthetic thought that accompanied this new naturalism see David Summers, *The Judgment of Sense: Renaissance Naturalism and the Rise of Aesthetics* (Cambridge: Cambridge University Press, 1990).

33. On van Eyck's eucharistic realism see Heike Schlie, *Bilder des Corpus Christi: sakramentaler Realismus von Jan van Eyck bis Hieronymus Bosch* (Berlin: Mann, 2002).

34. On Hebrew inscriptions in van Eyck's oeuvre see Jacques Paviot, "Les inscriptions grecques et hébraïques dans les tableaux eyckiens," *Revue belge d'archéologie et*

d'histoire de l'art 75 (2006): 53–73. The high priest's phylacteries are also a visual "literalization" of biblical text, referring to Matthew's condemnation of the Pharisees (Matt. 23:5: *dilatant phylacteria*). On Nicholas of Lyra's importance as an exegete in the later Middle Ages see most recently Deena Copeland, *The Insight of Unbelievers: Nicholas of Lyra and Christian Reading of Jewish Text in the Later Middle Ages* (Philadelphia: University of Pennsylvania Press, 2007). On Nicolas's illustrations see Felipe Pereda, "Le origini dell'architettura cubica: Alfonso de Madrigal, Nicola da Lira e la Querelle Salomonista nella Spagna del Quattrocento," *Annali di Architettura* 17 (2005): 21–52. My observations on the artist's literalizing biblicism in his representation of the *ephod* are based on Felipe Pereda's discussion of the same in "Eyes That They Should Not See."

35. On Hussite iconoclasm see Norbert Schnitzler, *Ikonoklasmus—Bildersturm: Theologischer Bilderstreit und ikonoklastisches Handeln während des 15. a und 16. Jahrhundert* (Munich, 1996), 51–60; "Faules Holz—Toter Stein: Thesen zum Bilderkult des Mittelater aus ikonoklastischer Perspektive," in *Pictura quasi fictura: die Rolle des Bildes in der Erforschung von Alltag und Sachkultur des Mittelalters und der frühen Neuzeit* (Vienna: Verlag der Österreichischen Akademie der Wissenschaften, 1996), 175–90. František Šmahel, *Husitské čechy: Struktury—procesy—ideje* (Hussite Bohemia: Structures—Processes—Ideas) (Prague: Lidové noviny, 2001), 349–50; Milena Bartlová, *Poctivé obrazy: Deskové malířství v čechách a na Moravě 1400–1460* (Devotional Images: Board Painting in Bohemia and Moravia 1400–1460] (Prague: Argo, 2001), 44–50. (*Non vidit.*) See also Horst Bredekamp, *Kunst als Medium sozialer Konflikte: Bilderkämpfe von der Spätantike bis zur Hussitenrevolution* (Frankfurt am Main: Suhrkamp, 1975), chap. 3.

36. "Projective identification" came to play an important role in Melanie Klein's thinking about what she called the paranoid-schizoid position, and the term occurs frequently in her writings. See, for example, her "Notes on Some Schizoid Mechanisms" of 1946, republished in Melanie Klein, *The Writings of Melanie Klein: Envy and Gratitude and Other Works (1946–1963)*, vol. 3, ed. Roger Money-Kyrle (New York: Free Press, 1975), 8. In the sense that I am pointing to a pictorial metadiscourse, my argument is similar to that of Rudolf Preimesberger, who pointed to the role of metadiscourses (he does not take up Judaism) in artistic claims to pictorial knowledge as a form of truth. See, for example, his "Zu Jan van Eycks Diptychon der Sammlung Thyssen-Bornemisza," *Zeitschrift für Kunstgeschichte* 54 (1991): 459–89. The essay is now available in English in his *Paragons and Paragone* (Los Angeles: Getty Research Institute, 2011), 23–52. My argument is more ambivalent than his, insofar as the metadiscourse I point to is pursued through categories that themselves solidify into dogmatic discourses, limiting the "reflexivity" they claim to facilitate.

37. On this possible (even probable) journey see the sources assembled by Pereda, "Eyes That They Should Not See," 119.

38. On the convert from Lleida see Archivo Municipal de Lleida, Llibres de Crims num. 803, fol. 115v–122r (Nov. 17, 1407). On the retable, Carlos Espí Forcén, *Recrucificando a Cristo*.

39. *Católica Impugnación*, ed. F. Márquez and F. Martín Hernández (Barcelona: Juan Floris, 1961), 189. This paragraph and the next owe a great deal to Felipe Pereda's *Las imágenes de la discordia: Política y poética de la imagen sagrada en la España del 400* (Madrid: Marcial Pons, 2007), 27–144. The translation is from the same author's "Through a Glass Darkly: Paths to Salvation in Spanish Painting at the Outset of the Inquisition," in *Judaism and Christian Art: Aesthetic Anxieties from the Catacombs to the Present*, ed. Herbert L. Kessler and David Nirenberg (Philadelphia: University of Pennsylvania Press, 2011), 263–90, here 270–72.

40. Thomas Aquinas: ST III q. 25, a. 3. Alfonso de Madrigal is discussed by Pereda, *Imagenes*, 62.

41. "Iten, porque es cosa razonable que las casas de los fieles cristianos sean munidas y guardadas de la memoria de la pasión de nuestro Redentor Jesucristo y de su bendita Madre, queremos y ordenamos que cada fiel cristiano tenga en la casa de su morada alguna imagen pintada de la cruz, en que nuestro Señor Jesucristo padeció, y algunas imágenes pintadas de nuestra Señora o de algunos santos o santas, que provoquen y despierten a los que allí moran a devoción." Hernando de Talavera, *Católica Impugnación*, 186. The translation is Pereda's, "Through a Glass Darkly," 264.

42. Donosa Ruiz: "Nunca tuvo ni tiene ni costumbró tener en su casa oratorio de la Virgen María ni de Jhu. Xristo, ni de sus santos, segunt que xristianos costumbran tener e delant de los quales fazen oración." B. Llorca, "La Inquisición española y los conversos judíos y marranos," *Sefarad* 8 (1942), 357–89. Edicts on images: "Petición presentada en el Cabildo de Sevilla, el 18 de Septiembre de 1480" (Actas Capitulares del Arch. Municipal de Sevilla 45–47), in J. Gestoso y Pérez, *Ensayo de un diccionario de artífices que florecen en Sevilla durante el siglo XIII al XVIII*, 3 vols. (Sevilla: En la oficina de la Andalucía moderna, 1899); and more recently C. Rallo Grus, *Aportaciones a la técnica y estilística de la pintura mural en Castilla a final de la Edad Media: Tradición e influencia islámica* (Madrid: Universidad Complutense de Madrid, Servicio de Publicaciones, 2002), 451–52. These topics are discussed, with additional examples, in Pereda, *Imágenes*.

43. J. Bruyn, *Van Eyck Problemen (De Levensbron-Het werk van een leerling van Jan Van Eyck)* (Utrecht: Dekker and Gumbert, 1957); and more recently Leslie Ann Blacksberg, "Between Salvation and Damnation: The Role of the Fountain in the 'Fountain of Life,'" in *Het Wellende Water: De bron in tekst en beeld in de middeleeuwse Nederlanden en het Rijnland*, ed. B. Baert and V. Fraeters (Louvain: Univ. Pers Louvain, 2005), 157–73. See Pereda's review of the evidence in "Eyes That They Should Not See," 117–23.

44. Larry Silver, *The Paintings of Quinten Massys: With Catalogue Raisonné* (Montclair: Allanheld and Schram, 1984), 94–95; M. J. Friedländer, *Altniederlandische Malerei VII, Quentin Massys* (Berlin: P. Cassirer, 1929), 51–52.

45. John Shearman points out the influence of Dürer and helpfully discusses (in terms very different from mine) this painting's address to the viewer. See his *Only Connect—: Art and the Spectator in the Italian Renaissance. The A. W. Mellon Lectures in the Fine Arts, 1988* (Princeton: Princeton University Press, 1992), 38–39.

46. Leon Battista Alberti, *De Pictura* (1435), trans. Cecil Grayson (London: Penguin, 1991), 78.

47. The inscription reads clockwise from the top: "o vos omnes qui / transitis per viam / atendite videte / si est dolor sicut dolor meus." I have not been able to determine the dating of the frame. *Cf.* Lam. 1:12: "O vos omnes qui transitis per viam, attendite, et videte si est dolor sicut dolor meus! Quoniam vindemiavit me, ut locutus est Dominus, in die irae furoris sui." For a similar inscription on an Italian Lamentation and Crucifixion see Millard Meiss, *Painting in Florence and Siena after the Black Death: The Arts, Religion, and Society in the mid-Fourteenth Century* (Princeton: Princeton University Press, 1951), 122.

48. Erwin Panofsky, *Early Netherlandish Painting*, vol. 1 (New York: Harper & Row, 1971), 137–39. My suggestion builds on that of Wolfgang Kemp, "Praktische Bildbeschreibung: Über Bilder in Bildern, besonders bei Van Eyck und Mantegna," in *Beschreibungskunst—Kunstbeschreibung: Ekphrasis von der Antike bus zur Gegenwart*, ed. Gottfied Boem and Helmut Pfotenhauer (Munich: Wilhelm Fin Verlag, 1995), 99–120. The subject of shadow and grisaille is a vast one, on which see especially Victor I. Stoichita, *A Short History of the Shadow* (London: Reaktion Books, 1997), who comments on pp. 67–71 on the passage from Luke.

49. I know of no work on the relationship between the sculptural and the painterly in this painting. The specific program of its architectural sculpture is itself enigmatic, and the interaction it catalyzes between pagan past and Christian present demands interpretation (a demand heightened by the imperial flag on the soldier's lance). Rudolf Preimesberger studies brilliantly the mediatic claims explored by van Eyck's engagement with sculptural paintings in "Zu Jan van Eycks Diptychon." The article also devotes some pages to the question of mirrors in van Eyck's work, on which more shortly. Its engagement with our topics, however, is minimal.

50. And not only Netherlandish: E. H. Gombrich long ago pointed out the place of the mirror in Leonardo's thought about painting in his *Art and Illusion: A Study in the Psychology of Pictorial Representation* (Princeton: Princeton University Press, 1969), 96–97.

51. *Histoire de Charles Martel*, vol. 3, Bibliothèque Royale de Belgique, Brussels, ms. 8, fol. 7r.

52. The analogy with poetry is relevant. Massys may have belonged to the Antwerp circle known as the "Rhetoricians" (*rederijkers*), whose poems often staged similar choices ("Gold is now most praised in the world"; "What good is gain to the greedy / when each man is certain to die. . . .") On *rederijkers* see J. J. Mak, *De rederijkers* (Amsterdam, 1944); A. van Elslander, "Letterkundig leven in de Bourgondische tijd: de rederijkers," *Rederijkersstudien* 5 (1969): 3–20. G. Degroote, "De poezie der rederijkers," *Dietsche warande en Belfort* 48 (1948): 292–301, 362–72; A. van Dixhoorn, *Lustige geesten: Rederijkers en hun kamers in het publieke leven van de Noordelijke Nederlanden in de vijftiende, zestiende en zeventiende eeuw* (Amsterdam: Proefschrift, 2004); S. Mareel and S. Bussels, "Strategieën van overtuiging in het rederijkerstoneel en de beeldende kunsten in de vijftiende- en zestiende-eeuwse Nederlanden," *Desipientia:*

Zin & Waan: Kunsthistorisch Tijdschrift 15 (2008): 16–20. For a later pictorial representation see Jan Steen's mid-seventeenth-century painting at the Philadelphia Museum of Art, *Rhetoricians at a Window*. Several *rederijker* anthologies from roughly Massys's period survive. One was compiled circa 1530 by Jan van Doesborch: *De Refreinenbundel van Jan van Doesborch*, ed. C. Kruyskamp (Leiden: Brill, 1940). Another dates from 1524: *Jan van Styevoorts Refreinenbundel anno 1524*, ed. F. Lyna and W. van Eeghem (Antwerp: Z. J., 1929–30). It is unfortunate that my Dutch is not sufficient to study the poetic ontology of these writers in the following chapter, for they would provide an interesting comparison with the traditions I do explore.

53. Felipe Pereda brings to my attention Bret L. Rothstein's *Sight and Spirituality in Early Netherlandish Painting* (Cambridge: Cambridge University Press, 2005), where Rothstein provides a reading of the objects in the Petrus Christus painting that discovers in them "a survey of bourgeois aesthetic and financial interests" (p. 2) that resonates well with the mediation of attention I am attributing to Massys's *Moneychanger*.

54. For a very different reading of the painting's moral valence see Ulrike Middendorf, "Moralische Gesinnung," *Weltkunst* 75.8 (2005): 73–75. Especially helpful is Larry Silver, "Power and Pelf: A New-Found Old Man by Massys," *Simiolus* 9 (1977): 63–92. See also Jean C. Wilson, "Self-Representation and the Evolution of the Northern European Occupational Portrait: The Metropolitan Museum's Man Weighing Gold, ca. 1515," *Dutch Crossing* 23.2 (1999): 29–55, who discusses in detail a painting from Bruges roughly contemporary with that of Massys, and provides as well a brief survey of the genre.

55. For a survey of van Reymerswaele's work see the still foundational work by M. Friedlender, *Die altniederländische Malerei*, vol. 12 (Leiden: A. W. Sijthoff, 1935), 69–76, 183–85. On the moneychanger paintings see H. van Werveke, "Aantekeningen bij de zogenaamde Belastingpachters en Wisselaers van Reymerswaele," *Gentsche Bidragen tot de Kunstgeschiedenis* 12 (1949–50): 43–58; A. Mackor, "Marinus van Reymerswaele: Painter, Lawyer, and Iconoclast?" *Oud-Holland* 109 (1995): 191–200; A. Mackor, "Are Marinus' Tax Collectors Collecting Taxes?" *Bulletin de Musée National de Varsovie* 36 (1995): 3–13. Both authors analyze the writing in the account books painted by van Reymerswaele in order to show that they were copied from actual records. Versions of van Reymerswaele's moneychanger can be found today in Madrid, Dresden, Florence, and Munich. They were so popular that they are sometimes found copied in gallery paintings by others. Van Reymerswaele also painted genre pictures of two moneychangers (National Gallery, London, Louvre, St. Petersburg, Warsaw, Antwerp), as well as of tax collectors and lawyers. On the relationship between the London and the Paris tax collectors see Paul Ackroyd, "The Two Tax-Gatherers by Marinus van Reymerswaele: Original and Replica," *National Gallery Technical Bulletin* 24 (2003): 50–63.

56. Francis Bacon, *De usura sive foenore*, in *The Works of Francis Bacon*, vol. X (London: W. Baynes and Son, 1824), 107. In "Marinus' Tax Collectors" Mackor divides van Reymerswaele's tax collectors into three types based on the style of their hats.

57. From Silver, "Power and Pelf," citing I. Bergstrom, *Dutch Still-Life Painting in the 17th Century* (London: Faber and Faber, 1956), 7: "Een wockeraar, een molenaar, een wisselaar, en een tollenaar zijn de vier evangelisten van Lucifaar."

58. Orcagna's tryptich is today at the Uffizi Gallery in Florence.

59. The same is true of van Reymerswaele's other *Calling of St. Matthew*, at Ghent, although in this painting the right side is a more mixed space, less dominated by the figure of Jesus, so that the soteriological divide between the two sides is less stark.

60. Giovanni Pietro Bellori, *Le Vite dei pittori scultori e architetti moderni* (Rome, 1672), ed. Evelina Borea, (Turin: Einaudi, 1976). The earlier sources are gathered in Howard Hibbard, *Caravaggio* (New York: Harper & Row, 1983), 343–60.

61. L'APOLLO, di Ottavio Tronsarelli. In Roma. Con Licenza de' Superiori. Per Francesco Corbelletti. MDCXXXIV. Edited and translated by Jonathan Unglaub in "Caravaggio and the 'Truth in Pointing,'" in *Caravaggio: Reflections and Refractions*, ed. David Stone and Lorenzo Pericolo (Burlington: Ashgate, 2012), 149–76. In addition to the painting today in Paris, there is one from circa 1594 at the Pinacoteca Capitolina in Rome.

62. See Lorenzo Pericolo, "Visualizing Appearance and Disappearance: On Caravaggio's London Supper at Emmaus," *The Art Bulletin* 89 (2007): 519–39. Cardinal Paleotti was one of the authors of the Council of Trent's defense of devotional images against the criticisms of Protestant reformers. His *Discorso intorno alle imagine sacri et profane* was published in Italian in 1582, in Latin in 1594, and in English as *Discourse on Sacred and Profane Images*, trans. William McCuaig (Los Angeles: Getty Publications, 2012). Paolo Prodi's introduction to this translation provides an excellent entry into a subject with a large bibliography. See also Prodi's *Ricerche sulla teorica delle arti figurative nella Riforma Cattolica* (Rome: Edizioni di storia e letteratura, 1962); reprinted with postface in his *Arte e Pietà nella Chiesa Tridentina* (Bologna: Il Mulino, 2013).

63. For a recent summary of and intervention in these debates see Michael Fried, *The Moment of Caravaggio* (Princeton: Princeton University Press, 2010), 197–201, with relevant bibliography on p. 285. My point here is quite different from, but compatible with, Wolfram Pichler's emphasis on *dubio* and redoubling in his "Il dubbio e il doppio: le evidenze in Caravaggio," in *Caravaggio e il suo ambiente: Richerche e interpretazioni*, ed. Sybille Ebert-Schifferer and Elisabeth Kieven (Milan: Silvana Editoriale, 2007), 9–34.

64. My thanks to Larry Silver for bringing this painting to my attention.

65. Antoine Arnauld and Pierre Nicole, *La logique ou l'art de penser* (Paris: Flammarion, 1970 [1662]), part 3, chap. 20 ("On Faulty Reasonings"), 339–40. The chapter draws much, including an antipharisaic flavor, from Augustine's *De doctrina* (cited, e.g., on 338). On the *Logique* see Louis Marin, *La critique du discours* (Paris: Minuit, 1975), 67–74; Elena Russo, *Styles of Enlightenment: Taste, Politics, and Authorship in Eighteenth-Century France* (Baltimore: Johns Hopkins University Press, 2007), 96. "It is pharisaic": A. Arnauld, *De la Frequente Communion* (Paris: Vitré, 1643), 169: "c'est estre pharisien que d'examiner le dehors, avant que d'avoir examiné le dedans."

Michel Foucault outlines his periodization in *The Order of Things: An Archaeology of the Human Sciences* (New York: Random House, 1994), 58–67, here 65.

66. René Descartes, *Principia Philosophiae* (Amsterdam, 1644), I.68 and I.69. On the debate over color see Bernard Teyssèdre, *Roger de Pile et les débats sur le coloris au siècle de Louis XIV* (Lausanne-Paris: Bibliotheque des Arts, 1964); Jacqueline Lichtenstein, *The Eloquence of Color: Rhetoric and Painting in the French Classical Age* (Berkeley: University of California Press, 1993). There are many non-French examples of this view, such as John Dryden's "Poetry and Painting" on expression in poetry, and color in painting as "the bawd" of design. See also Ricardo Nirenberg, "Metaphor: The Color of Being," in *Contemporary Poetics*, ed. Louis Armand (Evanston: Northwestern University Press, 2007), 153–74. Saint Bernard's quote is from Bernard of Clairvaux, *Apologia ad Guillelmum abb.*, PL 182, col. 915: "et eo creditor sanctior, quo coloratior."

67. On these debates see Russo, *Styles of Enlightenment.*

68. E. H. Gombrich, "The Father of Art History," in *Tributes: Interpreters of Our Cultural Tradition* (Ithaca: Cornell University Press, 1984), 51–69.

69. *The Earliest System-Programme* is translated in H. S. Harris, *Hegel's Development: Towards the Sunlight, 1770–1801* (Oxford: Clarendon Press, 1972). German text in *Mythologie der Vernunft*, ed. C. Jamme and H. Schneider (Frankfurt: Suhrkamp, 1984). I quote the list of basic dichotomies from Hegel's first published work, *Differenz des Fichteschen und Schellingischen Systems der Philosophie*, ed. Hartmut Buchner and Otto Pöggeler, *Gesammelte Werke*, vol. 4 (Hamburg: Meiner, 1968), 13; trans. H. S. Harris and Walter Cerf, *The Difference between Fichte's and Schelling's Systems of Philosophy* (Albany: State University of New York Press, 1977), 90. "The dead concept": *Aesthetics, Lectures on Fine Art*, 2 vols., trans. T. M. Knox (Oxford: Clarendon, 1975), 1:53–54; *Vorlesungen über die Ästhetik*, ed. E. Moldenhauer and K. M. Michel, 3 vols. (Frankfurt: Suhrkamp, 1970), 1:80. "Unity of concept" and the Idea: *Science of Logic*, trans. A. V. Miller (Oxford: Oxford University Press, 1969), 756–57; *Wissenschaft der Logik* (Hamburg: Felix Meiner, 1971), 2:408.

70. "Stripping off" is a quote from Hegel's *Lectures on the Philosophy of Religion*, 3 vols., trans. E. B. Speirs and J. B. Sanderson (New York: Humanities Press, 1962), 1:23; in German, Georg Lasson, ed., 2 vols. (Hamburg: Felix Meiner, 1974), 1:35. He delivered these lectures late in his career but made a similar point in his early *The Difference between Fichte's and Schelling's Systems*, 90–91 (English), 13–14 (German), as well as in his draft "Fragments of a Philosophical System" from the same year. "Jewish principle" is from "The Spirit of Christianity and Its Fate" of 1799: English in *Early Theological Writings*, trans. T. M. Knox (Philadelphia: University of Pennsylvania Press, 1971), 259*ff.*; German in *Hegels theologische Jugendschriften* (Tübingen: J. C. B. Mohr, 1907), 243*ff.*

71. The quotes are from *Aesthetics*, I, 8, 9, 111.

72. "Prophet of Orient": *Heines Werke*, ed. Helmut Holtzhauer, vol. 5 (Berlin: Aufbau Verlag, 1968), 197–98.

73. The ongoing necessity of art for Hegel is suggested by claims like the one

in the *Jena Phenomenology* that "the task nowadays consists not so much in purging the individual of an immediate, sensuous mode of apprehension, and making him into a substance that is an object of thought and that thinks, but rather in just the opposite, in freeing determinate thoughts from their fixity so as to give actuality to the universal, and impart to it spiritual life" (sec. 33, 19–20).

74. Deadening necrophilia: The centrality of Hegel's concern with the life and death of norms, and their deadening and enlivening potential, has long been recognized, though the exemplary role played by "Judaism" in that centrality is rarely noted. Hegel's colleague and contemporary Friedrich Schlegel had earlier (1803–1805) concluded his own study of the Old Masters with a similar warning to contemporary artists against the two false paths by which they sought to recapture their predecessors' greatness, that of "flight to certain merely Jewish objects of luxury from the Old Testament" or to "the field of Greek fables": "Zuflucht zu manchen blos jüdischen Prachtgegenständen des alten Testaments, oder zu einzelnen Abschweifungen ins Gebiet der griechischen Fabel. . . ." See his *Gemälde alter Meister*, ed. Hans Eichner and Norma Lelless (Darmstadt: Wissenschaftliche Buchesellschaft, 1984), 118.

75. Maurice Raynal, "Conception and Vision," in *A Cubism Reader: Documents and Criticism, 1906–1914*, ed. Mark Antliff and Patricia Leighten, trans. Jane Marie Todd (Chicago: University of Chicago Press, 2008), 320.

76. For an extended study of these aspects of Matisse's work see Todd Cronan, *Against Affective Formalism: Matisse, Bergson, Modernism* (Minneapolis: University of Minnesota Press, 2013). The quote is from p. 2. On Ensor see Andrei Pop, "Masks, Modernity and Egoism: Theatrical Practice in James Ensor and Maurice Maeterlinck," in *The Art of Theatre: Word, Image and Performance in France and Belgium, c. 1830–1910*, ed. Claire Moran (Oxford: Peter Lang, 2013), 287–305. On more general suspicion of the ocular see Martin Jay, *Downcast Eyes: The Denigration of Vision in Twentieth-Century French Thought* (Berkeley: University of California Press, 1993).

77. "Dream": see Jacques Derrida, *The Truth in Painting*, trans. Geoff Bennington and Ian McLeod (Chicago: University of Chicago Press, 1987), 73.

78. Hitler and Goebbels are both cited in Olaf Peters, "From Nordau to Hitler," in *Degenerate Art: The Attack on Modern Art in Nazi Germany, 1937*, ed. Olaf Peters (Munich, London, and New York: Neue Gallerie and Prestel Verlag, 2014), 27, 32.

79. Contemporary sources on the exhibition are vast and include a guide: Fritz Kaiser, *Führer durch die Ausstellung Entartete Kunst* (Berlin: Verlag für Kultur- und Wirtschaftswerbung, 1937). For historical and art historical research on the exhibition I have depended on *Die Bildenden Künste im Dritten Reich: eine Dokumentation*, ed. Joseph Wulf (Gütersloh: Sigbert Mohn Verlag, 1963); *Die "Kunststadt" München 1937: Nationalsozialismus und "Entartete Kunst,"* ed. Peter-Klaus Schuster (Munich: Prester-Verlag, 1987); *"Degenerate Art": The Fate of the Avant-Garde in Nazi Germany*, ed. Stephanie Barron (Los Angeles: Los Angeles County Museum of Art, 1991); Jonathan Petropoulos, *Art as Politics in the Third Reich* (Chapel Hill: University of North Carolina Press, 1996); Eric Michaud, *The Cult of Art in Nazi Germany*, trans.

Janet Lloyd (Stanford: Stanford University Press, 2004). On the difficulty of selecting works for the "Great German Art" exhibit, and on the interrelationship of the two exhibits, see Olaf Peters, "Genesis, Conception, and Consequences," in *Degenerate Art: The Attack on Modern Art in Nazi Germany, 1937*, ed. Olaf Peters, 106–25.

80. In this paragraph and the previous I am summarizing Bernhard Fulda and Aya Soika, "Emil Nolde and the National Socialist Dictatorship," in *Degenerate Art: The Attack on Modern Art in Nazi Germany, 1937*, 186–95. The material on *Der ewige Jude* is from the same text in Karl Stamm, "'Degenerate Art' on the Screen," 196–205, here 202–3.

81. Max Nordau, *Degeneration* (New York: Howard Fertig, 1968). On Nordau's theory as a defense against antisemitism see Christoph Schulte, *Psycopathologie des Fin de Siècle: Der Kulturkritiker, Arzt und Zionist Max Nordau* (Frankfurt am Main: Fischer, 1997), 210–12.

82. Hans Günther, *Rasse und Stil*, 2nd ed. (Munich: J. F. Lehmann, 1927); Paul Schultze-Naumburg, *Kunst und Rasse* (Munich: J. H. Lehmann, 1928). Hildegard Brenner's *Die Kunstpolitik des Nationalsozialismus* (Reinbek bei Hamburg: Rowohlt, 1963) is still foundational on this topic.

83. Heinrich Wölfflin, *Italien und das deutsche Formgefühl* (Munich: F. Bruckmann, 1931). English trans. *The Sense of Form in Art: A Comparative Psychological Study*, trans. A. Muehsam and N. Shatan (New York: Chelsea Publishing Co., 1958).

84. Joseph Goebbels, *Michael: Ein deutsches Schicksal in Tagebuchblättern* (Munich: Franz Eher, 1929), cited by Neil Levi, *Modernist Form and the Myth of Jewification* (New York: Fordham University Press, 2014), 59, himself citing from Donald E. Gordon, *Expressionism: Art and Idea* (New Haven: Yale University Press, 1987), 179, in turn citing Frank Whitford, "Radical Art and Radical Politics," in *Germany in Ferment: Exhibition of Paintings, Prints, Sculpture, 1900–1935* (Durham: Durham University Press, 1970), 5. Georg Lukács's contemporary analysis of Goebbels's relationship to Expressionism and Expressionism's relationship to Fascism well understood this commonality. See his "Expressionism: Its Significance and Decline," in *Essays in Realism*, trans. David Fernbach (London: Lawrence and Wishart, 1980), 77–113.

85. See Philipp Stauff's *Semi-Kürschner, oder Literarisches Lexicon* (Berlin: self-published, 1913), i–xi, on "The Alien Element [*Das Fremdtum*] in German Art: or Paul Cassirer, Max Liebermann, etc." Goebbels's 1936 edict is cited in Wulf, *Bildenden Künste*, 119.

86. Gerhard Richter and Sigmar Polke made a very similar point in 1964, in a fictional interview in which Richter explains that he no longer paints because his paintings killed so many in the concentration camps, but that now merely articulating the thought of his painting renders its hearer infertile and insane. See "Interview between John Anthony Thwaites and Gerhard Richter, Written by Sigmar Polke, October, 1964," in Gerhard Richter, *Writings, 1961–2007*, ed. Dietmar Elger and Hans Ulrich Obrist, trans. David Britt (New York: D. A. P., 2009), 24–25.

87. Max Horkheimer and Theodor W. Adorno, *Dialectics of Enlightenment* (New York: Continuum, 1972), 186.

2. Every Poet Is a Jew

1. Marina Tsvétayeva, "Poem of the End": "V som christianejsem iz mirov / Poety—zidy!"; trans. David McDuff in *Marina Tsvétaeva: Selected Poems* (Newcastle upon Tyne: Bloodaxe Books Ltd., 1987). Paul Celan's quotation (in Cyrillic) serves as epigraph to the poem "And with the Book from Tarussa," in Paul Celan, *Gesammelte Werke in fünf Bänden*, ed. Beda Allemann and Stefan Reichert with Rolf Bücher, vol. 1 (Frankfurt a. M.: Suhrkamp Verlag, 1983), 278. On the context of the citation see Eric Kligerman, *Sites of the Uncanny: Paul Celan, Specularity, and the Visual Arts* (Berlin: Walter de Gruyter, 2007), 11. Other poems in the collection also refer to Tsvétayeva's work, e.g., "Hinausgekrönt." For a commentary on the collection see *Die Niemandsrose: Kommentar*, ed. Jürgen Lehman with Christine Ivanovic (Heidelberg: Universitätsverlag C. Winter, 1996; 2nd ed. 1997).

2. *Kierkegaard's Journals and Notebooks*, vol. 3, ed. Bruce H. Kirmmse (Princeton: Princeton University Press, 2007), 234.

3. See also *Phaedrus* 245A. Plato's principal engagements with poets and poetry take place in the *Ion* and *The Republic*. For a useful summary of the issue and compendium of texts see Penelope Murray, *Plato on Poetry* (Cambridge: Cambridge University Press, 1996). For an expansive engagement with Plato's views on mimesis and their consequences see Stephen Halliwell, *The Aesthetics of Mimesis*, esp. 37–71.

4. Augustine on Varro: *De civitate Dei* 6.10, "Hanc libertatem Varro non habuit; tantum modo poeticam theologian reprehendere ausus est, ciuilem non ausus est, quam iste concidit." "Varro did not have this freedom of speech. He dared to condemn in this way only the poetic theology, and did not dare the political." Plato and the Platonists' condemnations are mentioned at *De civitate Dei* 2.14, 9.7 and elsewhere. For literature on Christian attitudes toward pagan religion and poetry more broadly, see R. P. C. Hanson, "The Christian Attitude to Pagan Religions up to the Time of Constantine the Great," in *Aufstieg und Niedergang der römischen Welt: Geschichte und Kultur Roms im Spiegel der neueren Forschung*, ed. Hildegard Temporini and Wolfgang Haase (Berlin: Walter de Gruyter, 1980), 910–73; K. O. Sanders, "The Challenge of Homer: School, Pagan Poets and Early Christianity," in *Poetry and Exegesis in Premodern Latin Christianity: The Encounter between Classical and Christian Strategies of Interpretation*, ed. W. Otten and K. Pollmann (Leiden: Brill, 2007). For an elegant summation of "The Place of Poetry in Latin Christianity" see W. Evenepoel's article by that title in *Early Christian Poetry: A Collection of Essays*, ed. Jan den Boeft and Antonius Hilhorst (Brill: Leiden, 1993), 35–60. (My thanks to Shadi Bartsch-Zimmer for this and other references.)

5. Paulinus of Nola, Carm. 10 (a poem addressed to Ausonius), lines 35–40, CSEL 30, 25, on *uis sophorum callida, ars rhetorum*, and *figmenta uatum*.

6. Augustine, *De doctrina* IV.5.7, citing Cicero, *De Inventione* I.1; *De doctrina* 4.14.30.

7. For Augustine on rhetoric see also *De civitate Dei* 11.18; *De doctrina* II.6 (7, 8) and IV.11 (26). On the consequences of Augustine's views for later aesthetic theory in the West see Joachim Küpper, "'Uti' und 'frui' bei Augustinus und die Problematik

des Genießens in der ästhetischen Theorie des Okzidents," in Wolfgang Klein and Ernst Müller, eds., *Genuß und Egoismus: Zur Kritik ihrer geschichtlichen Verknüpfung* (Berlin: Verlag, 2002), 3–29. Juvencus in Michael Roberts, *Biblical Epic and Rhetorical Paraphrase in Late Antiquity* (Liverpool: Francis Cairns, 1985), 69–70.

8. Antipode: Jerome, Epist. 53.10, CSEL 54.463. Paulinus's song: Ps. Paulinus Carm. 32 5–8, CSEL 30.330: "et ne displiceat quod talia carmina pango, / Dauid ipse deum modulata uoce rogauit, / quo nos exemplo pro magnis parua canemus, / dicentes quae sunt fugienda sequenda colenda." The association with David is common. See also Hilary, *Liber hymnorum*, ed. Walther Bulst, *Hymni Latini antiquissimi LXXV* (Heidelberg: F. H. Kerle, 1956), 31–33; Paulinus of Nola, Carm. 6.13–26 (CSEL 30.8).

9. Lactantius Inst. 1.1.10, CSEL 19.3. For a defense of the figurative power of poetry more specifically, see his Inst. 1.11.24, CSEL 19.40. On the mixture of poetry and music, which he says is even more dangerous as a form of "aurium uoluptas," Inst. 6.20–21, CSEL 19.562. Compare this lust of the ears to the visual lust of the eyes from the previous chapter. Specifically on Lactantius see Wolfgang Kirsch, "Die Umstrukturierung des lateinischen Literatursystems im Zeichen der Krise des 3. Jahrhunderts," *Philologus* 132 (1988); E. Messmer, "Laktanz und die Dichtung" (dissertation, Munich, 1974). Reinhart Herzog places Lactantius within the broader tradition of Christian engagement with classical poetry in his *Die Bibelepik der lateinischen Spätantike: Formgeschichte einer erbaulichen Gattung* I (Munich: W. Fink, 1975). See more recently Eberhard Heck, "Vestrum est—poeta noster: Von der Geringschätung Vergils zu seiner Aneignung in der frühchristlichen lateinischen Apologetik," *Museum Helveticum* 47 (1990): 102–20.

10. Sedulius, "Epistula ad Macedonium," in *Sedulii Opera Omnia*, ed. Johann Huemer, CSEL 10 (Vienna: Apud C. Geroldi filium, 1885), 4–5. The translation is Anna Lisa Taylor's from her *Epic Lives and Monasticism in the Middle Ages, 800–1050* (Cambridge: Cambridge University Press, 2013), 11–12.

11. *De propio ingenio*: Tertullian, Apol. 39.18, CCSL 1.153. Augustine on his own poetic compositions: Retract. 1.19[20], CSEL 36.96–97. On the Donatists' reproach see Augustine, Epist. 55.18.34 (CSEL 34.1.209). "Defensive weapon" is Fontaine's characterization of Ambrose's hymns, at *op. cit.* (1981), 82, 227. Ambrose mentions criticism of his hymns ("deceptum populum") and defends their purpose and success in Epistle 75A ("Sermo contra Auxentium de basilicis tradendis"), 34, CSEL 82.105. Augustine (*Confessions* 9.7.15) presents this moment of Ambrose's episcopacy as a watershed in the place of psalmody within the Church. "Every deadly delight" is from Augustine's *De doctrina*, 2.7.10 (CCSL 32.37). Augustine does occasionally comment on other Christian poets. See his remarks on Paulinus of Nola in Epist. 26.5 to Licentius (written in 395), CSEL 34.1.88: but note, the letter is explicitly written against Licentius's own poetry, which is, according to Augustine, insufficiently focused on eternal things. Other early Christian poets, such as Sedulius, were also explicit about the criticism they encountered, and about the limitations of their form. See Evenopoel, "The Place of Poetry," 48.

12. Braga: "Item placuit, ut extra psalmos, vel canonicarum scripturarum novi & veteris testamenti, nihil poetice compositum in ecclesia psallatur. . . ." For the text of the council see *Sacrorum Conciliorum Nova, et Omnium Amplissima Collectio*, ed. J. D. Mansi, vol. 9 (Florence: Expensis Antonii Zatta Veneti, 1763), 773–83, here 778. Toledo: *La Colección Canónica Hispana*, ed. Gonzalo Martínez Díez and Félix Rodríguez, vol. 5, *Concilios Hispanos, Segunda Parte* (Madrid: CSIC, 1992), canon XIII, 201–3 (specifically defending Hilary's and Ambrose's poems about martyrs, in part by citing Col. 3:16). The contrast between the two councils was long ago remarked by William John Blew, *Hymns and Hymn Books, with a Few Words on Anthems: A Letter to the Rev. William Upton Richards* (London: Rivingtons, 1858), 24–26.

13. More optimistic: Lactantius, *Epitome Divinarum Institutionum*, ch. 11, 12; Macrobius, *Commentum ad Somnium Scipionis*, I.2.11; Isidore of Seville, *Etymologiae* VIII.7.10.

14. Paulinus's poem: 20.28–30, CSEL 30.144. *Cf.* trans. P. G. Walsh, quoted in Evenopoel, "The Place of Poetry," 45. On the development of this space from early Christianity into the Middle Ages see Paul Klopsch, *Einführung in die Dichtungslehren des lateinischen Mittelalters* (Darmstadt: Wissenschaftliche Buchgesellschaft, 1980); and especially Jacques Fontaine, *Naissance de la poésie dans l'Occident chrétien: Esquisse d'une histoire de la poésie chrétienne du IIIe au Vie siècle* (Paris: Études Augustiniennes, 1981).

15. Sidonius Apollinaris, Epist. 9.12.1, ed. A. Loyen, vol. 3, p. 160; *cf.* Epist 9.16.55–6, p. 181. For English-speaking readers interested in deeper approaches to Late Antique poetry, the works of Michael Roberts are an important place to start, inter alia: *Biblical Epic and Rhetorical Paraphrase in Late Antiquity* (Liverpool: F. Cairns, 1985); *The Jeweled Style: Poetry and Poetics in Late Antiquity* (Ithaca: Cornell University Press, 1989); *Poetry and the Cult of Martyrs* (Ann Arbor: University of Michigan Press, 1993).

16. Thomas Aquinas, *Summa Theologica* I.II.101, on the ceremonial precepts: "quod sicut poetica non capiuntur a ratione humana propter defectum veritatis, qui est in eis, ita etiam ratio humana perfecte capere non potest divina propter excedentem ipsorum veritatem, et ideo utrobique opus est repraesentatione per sensibiles figuras." *Op. cit.* I.I.9 on metaphor in scripture: "Procedere autem per similitudines varias, et repraesentationes, est proprium Poeticae. . . ." "No purpose": Thomas Aquinas, *Quodlibetal Questions* 7.6.16.

17. On epic see most recently Taylor, *Epic Lives and Monasticism*. Bernard's commentary: Bernardus Sylvestris, *Commentary on the First Six Books of Virgil's "Aeneid,"* trans. Earl Schreiber and Thomas Maresca (Lincoln: University of Nebraska Press, 1979), here xxviii. For Horace's dictum see his *Satires, Epistles, and Ars Poetica*, ed. H. Rushton Fairclough, Loeb Classical Library (Cambridge: Harvard University Press, 1966), 478. "Moral ends": the words are Conrad of Hirsau's, who asserted that orientation toward such ends distinguished fictions like those of Aesop from the "lying fictions" of poets like Terence and Plautus. Conrad and Alexander Neckam are cited in Eleanor Johnson, *Practicing Literary Theory in the Middle Ages: Ethics and the Mixed Form in Chaucer, Gower, Usk, and Hoccleve* (Chicago: University of Chicago Press, 2013), 2, 5. On these issues more generally see A. J. Minnis and A. B. Scott, eds.,

Medieval Literary Theory and Criticism, 1100–1375: The Commentary Tradition (Oxford: Clarendon, 2000).

18. For a now canonical statement see Ernst Robert Curtius, *Europäische Literatur und lateinisches Mittelalter*, 4th ed. (Berne: Francke, 1963), "Poesie und Theologie," 221–234 [*European Literature and the Latin Middle Ages* (Princeton, 1953)]. On the relationship between these defenses of poetry see Alastair J. Minnis, "The Transformation of Critical Tradition: Dante, Petrarch, and Boccaccio," in *Medieval Literary Theory and Criticism, c. 1000–c. 1375*, ed. A. J. Minnis and A. B. Scott, 2nd ed. (Oxford, 1998); *The Cambridge History of Literary Criticism: Vol. 2, The Middle Ages*, ed. A. J. Minnis and Ian Johnson (Cambridge: Cambridge University Press, 2005); and Joachim Küpper, "Zu einigen Aspekten der Dichtungstheorie in der Frührenaissance," in *Renaissance: Konzepte einer Epoche im Dialog der Disziplinen*, ed. Andreas Kablitz and Gerhard Regn (Heidelberg: C. Winter, 2005). Though in this chapter Dante must stand for all, I am sorry to neglect the place of Boccaccio and Petrarch in this debate. Readers may wish to turn to Giovanni Boccaccio's *Geneologia deorum gentilium libri*, ed. V. Romano (Bari: Laterza 1951), especially the preface and books 14–15; Petrarch's *Invective contra medicum* [ed. A. Bufano, in *Opere latine di Francesco Petrarca*, vol. 2 (Turin: Unione Tipografico–Editrice Torinese, 1975)], *Familiares* 10.4, "de proportione inter theologiam et poetriam" [ed. V. Rossi, *Le familiari* (Florence: Le lettere, 1997)], and his *Collatio laureationis* [ed. C. Godi, "La *Collatio laureationis* del Petrarca nelle due redazioni," *Studi petrarcheschi* 5 (1988), 1–56].

19. "Letter to Cangrande della Scala" [Latin text in Dante Alighieri, *Tutte le opere*, ed. Luigi Blasucci (Florence: Sansoni, 1965), 341–52]. On these issues see August Buck, *Italienische Dichtungslehren vom Mittelalter bis zum Ausgang der Renaissance* (Tübingen: M. Niemeyer, 1952), 33–53; and Otfried Lieberknecht, *Allegorese und Philologie: Überlegungen zum Problem des vierfachen Schriftsinns in Dante's Commedia* (Stuttgart: Steiner, 1999), who discusses Dante's authorship of the letter on pp. 4*ff*. On the "fourfold meaning" of scripture Henri de Lubac remains fundamental: *Exégèse médiévale, les quatre sens de l'Ecriture*, 4 vols. (Paris: Éditions Montaigne 1959–64).

20. The translation is from Dante Alighieri, *Dantis Alagherii Epistolae*, ed. and trans. Paget Jackson Toynbee (Oxford: Clarendon Press, 1920), 199–200.

21. "Mester es sin pecado" is from the anonymous *Libro de Alexandre* 1, ed. Jesús Cañas, 5th ed. (Catedra: Madrid, 2007), 130. On parallel formulations in the *Libro de Apolonio*, a near contemporary work from the same genre, see A. D. Deyermond, "Mester es sen Pecado," *Romanische Forschungen* 77 (1965): 111–16.

22. For Albert's definition of metaphor see *Alberici Casinensis Flores rhetorici*, ed. M. Inguanez and H. M. Willard (Montecassino: Arti grafiche e fotomeccaniche Sansaini, 1938), 45.

23. Gonzalo de Berceo, *Milagros de Nuestra Señora*, ed. A. G. Solalinde (Madrid: Espasa-Calpe, 1978), Milagro 25, 791b.

24. The hope that the poet's verses will please God (or in this case Mary) and produce salvation for the poet is an ancient one in Christian poetry: see, e.g., Juvencus, Praef. 22, CSEL 24.2; Prudentius, Praef. and Epil.

25. *Enterpretador*: the word is not very common in the medieval Castilian corpus. It derives from the Latin *interpres*, whose etymology is obscure. Among early philologists F. E. J. Valpy defined it as an agent between two parties, deriving it from *inter+praestare* or *inter+pretium*, or from Greek *prates*, a vendor: *An Etymological Dictionary of the Latin Language* (London: Baldwin and Longman, 1828), 208. A. Ernout and A. Meillet suggest a derivation from a lost Latin word similar to *pretium*, price, a verb that they surmise meant to buy or sell. See their *Dictionaire étymologique de la langue latine: histoire des mots*, 3rd ed. (Paris: Klinksiek, 1939), 492. Regardless of etymology, there are numerous early attestations in which the Latin word carries the meaning of a businessman, or a commercial or political go-between.

26. I owe the observation to my many conversations with Laura Fernández Fernández. Ana Domínguez Rodriguez's valuable article on the king's representation as Mary's troubadour does not comment on this aspect of the representation: "Imágenes de un rey trovador de Santa María (Alfonso X en Las Cantigas)," in *Il medio Oriente e l'Occidente nell'Arte del XIII secolo: Atti del XXIV Congresso Internazionale di Storia dell'Arte* (Bologna, 1979), ed. Hans Belting (Bologna: CLUEB, 1982), 229–39.

27. Well lettered: "clérigo bien letrado, / todo su ministerio tenié bien decorado" (11. 1800 cd). The confusion of Apelles as Jewish is not unique to the Castilian tradition or to this author. In the Latin *Alexandreis*, for example, Gaultier de Lille (or Châtillon) writes of the talents of "Hebraeus Apelles" (beginning at Book 4, line 176). We know from manuscripts that the passage intrigued later readers. The fourteenth-century British Library manuscript Ad. 18,217 contains, among other things, the *Alexandreis*, with the section on Apelles (Book 4, lines 176–274) extracted and copied again later in the manuscript (fols. 118–132b), with additional commentary. On this manuscript see the *Catalogue of Romances in the Department of Manuscripts in the British Museum*, H. L. D. Ward and J. A. Herbert (London: British Museum, 1883), 99–100. For a recent study of Apelles as a figure through which the poet explores questions of representation see Clara Pascual Argente, "'El Cabdal Sepulcro': Word and Image in the *Libro de Alexandre*," *La Corónica* 38 (2010): 71–98.

28. "tant avié buen engeño e sotil coraçon" and "Por su sotil engeño que tant' apoderava / a maestre Nectánabo dizién que semejava, / e que su fijo era grant roído andava": *Libro de Alexandre*, stanzas 17 and 19. The condemnation for "sobervia" and the plot to poison: stanzas 2324–2329. For an exploration of the Judaizing stigma of this type of learning and of words like *sotil engeño* in medieval Castilian culture see David Nirenberg, "'Judaism,' 'Islam,' and the Dangers of Knowledge in Christian Culture, with Special Attention to the Case of King Alfonso X, 'the Wise,' of Castile," in *Mapping Knowledge: Cross-Pollination in Late Antiquity and the Middle Ages* (Arabica Veritas, 1), ed. C. Burnett and P. Mantas-España (Cordoba: Oriens Academica, 2014), 253–76.

29. "Non podrié peor fuego en su cuerpo entrar, / enveninó las venas que pudo alcançar, / en lugar de guarir, fízolas peorar." [2617]

30. "La gloria deste mundo, quien bien quiere asmar, / Más que la flor del campo

non la deve preçiar, / Ca quando omne cuida más seguro estar, / Échalo de cabeça en el peor lugar." [2671]

31. All references are from the *Cancionero de Juan Alfonso de Baena*, ed. Brian Dutton and Joaquín González Cuenca (Madrid: Visor Libros, 1993); henceforth *Cancionero*. Poems from *cancioneros* other than that of Baena will be cited from Brian Dutton's *El Cancionero del Siglo XV, c. 1360–1520*, 7 vols. (Salamanca: Universidad de Salamanca, 1990–1991). On attitudes toward Jews and converts in the *cancionero* see (in addition to the works cited to follow) Stanley Rose, "Anti-Semitism in the 'Cancioneros' of the Fifteenth Century: The Accusation of Sexual Indiscretions," *Hispanófila* 26 (1983): 1–11; Stanley Rose, "Poesía antijudía y anticonversa en la poesía artística del siglo XV en España" (PhD diss., Catholic University of America, 1975); Gregory S. Hutcheson, "Marginality and Empowerment in Baena's Cancionero" (PhD diss., Harvard University, 1993). The literature on the *cancionero* is vast, but two recent collections may serve as a starting point: *Poetry at Court in Trastamaran Spain: From the Cancionero de Baena to the Cancionero General*, ed. E. Michael Gerli and Julian Weiss (Tempe: Medieval & Renaissance Texts & Studies, 1998); *Juan Alfonso de Baena y su Cancionero: actas del I Congreso Internacional sobre el Cancionero de Baena, Baena, del 16 al 20 de febrero de 1999*, ed. Jesús L. Serrano Reyes and Juan Fernández Jiménez (Córdoba: M. I. Ayuntamiento de Baena, Delegación de Cultura, 2001). What follows in this section is a much compressed summary of arguments found in my "Figures of Thought and Figures of Flesh: 'Jews' and 'Judaism' in Late Medieval Spanish Poetry and Politics," *Speculum* 81 (2006): 398–426. Readers may look there for much more extensive notes and bibliography.

32. It is entirely on the evidence of these poems that Baena's status as converso rests. The eggplant quotes are from poems by Diego de Estuniga (#424) and Juan García (#384). The reference to *adefyna* is by Juan de Guzmán (#404) and the baptismal allusion by Ferrand Manuel (#370). For allusions to Baena's sexual encounters with Jewesses see, inter alia, the same poem by Juan García: "Con judia Aben Xuxena / o Cohena / bien me plaze que burledes. . . ." For the Mariscal's insult see #418. (Allusions to interfaith sexual dalliance are very common in the *cancionero*, some penned by Baena himself, e.g., #449. 'Juan Bautista Avalle-Arce considered the possibility of a *morisco* as well as a converso background for Juan Alfonso in "Sobre Juan Alfonso de Baena," *Revista de Filología Hispánica* 7 (1945): 141–47. José María Azáceta opted for converso in his *Cancionero: Edición Crítica*, vol. 1 (Madrid: Consejo Superior de Investigaciones Científicas, 1966), v, 4, and accompanying notes. Dutton and Gonzalez Cuenca, the most recent editors, begin by accepting the poetic evidence of Baena's converso status only "provisionalmente" but end by treating it as certainty: *Cancionero*, xv, xviii. On eggplant see my *Anti-Judaism: The Western Tradition* (New York: W. W. Norton, 2013), 230–31.

33. The quote is from Théodore de Puymaigre, *La cour littéraire de don Juan II, roi de Castille* (Paris: A. Franck, 1873), 131. For similar arguments see Francisco Cantera Burgos, "El Cancionero de Baena: Judíos y conversos en él," *Sefarad* 27 (1967): 71–111; Julio Rodríguez-Puértolas, *Poesía de protesta en la edad media castellana: historia y*

antología (Madrid: Editorial Gredos, 1968), 216–24; Cristina Arbós, "Los cancioneros castellanos del siglo xv como fuente para la historia de los judíos españoles," in *Jews and Conversos: Studies in Society and the Inquisition*, ed. Yosef Kaplan (Jerusalem: Magnes Press, 1985), 77–78; Gregory S. Hutcheson, "'Pinning Him to the Wall': The Poetics of Self-Destruction in the Court of Juan II," *Disputatio* 5 (2002): 87–102, esp. 92–95. *Cf.* José Amador de los Ríos, *Estudios históricos, políticos y literarios sobre los judíos de España* (Madrid: Imp. de M. Díaz, 1848), 425*ff*.

34. As Charles Fraker concedes in his review of Wolf-Dieter Lange's *El fraile trobador: Zeit, Leben und Werk des Diego de Valencia de León (1350?–1412?)* (Frankfurt am Main: V. Klostermann, 1971): "Thus one more supposed New Christian gets stricken from the canon." *Hispanic Review*, 42.3 (1974): 341–43, here 341.

35. For the specific context of these debates in Iberia see especially Karl Kohut, "Zur Vorgeschichte der Diskussion um das Verhältnis von Christentum und antiker Kultur im spanischen Humanismus: die Rolle des *Decretum Gratiani* in der Übermittlung patristischen Gedankengutes," *Archiv für Kulturgeschichte* 55 (1973): 80–106; and his "Der Beitrag der Theologie zum Literaturbegriff in der Zeit Juans II von Kastilien: Alonso de Cartagena (1384–1456) und Alonso de Madrigal, genannt el Tostado (1400?–1455)," *Romanische Forschungen* 89 (1977): 183–226; and *Las teorías literarias en España y Portugal durante los siglos XV y XVI* (Madrid: Consejo Superior de Investigaciones Científicas, 1973). On Saint Vincent Ferrer's opposition to the extension (such as Dante's) of allegorical truth claims from scripture to poetry see Pedro Catedra, "La predicación castellana de San Vicente Ferrer," *Boletín de la Real Academia de Buenas Letras de Barcelona* 39 (1983–1984): 235–309, esp. 278, citing Biblioteca Nacional, Madrid, ms. 9,433, fol. 33r–43r. For Castilian appropriations of Petrarch's and Boccaccio's defenses of poetry see inter alia J. Piccus, "El traductor español de *De genealogia deorum*," in *Homenaje a Rodríguez-Moñino*, vol. 2 (Madrid: Editorial Castalia, 1966), 59–75; Hernando de Talavera, "Invectivas contra el médico rudo e parlero," ed. P. Cátedra, in *Petrarca: Obras,* I: *Prosa*, ed. F. Rico et al. (Madrid: Alfaguara, 1978), 369–410.

36. ". . . doctrinas que non tienen el valor por la autoridat de quien las dixo nin han seso moral nin mitico, mas solamente en ellas se cata lo que la simple letra significa. . . ." Cited in Kohut, "Der Beitrag der Theologie," 196. For the eulogy see the "Coplas que hizo Hernán Perez de Gusman a la muerte del obispo de Burgos, don Alonso de Cartagena," *Cancionero Castellano del siglo XV*, vol. 1, ed. R. Foulché-Delbosc, *Nueva Biblioteca de Autores Españoles*, vol. 19 (Madrid: Bailly-Bailliere, 1912), 676.

37. Kohut, "Der Beitrag der Theologie," 206, 220–21.

38. The only works I know of that treat the *Cancionero* of Baena in this context are those of Karl Kohut, "La teoría de la poesía cortesana en el Prólogo de Juan Alfonso de Baena," *Actas del coloquio hispano-aleman Ramón Menendez Pidal* (Madrid: Niemeyer, 1982): 120–37, here 131, note 27; and Lange, *El fraile trobador*, 101*ff*.

39. *Cancionero*, 1. The rubric is discussed in a number of poems, most notably by Baena, #359, p. 639, vv. 9–10; and Manuel de Lando, #253, pp. 451–52, vv. 17–24, and #257, pp. 456–58, couplet 11. For a good summary and revision of the scholarly

debates over the meaning of this theme of *gracia* in the *cancionero* see Julian Weiss, *Poet's Art: Literary Theory in Castile, c. 1400–60* (Oxford: Oxford University Press, 1990), 25–40.

40. See #359, 639, ll. 1–4, 9–12: "Ferrand Manuel, por que se publique / la vuestra çiençia de grant maravilla, / en esta grant cort del Rey de Castilla / conviene forçado que alguno vos pique. . . ." "Fernand Manuel, pues unicuique / data est graçia doblada e senzilla, non se vos torne la cara amarilla / por que mi lengua vos unte o salpique." As Baena puts it in the challenge he issued to Villasandino and Lando in 1423: "que pierdan malenconía / e tomen plazentería, / sin enojo e sin zizaña, / ca la burla non rascaña" (#357, lines 28–30). The "truth claims" of these insults deserve to be studied in the light of Jean-Claude Milner's *De la syntaxe à l'interprétation: Quantités, insultes, exclamations* (Paris: Seuil, 1978), 174–223. My thanks to G. Agamben for drawing my attention to this aspect of Milner's work.

41. Lando to Baena, #360, 639–40, here ll. 6–8. Baena to Lando, #363, 641–42. Note Baena's claim that insult specifically enables good poetry: "Fernand Manuel, por que versefique / donaires mi lengua sin raça e polilla, / sabed que vos mando de mula pardilla / dozena de festes en el quadruplique" (ll. 9–12: *festes*: *cagajones*, horse turds). For a comment on the use of the word *raça*, race, to signify (poetic) defect see David Nirenberg, "Was There Race before Modernity? The Example of 'Jewish' Blood in Late Medieval Spain," in *Neighboring Faiths: Christianity, Islam, and Judaism in the Middle Ages and Today* (Chicago: University of Chicago Press, 2014), 169–90, here 181.

42. "Señor, este vil borrico frontino, / torçino e relleno de vino e de ajos, / sus neçios afanes e locos trabajos / es porque l'tengo por trobador fino; en esto se enfinge el suzio cohino / e con muchos buenos levanta baraja; e quien reçelasse su parlar de graja / más negro sería que cuervo marino. // Quien non es capaz bastante nin dino / de aquesta çiençia de que se trabaja, / su argumentar non vale una paja, / nin un mal cogombro, tampoco un pepino."

43. See #270, 470, Alfonso de Moraña against Ferrán Manuel de Lando.

44. See #140, Alfonso Álvarez de Villasandino against Alfonso Ferrández Semuel: "nunca serviste amor / nin fuste en su conpañia." To this charge Alfonso Álvarez adds that his target is an apostate Jew with a big nose, a *meshumad*. For a suggestive study on the place of love in the production of poetry and nobility in Castile during this period see Julian Weiss, "Álvaro de Luna, Juan de Mena and the Power of Courtly Love," *Modern Language Notes* 106 (1991): 241–56.

45. *Baena*, #501, 343. F. Cantera Burgos is among those who move from vocabulary to sociology: "Ya adelantamos que se ignora la ascendencia de Fray Diego y desde luego sorprende en él el amplio conocimiento que del vocabulario hebreo hace gala. Nada nos chocaría, pues, que . . . poseyera amplios contactos judaicos, quizá inclusos familiares," *El Cancionero de Baena*, 103. Charles F. Fraker's phrasing and conclusion are almost identical: *Studies on the Cancionero de Baena* (Chapel Hill: University of North Carolina Press, 1996): 9–10, note 2. But *cf.* Lange's conclusive rebuttal in *El fraile trobador*.

46. His verse to Queen Isabel: Dutton MP2–81. In ID0181, PN10–33, Montoro deploys the "killers of Christ" motif in order to playfully threaten the Corregidor of Cordoba: the lineage that could deal with Christ will be able to deal with the Corregidor as well. In another poem (Dutton ID6767, "Otra del ropero a su cauallo") Montoro's own horse reproaches him as a renegade Jew who is torturing the horse just as he and his people had crucified Christ. See *Cancionero de Antón de Montoro*, ed. Emilio Cotarelo y Mori (Madrid: José Perales y Martínez, 1900), 220. On converso self-mockery see inter alia Francisco Márquez Villanueva, "Jewish 'Fools' of the Spanish Fifteenth Century," *Hispanic Review* 50 (1982): 385–409. On Montoro's poem to Isabel see Barbara F. Weissberger's "'Deceitful Sects': The Debate about Women in the Age of Isabel the Catholic," in *Gender in Debate from the Early Middle Ages to the Renaissance*, ed. Thelma S. Fenster and Clare A. Lees (New York: Palgrave Macmillan, 2002), 207–35, here 214–19. See also the review essay of E. Michael Gerli, "Antón de Montoro and the Wages of Eloquence: Poverty, Patronage, and Poetry in 15th-C. Castile," *Romance Philology* 48 (1994–1995): 265–76.

47. H. de Vocht, "Rodrigo Manrique's Letter to Vives," in *Texts and Studies about Louvain Humanists in the First Half of the Sixteenth Century*, Monumenta Humanistica Lovaniensia 4 (Louvain: Librairie universitaire, 1934), 427–58, here 435.

48. Many of the analogues were gathered by C. Brown in *A Study of the Miracle of Our Lady Told by Chaucer's Prioress*, Chaucer Society (series 2) 45 (London: Paul, Trench, Trübner and Company, 1910); and his "The Prioress' Tale," in W. F. Bryan and G. Dempster, eds., *Sources and Analogues of Chaucer's Canterbury Tales* (London: Routledge & K. Paul, 1941), 447–85.

49. On the Vernon Manuscript and its version of the miracle of the singing boy see Anthony Bale, *The Jew in the Medieval Book: English Antisemitism, 1350–1500* (Cambridge: Cambridge University Press, 2006), 75–81.

50. See among many others Louise O. Fradenburg, "Criticism, Anti-Semitism, and the 'Prioress's Tale,'" *Exemplaria* 1 (1989): 69–115; L. Besserman, "Ideology, Antisemitism, and Chaucer's 'Prioress's Tale,'" *Chaucer Review* 36 (2001): 48–72.

51. On these issues see the textual notes in *The Riverside Chaucer*, 3rd ed., ed. Larry Benson (Oxford: Oxford University Press, 2008), 1121; and N. F. Blake, *The Textual Tradition of the Canterbury Tales* (London: Edward Arnold, 1985), 24–43.

52. *The Riverside Chaucer*, 208, lines 413–34.

53. Lisa Lampert notes the contrast between the Shipman and the Prioress to a different but very helpful end in *Gender and Jewish Difference from Paul to Shakespeare* (Philadelphia: University of Pennsylvania Press, 2004), 72.

54. For some of those hints see Lee Patterson, "'Living Witnesses of Our Redemption': Martyrdom and Imitation in Chaucer's Prioress's Tale," *Journal of Medieval and Early Modern Studies* 31 (2001): 507–60.

55. It is often noted that in the Prioress's tale the Jews are gleefully condemned to a gruesome death in what a medieval audience would have understood as decidedly Old Testament terms: "Yvele shal have that yvele wol deserve": an eye for an eye, a tooth for a tooth.

56. For a collection of such commentary see Geoffrey Chaucer, *The General Prologue*, ed. Malcolm Andrew and Daniel J. Ransom (Norman: University of Oklahoma Press, 1993), 167–68.

57. David Nirenberg, "Shakespeare's Jewish Questions," *Renaissance Drama* 38 (2010): 77–113.

58. George Herbert, *The Complete English Poems*, ed. John Tobin (London: Penguin, 1991), 160–61.

59. For Pietro Aretino's boast, see Pietro Aretino, *Lettere*, 2 vols., ed. Paolo Procaccioli (Milan: Rizzoli, 1991), 1:199 (dated May 15, 1537).

60. For Arnauld and Nicole see the sources in chapter 1.

61. "Untainted by all self-concern": "Explication des maximes des saints," in *Oeuvres*, ed. Jacques Le Brun, 2 vols. (Paris: Gallimard, 1983) 1:1011. "We must write": "Discours à l'Académie française" (1683), in *Oeuvres*, 1:535–36. *The Lettre à l'Académie* (1714), ed. Ernesta Calderini (Geneva: Droz, 1970), 78–79, praises Raphael for hiding his skill "in order to deceive the spectator and have him take his painting for Jesus Christ himself transfigured on the Thabor." Poussin is praised in "Dialogue des morts." "Salvation" versus "vainglory": *Lettre à l'Académie*, 51. "The poet disappears": "Dialogue sur l'éloquence" (1718), in *Oeuvres*, 1:35. I have been guided here by Russo, *Styles of Enlightenment*, 85–112.

62. Among many formulations of this point in the Lectures on Fine Arts see *Aesthetics*, 104.

63. "Most perfect art": *Philosophie der Kunst oder Ästhetik. Nach Hegel. Im Sommer 1826. Mitschrift Friedrich Carl Hermann Victor von Kehler*, ed. A. Gethmann-Siefert and B. Collenberg-Plotnikov (Munich: Wilhelm Fink Verlag, 2004), 197; *Aesthetics*, 89. "Absolute and true," "richest and most unrestricted": *Aesthetics*, 626–27.

64. "Free spiritual subject" and "negative" relation to the absolute: *Philosophie der Kunst oder Ästhetik*, 90–91; *Aesthetics*, 321.

65. Hegel on Islam and poetry: *The Philosophy of History, by G. W. F. Hegel*, trans. J. Sibree, from the 2nd ed. (New York: Collier & Son, 1902), 454; Goethe's *West-östlicher Divan* is mentioned as the heir to Arabic poetry on p. 456. But compare *Aesthetics*, 557, 978. Hegel was far from unique in lumping together Jews and Muslims in one aesthetic category. *Cf.* Immanuel Kant, *The Critique of Judgment*, trans. Werner S. Pluhar (Indianapolis: Hackett, 1987), 135.

66. Psalms: *Philosophie der Kunst oder Ästhetik*, 91. Compare *Aesthetics*, 364.

67. Heinrich Heine, "Ludwig Börne: Eine Denkschrift," Books 1 and 2, in *Ludwig Börne und Heinrich Heine, ein deutsches Zerwürfnis*, ed. Hans Magnus Enzensberger (Nördlingen: Franz Greno, 1986). For the attributes Heine assigns to Nazarenes/Jews and to Hellenes, 128; for the "Zweykampf" between Hellenism and Judaism, 127; for "Der Jude Pustkuschen . . . pharisäisches Zeter . . . ," 158; for "Shakespeare," 157. Heine relates Shakespeare's Englishness to Jesus' Jewishness in "Shakespeare's Maidens and Women," translated by Charles Godfrey Leland in *The Works of Heinrich Heine*, vol. 1 (London: William Heinemann, 1906), 249. Hegel's Greece as a union of real and ideal: *Philosophy of History*, 215, 238.

68. Matthew Arnold, *Culture and Anarchy: An Essay in Political and Social Criticism* (London: Smith, Elder and Co., 1869). The terms Philistine and Hebraizing are everywhere in that book, such as in the introduction (lviii–lix), with its criticism of the English nation as "Hebraizing Philistines." James Joyce, *Ulysses* (New York: Random House, 1934), 492. Thomas Mann, *Rede und Antwort* (Berlin: S. Fischer, 1922), 382.

69. On this utility see now Levi, *Modernist Form*.

70. Julius Bab, "Der Anteil der Juden an der deutschen Dichtung der Gegenwart," *Kölnische Zeitung*, September 17, 1911. The debate is extensively discussed by Rachel Seelig in her "Between Center and Periphery: Transnational Jewish Literature in Weimar Berlin" (PhD diss., University of Chicago, 2011), 89–95.

71. For these citations see Ludwig Strauss, "Beitrag zur Kunstwart-Debatte," *Gesammelte Werke in vier Bänden*, ed. Tovia Rübner and Hans Otto Horch, vol. 4 (Göttingen: Wallstein Verlag, 1998), 445; Ludwig Strauss, "Ein Dokument der Assimilation," *Die Freistatt* 1.14 (April 1913): 15–16; Seelig, "Between Center and Periphery," 94.

72. Walter Benjamin, "Goethes Wahlverwandtschaften" (ca. 1919–22), in *Walter Benjamin, Gesammelte Schriften*, ed. Rolf Tiedemann and Hermann Schweppenhäuser, vol. I.1 (Frankfurt: Suhrkamp, 1991), 195.

73. I will briefly address Heidegger's conviction in the next chapter. The quote is from *Martin Heidegger: Letters to His Wife, 1915–1970*, ed. Gertrud Heidegger, trans. R. D. V. Glasgow (London: Polity, 2010), 225. *'Mein liebes Seelchen': Briefe Martin Heideggers an seine Frau Elfride 1915–1970*, ed. Gertrud Heidegger (Munich: Deutsch Verlags-Anstalt, 2005), 279. For a very different way of dealing with a related terror see Eric Santner, *My Own Private Germany: Daniel Paul Schreber's Secret History of Modernity* (Princeton: Princeton University Press, 1996), xi–xii.

74. The original title page of the thesis is lost, but the Heidelberg library replacement page gives it as "Wilhelm von Schütz als Dramatiker: ein Beitrag zur Geschichte des Dramas der romantischen Schule." False synthesis (*Aufhebung*), "irony," etc., at 17*ff.*; "new type of Philistinism" at 23–26. It should be noted that despite Goebbels's critique of the Romantics' corruption by philosophy, many of his own key concepts (such as the national literary folk spirit) were in fact developed by the Romantics in their own attempts to criticize "reason." See among others Erich Auerbach's essay of 1949, "Vico and Aesthetic Historicism," in his *Scenes from the Drama of European Literature* (Gloucester: Peter Smith, 1973), 186–87.

75. Houston Stewart Chamberlain, *Die Grundlagen des neunzehnten Jahrhunderts*, vol. 1 (Munich: Verlagsanstalt F. Bruckmann, 1903), 457–58. Also quoted by Steven Edward Aschheim, "The Jew Within: The Myth of Judaization in Germany," in his *Culture and Catastrophe: German and Jewish Confrontations with National Socialism* (London: MacMillan, 1996), 45–68, here 58.

76. Jacques Derrida, "A Testimony Given," in *Questioning Judaism: Interviews by Elizabeth Weber*, trans. Rachel Bowlby (Stanford: Stanford University Press, 2004), 43. Later in the same interview Derrida himself alludes to Marina Tsvétayeva's poem.

3. Judaism as Political Concept

1. "The Letter to M. d'Alembert on the Theatre" (1758), in *Politics and the Arts*, ed. and trans. Allan Bloom (Ithaca: Cornell University Press, 1968), 79.

2. Plotinus, *Enneads* I. 2 .7 19–27. See also John Dillon, "An Ethic for the Late Antique Sage," in *The Cambridge Companion to Plotinus*, ed. Lloyd P. Gerson (New York: Cambridge University Press, 1996), 315–35.

3. According to Aristotle the natural life of subsistence we share with animals, but the human has a higher goal: "born with regard to life, but existing essentially with regard to the good life," *Politics* 1252b, 30. *Cf.* 1278b, 23–31; 1252a, 26–35.

4. *Politics* 1254b.

5. *Nicomachean Ethics* 1177b. On good government and transcendence see also *Politics* 1279b.

6. Carl Schmitt, *Politische Theologie: Vier Kapitel zur Lehre von der Souveränität* (Munich: Duncker and Humblot 1922). The book is not known to have been in Kantorowicz's library. Nevertheless, before Schmitt's publication the phrase was rarely used in a positive sense in modern German scholarship: see in general Heinrich Meier, *The Lesson of Carl Schmitt: Four Chapters on the Distinction between Political Theology and Political Philosophy*, expanded ed. (Chicago: University of Chicago Press, 2011). Victoria Kahn refers to the allusion as "coy" in her illuminating pages dedicated to "Sacred Kingship and Political Fiction." See Victoria Kahn, *The Future of Illusion: Political Theology and Early Modern Texts* (Chicago: University of Chicago Press, 2014), 59.

7. Carl Schmitt, *Der Begriff des Politischen* (Berlin: Duncker and Humblot, 1932).

8. I am not here taking a position on whether Schmitt actively sought to establish a politics oriented toward transcendence, as Heinrich Meier suggests, or whether he was pragmatically looking for historically authoritative forms that might stabilize political institutions in a godless modernity. The former was undoubtedly true at certain stages in Schmitt's career, but the latter may also constitute an important aspect of Schmitt's thought, on which see David Bates, "Political Theology and the Nazi State: Carl Schmitt's Concept of the Institution," *Modern Intellectual History* 3 (2006): 415–42.

9. From Carl Schmitt's concluding remarks at a retreat for a Nazi high school youth organization (Tagung Reichsgruppe Hochschullehrer), in Carl Schmitt, ed., *Das Judentum in der Rechtswissenschaft: Ansprachen, Vorträge und Ergebnisse der Tagung der Reichsgruppe Hochschullehrer des NSRB am 3. und 4. Oktober 1936* (Berlin: Deutscher Rechts-Verlag, 1936), 28–34, here 33. See Meier, *The Lesson*, 152.

10. Carl Schmitt, *Der Nomos der Erde im Völkerrecht des Jus Publicum Europaeum* (Cologne: Greve, 1950), 33. Though his rhetoric of Judaism changed over the course of his long career, the basic shape of his critique did not. See, for example, his criticism of Hans Blumenberg in *Politische Theologie II, Die Legende von der Erledigung jeder Politischen Theologie* (Berlin: Dunker and Humblot, 1970), 113–14. "Satanic princes" is my own Johannine gloss on Schmitt's association. On the place of anti-Judaism

in Schmitt's thought see inter alia Meier, *The Lesson*, 151–58; Raphael Gross, *Carl Schmitt und die Juden* (Frankfurt a. M.: Suhrkamp, 2000).

11. Cut off: e.g., "for if you circumcise yourselves, Jesus Christ will avail you nothing," Gal. 5.2. On the word *to Judaize* see Róbert Dán, "Judaizare—the Career of a Term"; Gilbert Dagron, "Judäiser"—both cited in the introduction.

12. On these antinomies see the sources cited in the introduction.

13. Elsewhere Paul seems less monistic: *cf.* 1 Thess. 5:1–11, 1 Cor. 3:5–4:5, 15:24; 2 Thess. 1:1–12.

14. Paul believed that "what we aim for is not visible but invisible. Visible things are transitory, but invisible things eternal" (2 Cor. 4:17–18). But at the same time he did not treat the body as a "tomb," as so many ancient authors (including Philo) did, but as a sheltering tent (2 Cor. 5:1–4). And if the spiritual was higher, the physical was prior: "If there is a natural body, there is a spiritual body too. . . . But first came the natural body, not the spiritual one" (1 Cor 15:44–46). For modern scholarship on the relationship between matter and spirit in the historical Paul, see Troels Engberg-Pedersen, *Cosmology and Self in the Apostle Paul: The Material Spirit* (New York: Oxford University Press, 2010); and his *Paul and the Stoics* (Louisville: Westminster John Knox Press, 2000). See also Dale Martin, *The Corinthian Body* (New Haven: Yale University Press, 1999). Marie E. Isaacs discusses the deployment of the term *pneuma* in service of a "new particularism," and specifically in supersessionism and "anti-Jewish polemic," in *The Concept of Spirit: A Study of Pneuma in Hellenistic Judaism and Its Bearing on the New Testament* (London: Heythrop College, 1976), 144–45. On Philo's use of the trope of body as tomb see D. Winston, ed. and trans., "Philo and the Contemplative Life," in *Jewish Spirituality from the Bible through the Middle Ages*, ed. A. Green (New York: Crossroad, 1988), 198–231, here 212.

15. Tertullian, for example, opposed church and empire as castle of light to castle of darkness: *De idolatria* 19.1, CCSL 2:1120. Similarly for Hippolytus of Rome "the kingdom of this world" "rules through the power of Satan": *Eis ton Danila* 4.9, cited by Gerard E. Caspary, *Politics and Exegesis: Origen and the Two Swords* (Berkeley: University of California Press, 1979) 137–38. Caspary is himself citing from Erik Peterson, *Der Monotheismus als politisches Problem* (Leipzig: Jakub Hegner, 1935), 69; Peterson's book was a response to Schmitt's. The argument that earthly kingdoms are godly institutions for the utility of the pagan ungodly emerges in the second-century author Irenaeus, *Adversus Haereseos* 5.24.2. Those gathered at the Council of Antioch in 341 thought of earthly kings as "exterae potestates," neither demonic nor salvific but simply external and natural powers appointed for those who do not belong to the people of God: Mansi, *Sacrorum Conciliorum Nova et Amplissima Collectio*, vol. 2, 1131*ff.* Both these sources are cited by Caspary at p. 141. On the issues treated in the following paragraphs, Caspary, *Politics and Exegesis*, chapter 4, and L. Field Jr., *Liberty, Dominion, and the Two Swords* (Notre Dame: University of Notre Dame Press, 1998), are especially useful.

16. Pseudo-Cyprian, *Adversus Iudaeos* 42, 54, CCSL 4.271, 273, and *De montibus* 7, CSEL 3.3.111. See also Justin, *Dialogus* 41.1, and Melito of Sardis's *Homily on the Pas-*

sion. On debates over the dating (212?) and authorship of the *Adv. Iud*. see the works listed in Field, *Liberty*, 280, note 60.

17. *Com. Rom*. 9.25, 1226B, cited by Caspary, *Politics and Exegesis*, 142; H. Crouzel, *Théologie de l'image de Dieu chez Origène* (Paris: Aubier, 1954), 193–96.

18. This position is less antinomian than it sounds. Origen also stressed (tropologically) that all bodily things "bear the bodily image of the Prince of Bodies": *Com. Matt*. 17:27, 658*ff*. See Caspari, *Politics and Exegesis*, 155, note 64: "echonta tēn eikona tou tōn sōmatōn sōmatikēn." Or as the Latin has it, "imaginem enim Caesaris habet omnis res corporalis." Only Jesus' flesh did not bear upon it the stamp of the prince of this world: Caesar had no rights over him. Hence Jesus had to draw from the mouth of a fish the coin with which he paid the tax collector (Matt. 17:24*ff*.). On the fish see *Com. Matt*. 13:11, 208*ff*. On Peter and John, *Com. Rom*. 9:25, 1226B.

19. The quote is from Caspary, *Politics and Exegesis*, 9. Caspary uses the term *fleshly envelope* to refer to Origen's view of the relationship of state to church, 181. For examples of Origen's "Judaizing" political error see *Com. Matt*. 17:27, 659*ff*., where he calls those Christians who err by refusing to acknowledge the debts of the flesh "Pharisaei"; or his characterization in his commentary on Romans of pneumatics who resist the earthly powers with material force as Judaizing zealots.

20. A position eventually adopted as imperial law: *cf. Codex Iustinianus* 1.4, *De audentia episcopali* 26.5 (*Corpus iuris civilis*, ed. Theodore Mommsen et al., 3 vols., here 2.43). Ambrose's letter is preserved in two versions: the finished form (Ep. 74) and an original or earlier draft. I quote from the latter, Ep. 1a *extra collectionem*, in Ambrose, *Epistulae et acta*, ed. O. Faller and M. Zelzer, CSEL 82.1–4, 4 vols. (Vienna, 1968–1996), 3:162–77. See generally N. B. McLynn, *Ambrose of Milan: Church and Court in a Christian Capital* (Berkeley: University of California Press, 1994), 298–315.

21. Augustine of Hippo, *Sermones*, in PL, vol. 38, column 56, "Behold, the Jew is slave [*servus*] to the Christian," and 57, "Quomodo servi. . . ." In addition to slaves/servants Augustine developed many further metaphors. "Like milestones along the route the Jews inform the traveler, while they themselves remain senseless and immobile." "Milestones": *Sermo* 199.I.2, PL 38:1027. For other examples see Cohen, *Living Letters of the Law: Ideas of the Jew in Medieval Christianity* (Berkeley: University of California Press, 1999). Compare Quran 62.5, with its image of the Jews as donkeys carrying books.

22. Augustine, *Enarrationes in Psalmos*, 59.17–19. For a recent English translation see Augustine, *Expositions of the Psalms*, trans. Maria Boulding (Hyde Park: New City Press, 2000).

23. Augustine, *Against Faustus the Manichee*, 12.9–13. On Augustine's use of Jews and Judaism in his anti-Manichaean writings see especially Paula Fredriksen, *Augustine and the Jews: A Christian Defense of Jews and Judaism* (New York: Doubleday, 2008). This exegesis was much cited in the Middle Ages, on which see Gilbert Dahan, "L'exégèse de l'histoire de Caïn et Abel du XIIe au XIVe siècle en occident," *Recherches de théologie ancienne et médiévale* 49 (1982): 21–89, here 25–27, and 50 (1983), 5–68.

24. Augustine, *De civitate Dei*, 3.6, 15.4–5, 7. His proof texts here come significantly

from Galatians (5:17) and Romans (7:17, 6:13). This link between Cain and the earthly city is mentioned briefly by Fredriksen (*Augustine and the Jews*, 346–47), but she does not refer it to the problem of Jewish political or legal status. Instead she reads *The City of God* as beginning to dissociate Jews from Cain (so that Augustine can redeem the idea of "wandering" [*peregrinatio*]). (But note that in *De doctrina Christiana* Augustine describes the Jews as submitting the soul to the flesh.) On the contrast between these two treatments of Cain in Augustine see Peter Brown, *Augustine of Hippo: A Biography* (London: Faber & Faber, 1967), 321. Lies: "Nunc propter tres theologias, quas Graeci dicunt mythicen, physicen politicen, Latine autem dici possunt fabulosa naturalis civilis," *De civitate Dei* 6.12. Of political theology he writes (taking aim at Varro) that it is "mendosum."

25. Erik Peterson, *Der Monotheismus als politisches Problem*.

26. Laws of Edward: "quia ipsi Iudei et omnia sua regis sunt . . . tanquam suum proprium," in Leges Edwardi Confessoris 25, in *Die Gesetze der Angelsachsen*, ed. Felix Liebermann (Halle: Niemeyer, 1903/2007), 650. Alfonso II and Frederick II: David Abulafia, "'Nam Iudei servi regis sunt, et semper fisco region deputati': The Jews in the Municipal Fuero of Teruel (1176–7)," in *Jews, Muslims, and Christians in and around the Crown of Aragon: Essays in Honour of Professor Elena Lourie*, ed. Harvey Hames (Leiden: Brill, 2004), 97–123. (Abulafia argues strongly against giving the word *servi* the sense of slave in these twelfth- and thirteenth-century texts.) On the Capetians see Gavin Langmuir, "'Tanquam Servi': The Change in Jewish Status in French Law about 1200," in his *Toward a Definition of Anti-Semitism* (Berkeley: University of California Press, 1990).

27. John: "sicut res nostre proprie," "sicut nostrum proprium catallum," Carta Judaeorum Angliae et Normaniae, Charta 2 John, number 49, published in John Elijah Blunt, *A History of the Establishment and Residence of the Jews in England* (London: Saunders and Benning, 1830), 133. Bracton: see F. I. Schechter, "The Rightlessness of Medieval English Jewry," *Jewish Quarterly Review* 4 (1914): 128; F. W. Maitland and F. Pollock, *History of English Law before the Time of Edward I*, 2 vols. (Cambridge: Cambridge University Press, 1952), 1:472–73 [emphasis added]. For the expulsion text see David Abulafia, "The Servitude of Jews and Muslims in the Medieval Mediterranean: Origins and Diffusion," *Mélanges de l'École Française de Rome, Moyen Âge* 112 (2000): 687–714, here 691; John A. Watt, *The Jews, the Law, and the Church: The Concept of Jewish Serfdom in Thirteenth-Century England*, Studies in Church History, Subsidia 9 (Oxford: Ecclesiastical History Society, 1991), 153–72.

28. Ernst Kantorowicz, *The King's Two Bodies: A Study in Medieval Political Theology* (Princeton: Princeton University Press, 1997), 173. I've slightly altered the first words of the translation.

29. For a near contemporary representation of a three-headed Antichrist enthroned and surrounded by Jews see the moralized bible produced for the French monarchy circa 1225 and housed today at the Österreichische Nationalbibliothek, Ms. 2554, 43b.

30. On the role of Jews in Angevin England see the many essays of Robert Stacey,

especially "Parliamentary Negotiation and the Expulsion of the Jews from England," in vol. 6 of *Thirteenth-Century England*, eds. Michael Prestwich, Richard H. Britnell, and Robin Frame (Woodbridge: Boydell Press, 1997), 93–94; and "Anti-Semitism and the Medieval English State," in *The Medieval State: Essays Presented to James Campbell*, ed. John Robert Maddicott and David Michael Palliser (London: Hambledon Press, 2001), 163–77. See as well Robin R. Mundill, *England's Jewish Solution: Experiment and Expulsion, 1262–1290* (Cambridge: Cambridge University Press, 1998). For the cartoon see Michael Adler, *Jews of Medieval England* (London: Jewish Historical Society of England, 1939), plate 1. For exercises of *captio* by Capetian kings and magnates in France see Robert Chazan, *Medieval Jewry in Northern France: A Political and Social History* (Baltimore: Johns Hopkins University Press, 1973), 38–40, 73, 78–80; William C. Jordan, *The French Monarchy and the Jews: From Philip Augustus to the Last Capetians* (Philadelphia: University of Pennsylvania Press, 1989), 98–102.

31. Matthew Paris, *Chronica majora*, ed. Henry Richards Luard, 7 vols. (London: Rolls Series, 1872–1884), 5:487–88. Elsewhere Matthew Paris imagines Henry's debased coinage as effecting his "circumcision": see Willis Johnson, "Textual Sources for the Study of Jewish Currency Crimes in Thirteenth-Century England," *British Numismatic Journal* 66 (1997): 23.

32. Petrus Cantor, *Petri Cantoris Parisiensis Verbum adbreviatum*, CCCM, vols. A–C (CXCVI), ed. Monique Boutry (Turnhout: Brepols, 2012), A:292. I do not think it has yet been noted that Peter here is deliberately confusing Jewish and non-Jewish moneylenders, in order to describe the non-Jewish ones (with whom he seems principally concerned) as Jews: "Homines tam detestabiles nunc fiunt cubicularii principum et prelatorum, filios quorum pecunia fenebri interueniente in principes et prelatos Ecclesie promouerunt, ut sedeant cum principibus et solium glorie teneant [1 Kings 2:8] et cathedram. Hii etiam sunt loculi et sanguissuge principum, quia cum omnia suxerint, euomunt in fiscum, ut dicere possint principes ad sanguissugam talem: 'Macra cauum repetes quem' quondam 'macra subisti' [Horace, Epistles, 1, 7, 33]. Isti etiam nomen Iudeorum adepti sunt. Principes enim eos tuentes non permittunt eos super aliquo crimine accusari dicentes: 'Isti nostri Iudei sunt.' Immo peiores Iudeis sunt, quia Iudeus ex precepto legis non fenerabatur fratri [Deuteronomy 23:19], set tantum alieno ex permissione; iste autem et proximo et alieno contra preceptum Domini feneratur. Tales enim in detestacionem criminis, si clerici fuerint, non potest clericale priuilegium aduersus principes tueri." For an earlier edition see Petrus Cantor, *Verbum Abbreviatum*, PL 205, col. 158.

33. On the Theophilus miracle in the *Cantigas* see P. Patton, "Constructing the Inimical Jew in the *Cantigas de Santa María*: Theophilus's Magician in Text and Image," in *Beyond the Yellow Badge: Anti-Judaism and Antisemitism in Medieval and Early Modern Visual Culture*, ed. Mitchell B. Merback (Leiden: Brill, 2008), 233–56.

34. On the episcopal complaints see P. Linehan, "The Spanish Church Revisited: The Episcopal *Gravamina* of 1279," in *Authority and Power: Studies on Medieval Law and Government Presented to Walter Ullmann on His Seventieth Birthday*, ed. Brian Tierney and Peter Linehan (Cambridge: Cambridge University Press, 1980),

127–47. The quote is from 137. On the role of Jews in Alfonso's administration, and on the impact of the revolts upon these Jews, see Yitzhak Baer, *A History of the Jews in Christian Spain*, vol. 1 (Philadelphia: University of Pennsylvania Press, 1978), 120–37; J.-M. Nieto Soria, "Los judíos de Toledo en sus relaciones financieras con la monarquía y la Iglesia (1252–1312)," *Sefarad* 41 (1981): 301–19; 42 (1982), 79–102.

35. *Cantigas de Santa María*, Cantiga 209, "Muito faz grand' erro e en torto jaz, a Deus quen lle nega o ben que lle faz." W. Mettmann, *Cantigas de Santa María*, 3 vols. (Madrid: Castalia, 1986–1989), provides a good edition. The translation here is modified from that of K. Kulp-Hill, *Songs of Holy Mary of Alfonso X, the Wise* (Tempe: Arizona Center for Renaissance and Medieval Studies, 2000), 251. On Cantiga 209 see Francisco Prado Vilar, "*Iudeus Sacer*: Life, Law, and Identity in the 'State of Exception' Called 'Marian Miracle,'" in *Judaism and Christian Art: Aesthetic Anxieties from the Catacombs to Colonialism*, 115–42.

36. For a facsimile edition of this manuscript (Biblioteca Nazionale Centrale, MS Banco Rari 20) see Alfonso X el Sabio, *Cantigas de Santa María: Edición facsímil del códice B.R. 20 de la Biblioteca Centrale de Florencia, siglo XIII*, 2 vols. (Madrid: Edilan, 1989). The manuscript was conceived as the second volume of a single fully illustrated compilation of the *Cantigas* produced between 1275 and 1284. The first volume is Escorial, Biblioteca del Real Monasterio, MS. T.I.1, commonly known as *Codice Rico* and also available in facsimile edition: Alfonso X el Sabio, *Cantigas de Santa María: Edición facsímil del Códice T.I.1 de la Biblioteca de San Lorenzo de El Escorial: Siglo XIII*, 2 vols. (Madrid: Edilan, 1979).

37. The text was edited by Eloy Benito Ruano, "El memorial contra los conversos del bachiller Marcos García de Mora ('Marquillos de Mazarambroz')," in *Sefarad* 17 (1957): 314–51, here 320–21; and more recently, along with many other texts from the conflict, by Tomás González Rolán and Pilar Saquero Suárez-Somonte, *De la* Sentencia-Estatuto *de Pero Sarmiento a la* Instrucción *del Relator* (Madrid: Aben Ezra Ediciones, 2012), here 199–200.

38. For some examples among Luther's countless representations of the papacy as "Jewish" see "Lectures on the Epistle to the Hebrews," WA 57: 168. 5–11; "On the Jews and Their Lies," WA 53: 427–39. "Teufels Synagoga" is from "Wider das Bapstum zu Rom vom Teuffel gestifft," WA 54: 206–99, here 245. For a reproduction (without comment on the adaptation) of the pope-on-a-pig print, see Mark U. Edwards, *Luther's Last Battles: Politics and Polemics, 1531–1546* (Ithaca: Cornell University Press, 1983), 196; and WA 54. Wolfgang Harms, *Deutsche illustrierte Flugblätter des 16. und 17. Jahrhunderts*, vols. 1–4 and 7 (Tübingen: Max Niemeyer Verlag, 1980–1997); here vol. 2, 146, provides references to the numerous editions of the print. See also Petra Schöner, *Judenbilder im deutschen Einblattdruck der Renaissance: ein Beitrag zur Imagologie*. Saecula Spiritualia 42 (Baden-Baden: Valentin Koerner, 2002). On the Judensau see the classic work of Isaiah Shachar, *The Judensau: A Medieval Anti-Jewish Motif and Its History* (London: Warburg Institute, 1974). He specifically discusses Luther in relation to the Wittenberg Judensau at 30*ff*., 43–51, and plates 26–27.

39. Johann Eck, *See Ains Judenbuechlins verlegung: darin ain Christ, gantzer Christenhait zü schmach, will es geschehe den juden vnrecht in bezichtigung der Kristen kinder mordt* (Ingolstadt: Weissenhorn, 1542). "Judenvater" occurs at, e.g., fol. A IIIv and elsewhere. On the Augsburg preacher see the complaint of Sir Richard Morrison, English ambassador to the court of Charles V, in the *Calendar of State Papers, Spanish (1550–1552)*, ed. Royall Tyler (London: Institute of Historical Research, 1914), 236, 254. On Reformation and Counter-Reformation charges of "Judaism" see Nirenberg, *Anti-Judaism*, 246–68.

40. For my interpretation of *The Merchant of Venice* along the lines suggested here, see "Shakespeare's Jewish Questions." Readers interested in deeper explorations of Kantorowicz's reading of Richard II may turn to Lorna Hutson, "Imagining Justice: Kantorowicz and Shakespeare," *Representations* 106 (2009): 118–42; and Anselm Haverkamp, "Richard II, Bracton, and the End of Political Theology," *Law and Literature* 16 (2004): 313–26.

41. "Real humanism" is from Marx and Engels, *Werke*, 2.7. "Philosophy is nothing else": Karl Marx, *Economic and Philosophical Manuscripts of 1844*, trans. Martin Milligan (Mineola: Dover Publications Inc., 1961/2007), 145. Marx exempted only Ludwig Feuerbach from this critique. For the history of these debates see, among many others, Warren Breckman, *Marx, the Young Hegelians and the Origins of Radical Social Theory* (Cambridge: Cambridge University Press, 1999).

42. "Imitatio Christi": Compare Werner Hamacher, *Pleroma: Readings in Hegel* (London: Athlone Press, 1998), 199–200, who concludes that for Hegel "all of world history is an *imitatio Christi*." Hegel did not hide the Christological foundations of his thought: "It is in connection with a true understanding of the death of Christ that the relation of the subject as such in this way comes into view. . . . The highest knowledge of the nature of the Idea of Spirit is contained in this thought." *Lectures on the Philosophy of Religion*, trans. E. B. Speiers and J. B. Sanderson, 3 vols. (New York: Humanities Press, 1962), 3:96–97, 98. *Cf.* 2:220–24; and Hegel's *Phenomenology of Spirit*, trans. A. V. Miller (Oxford: Oxford University Press, 1977), 470–78. On the *Philosophy of Religion* as a Trinitarian demonstration of the rational structure of reality see Peter C. Hodgson's "Editorial Introduction" to the *Lectures on the Philosophy of Religion*, 3 vols. (Berkeley: University of California Press, 1984–1987), 1:63–64. See more generally Laurence Dickey, *Hegel: Religion, Economics, and the Politics of Spirit, 1770–1807* (Cambridge: Cambridge University Press, 1987).

43. Hegel tried to claim that love had its own "law" independent of any positive or external law. But his recourse to the mysterious appeal of "forgiveness" in chapter 6 of the *Phenomenology* suggests that he himself found the argument wanting.

44. The translations are my own, from the text in *Karl Marx–Friedrich Engels Werke*, vol. 1 (Berlin: Dietz, 1957), p. 360.

45. Roberto Esposito, *Bios: Biopolitics and Philosophy* (Minneapolis: University of Minnesota Press, 2008), 58, cited in Eric L. Santner, *The Royal Remains: The People's Two Bodies and the Endgames of Sovereignty* (Chicago: University of Chicago Press, 2011), 17. Santner's formulation is from p. xiii.

46. The quotes are from Slavoj Žižek, *In Defense of Lost Causes* (London: Verso, 2009), 4–5, 6.

47. Martin Buber, "The Validity and Limitations of the Political Principle," in *Pointing the Way*, ed. and trans. Maurice Friedman (New York: Schocken Books, 1957), 215. Here and in the paragraph that follows I am relying on material from Paul Mendes-Flohr's "Martin Buber and Martin Heidegger in Dialogue," *Journal of Religion* 94 (2014): 2–25.

48. M. Siegfried, *Abkehr vom Subjekt: Zum Sprachdenken bei Heidegger und Buber* (Freiburg im Breisgau: Verlag Karl Alber, 2010).

49. "Das Wort, das gesprochen wird," in *Martin Buber Werkausgabe*, Vol. 6: *Sprachphilosophische Schriften*, ed. Asher Biemann (Gütersloh: Gütersloh Verlagshaus, 2003), 109*ff.*

50. Heidegger, *Letters to His Wife*, 225. *"Mein liebes Seelchen,": Briefe Martin Heideggers an seine Frau Elfride*, 279.

51. Martin Buber, *Paths in Utopia* (New York: Macmillan, 1949), 134–35. My thanks to Samuel Hayim Brody for the reference. We will all learn to think anew about Buber's "theopolitics" from his dissertation, "This Pathless Hour: Messianism, Anarchism, Zionism, and Martin Buber's Theopolitics Reconsidered" (PhD diss., University of Chicago, 2013).

52. Žižek, *In Defense of Lost Causes*, 4.

53. Friedrich Nietzsche, *The Gay Science* (Leipzig: E. W. Fritzsch Verlag, 1887), 121.

54. Friedrich Nietzsche, *Beyond Good and Evil*, trans. Walter Kaufmann (New York: Vintage, 1989), 1–2.

55. Following Nietzsche, Foucault used the term *genealogy* to describe his antithetical alternative to the histories produced by this fantasy, a history that does not "go back in time to restore an unbroken continuity that operates beyond the dispersion of forgotten things . . . [that] does not resemble the evolution of a species or map the destiny of a people." See Michel Foucault, "Nietzsche, Genealogy, History," in *Language, Counter-Memory, Practice*, ed. D. Bouchard (Ithaca: Cornell University Press, 1977), 154, 162; and also his "Il faut défendre la société," Cours au Collège de France, 1976 (Paris: Gallimard/Seuil, 1997), 10. "Masks": I take the liberty of personifying concepts here, a liberty authorized by Nietzsche's aphorism in *Beyond Good and Evil*, section 40, on the mask as a necessary form of presentation for every "great spirit."

56. Karl Marx, *Economic and Philosophical Manuscripts of 1844*, 145.

BIBLIOGRAPHY

Abulafia, Anna. "An Eleventh-Century Exchange of Letters between a Christian and a Jew." *Journal of Medieval History* 7, no. 2 (1981): 153–74.

Abulafia, David. "'Nam Iudei servi regis sunt, et semper fisco regio deputati': The Jews in the Municipal Fuero of Teruel (1176–7)." In *Jews, Muslims, and Christians in and around the Crown of Aragon: Essays in Honour of Professor Elena Lourie*. Edited by Harvey Hames, 97–123. Leiden: Brill, 2004.

———. "The Servitude of Jews and Muslims in the Medieval Mediterranean: Origins and Diffusion." *Mélanges de l'École Française de Rome, Moyen Âge* 112 (2000): 687–714.

Ackroyd, Paul. "The Two Tax-Gatherers by Marinus van Reymerswaele: Original and Replica." *National Gallery Technical Bulletin* 24 (2003): 50–63.

Adémar of Chabannes. *Chronicon*. Edited by P. Bourgain (CCCM, 129). Turnhout: Brepols, 1999.

Adler, Michael. *Jews of Medieval England*. London: Jewish Historical Society of England, 1939.

Albert of Montecassino. *Alberici Casinensis Flores rhetorici*. Edited by M. Inguanez and H. M. Willard. Montecassino: Arti grafiche e fotomeccaniche Sansaini, 1938.

Alberti, Leon Battista. *De Pictura*. Translated by Cecil Grayson. London: Penguin, 1991.

Alfonso X el Sabio. *Songs of Holy Mary of Alfonso X, the Wise*. Translated by Kathleen Kulp-Hill. Tempe: Arizona Center for Renaissance and Medieval Studies, 2000.

———. *Cantigas de Santa María: Edición facsímil del códice B. R. 20 de la Biblioteca Centrale de Florencia, siglo XIII*. 2 vols. Madrid: Edilán, 1989.

———. *Cantigas de Santa María*. 3 vols. Edited by W. Mettmann. Madrid: Castalia, 1986–1989.

———. *Cantigas de Santa María: Edición facsímil del códice T.I.1 de la Biblioteca de San Lorenzo de El Escorial, siglo XIII*. 2 vols. Madrid: Edilán, 1979.

Alighieri, Dante. *Tutte le opere*. Edited by Luigi Blasucci. Florence: Sansoni, 1965.

———. *Dantis Alagherii Epistolae*. Edited and translated by Paget Jackson Toynbee. Oxford: Clarendon Press, 1920.

Alpert of Metz. *De Diversitate Temporum*. Edited by G. H. Pertz (MGH SS 4). Hannover: Impensis Bibliopolii Avlici Hahniani, 1841.

Amador de los Ríos, José. *Estudios históricos, políticos y literarios sobre los judíos de España*. Madrid: Imp. de M. Díaz, 1848.

Ambrose. *Epistulae et acta*. Vol. 3. CSEL 82.1–4. Edited by O. Faller and M. Zelzer. Vienna: Hoelder-Pinchler-Temsky, 1968–1996.

Anastos, M. V. "The Argument for Iconoclasm as Presented by the Iconoclastic

Council of 754." In *Late Classical and Medieval Studies in Honor of A. M. Friend, Jr.*, edited by Kurt Weitzmann, 177–88. Princeton: Princeton University Press, 1955.

Aretino, Pietro. *Lettere*. Edited by Paolo Procaccioli. 2 vols. Milan: Rizzoli, 1991.

Arnauld, Antoine. *De la fréquente communion*. Paris: Vitré, 1643.

Arnauld, Antoine, and Pierre Nicole. *La logique ou l'art de penser*. Edited by Louis Marin. Paris: Flammarion, 1970.

Arbós, Cristina. "Los cancioneros castellanos del siglo xv como fuente para la historia de los judíos españoles." In *Jews and Conversos: Studies in Society and the Inquisition*, edited by Yosef Kaplan, 77–78. Jerusalem: Magnes Press, 1985.

Arduini, Maria Lodovica. *Ruperto di Deutz e la controversia tra cristiani ed ebrei nel secolo XII*. Edited by Rhabanus Haacke. Rome: Istituto storico italiano per il Medio Evo, 1979.

Arnold, Matthew. *Culture and Anarchy: An Essay in Political and Social Criticism*. London: Smith, Elder and Co., 1869.

Aschheim, Steven Edward. *Culture and Catastrophe: German and Jewish Confrontations with National Socialism*. London: MacMillan, 1996.

Auerbach, Erich. *Scenes from the Drama of European Literature*. Gloucester: Peter Smith, 1973.

Augustine. *Expositions of the Psalms*. Translated by Maria Boulding. Hyde Park: New City Press, 2000.

Avalle-Arce, Juan Bautista. "Sobre Juan Alfonso de Baena." *Revista de Filología Hispánica* 7 (1945): 141–47.

Azáceta, José María. *Cancionero: Edición Crítica*. Vol. 1. Madrid: Consejo Superior de Investigaciones Científicas, 1966.

Bab, Julius. "Der Anteil der Juden an der deutschen Dichtung der Gegenwart." *Kölnische Zeitung*, September 17, 1911.

Bacci, Michele. "The Berardenga Antependium and the *Passio Ymaginis* Office." *Journal of the Warburg and Courtauld Institutes* 61 (1998): 1–16.

Bacon, Francis. *The Works of Francis Bacon*. Vol. 10. London: W. Baynes and Son, 1824.

Baena, Juan Alfonso de. *Cancionero de Juan Alfonso de Baena*. Edited by Brian Dutton and Joaquín González Cuenca. Madrid: Visor Libros, 1993.

Baer, Yitzhak. *A History of the Jews in Christian Spain*. Philadelphia: University of Pennsylvania Press, 1978.

Bale, Anthony. *The Jew in the Medieval Book: English Antisemitism, 1350–1500*. Cambridge: Cambridge University Press, 2006.

Barron, Stephanie, ed. *"Degenerate Art": The Fate of the Avant-Garde in Nazi Germany*. Los Angeles: Los Angeles County Museum of Art, 1991.

Bartlová, Milena. *Poctivé obrazy: Deskové malířství v čechách a na Moravě 1400–1460*. Prague: Argo, 2001.

Bates, David. "Political Theology and the Nazi State: Carl Schmitt's Concept of the Institution." *Modern Intellectual History* 3 (2006): 415–42.

Bellori, Giovanni Pietro. *Le Vite dei pittori scultori e architetti moderni*. Edited by Evelina Borea. Turin: Einaudi, 1976.

Belting, Hans. *Likeness and Presence: A History of the Image before the Era of Art*. Translated by E. Jephcott. Chicago: University of Chicago Press, 1994.

Belting, Hans, and Christiane Kruse. *Die Erfindung des Gemäldes: das erste Jahrhundert der niederländischen Malerei*. Munich: Hirmer Verlag, 1994.

Benito Ruano, Eloy. "El memorial contra los conversos del bachiller Marcos García de Mora ('Marquillos de Mazarambroz')." *Sefarad* 17 (1957): 314–51.

Benjamin, Walter. *Walter Benjamin, Gesammelte Schriften*. Edited by Rolf Tiedemann and Hermann Schweppenhäuser. Frankfurt: Suhrkamp, 1991.

Berceo, Gonzalo de. *Milagros de Nuestra Señora*. Edited by A. G. Solalinde. Madrid: Espasa-Calpe, 1978.

Bergstrom, I. *Dutch Still-Life Painting in the 17th Century*. London: Faber and Faber, 1956.

Bernard of Clairvaux. *Patrologiæ cursus completus: sive bibliotheca universalis, integra, uniformis, commoda, oeconomica, omnium SS. patrum, doctorum, scriptorumque ecclesiasticorum. Series latina*. Vol. 182. Edited by J. P. Migne. Paris: Apud Garnier Fratres, 1854.

Besserman, L. "Ideology, Antisemitism, and Chaucer's 'Prioress's Tale.'" *Chaucer Review* 36 (2001): 48–72.

Blacksberg, Leslie Ann. "Between Salvation and Damnation: The Role of the Fountain in the 'Fountain of Life.'" In *Het Wellende Water: De bron in tekst en beeld in de middeleeuwse Nederlanden en het Rijnland*, edited by B. Baert and V. Fraeters, 157–73. Louvain: Univ. Pers Leuven, 2005.

Blake, N. F. *The Textual Tradition of the "Canterbury Tales."* London: Edward Arnold, 1985.

Blew, William John. *Hymns and Hymn Books, with a Few Words on Anthems: A Letter to the Rev. William Upton Richards*. London: Rivingtons, 1858.

Blunt, John Elijah. *A History of the Establishment and Residence of the Jews in England*. London: Saunders and Benning, 1830.

Boccaccio, Giovanni. *Geneologia deorum gentilium libri*. Edited by V. Romano. Bari: Laterza, 1951.

Breckman, Warren. *Marx, the Young Hegelians and the Origins of Radical Social Theory*. Cambridge: Cambridge University Press, 1999.

Bredekamp, Horst. *Kunst als Medium sozialer Konflikte. Bilderkämpfe von der Spätantike bis zur Hussitenrevolution*. Frankfurt am Main: Suhrkamp, 1975.

Brenner, Hildegard. *Die Kunstpolitik des Nationalsozialismus*. Reinbek bei Hamburg: Rowohlt, 1963.

Brody, Samuel Hayim. "This Pathless Hour: Messianism, Anarchism, Zionism, and Martin Buber's Theopolitics Reconsidered." PhD diss., University of Chicago, 2013.

Brown, Carleton. "The Prioress' Tale." In *Sources and Analogues of Chaucer's*

"Canterbury Tales," edited by W. F. Bryan and G. Dempster, 447–85. London: Routledge & K. Paul, 1941.

———. *A Study of the Miracle of Our Lady Told by Chaucer's Prioress*. Chaucer Society (series 2) 45. London: Paul, Trench, Trübner and Company, 1910.

Brown, Peter R. L. "Images as a Substitute for Writing." In *East and West: Modes of Communication*, edited by Euangelos K. Chrysos and Ian Wood, 15–34. Leiden: Brill, 1999.

———. *Augustine of Hippo: A Biography*. London: Faber and Faber, 1967.

Brubaker, Leslie, and John F. Haldon. *Byzantium in the Iconoclast Era (c. 680–850): The Sources, an Annotated Survey*. Burlington: Ashgate, 2011.

Brubaker, Leslie, John F. Haldon, and Robert Ousterhout. *Byzantium in the Iconoclast Era (c. 680–850): A History*. Cambridge: Cambridge University Press, 2008.

Bruyn, J. *Van Eyck Problemen: de Levensbron, het werk van een leerling van Jan van Eyck*. Utrecht: Dekker and Gumbert, 1957.

Buber, Martin. *Martin Buber Werkausgabe*. Vol. 6: *Sprachphilosophische Schriften*. Edited by Asher Biemann. Gütersloh: Gütersloh Verlagshaus, 2003.

———. *Pointing the Way*. Edited and translated. by Maurice Friedman. New York: Schocken Books, 1957.

———. *Paths in Utopia*. New York: Macmillan, 1949.

Buck, August. *Italienische Dichtungslehren vom Mittelalter bis zum Ausgang der Renaissance*. Tübingen: M. Niemeyer, 1952.

Bulst, Walther. *Hymni Latini antiquissimi LXXV*. Heidelberg: F. H. Kerle, 1956.

Cañas, Jesús, ed. *Libro de Alexandre*. 5th ed. Madrid: Catedra, 2007.

Cantera Burgos, Francisco. "El Cancionero de Baena: Judíos y conversos en él." *Sefarad* 27 (1967): 71–111.

Caspary, Gerard E. *Politics and Exegesis: Origen and the Two Swords*. Berkeley: University of California Press, 1979.

Cátedra, Pedro. "La predicación castellana de San Vicente Ferrer." *Boletín de la Real Academia de Buenas Letras de Barcelona* 39 (1983–1984): 235–309.

Celan, Paul. *Gesammelte Werke in fünf Bänden*. Edited by Beda Allemann and Stefan Reichert. Vol. 1. Frankfurt: Suhrkamp Verlag, 1983.

Chamberlain, Houston Stewart. *Die Grundlagen des neunzehnten Jahrhunderts*. Vol. 1. Munich: Verlagsanstalt F. Bruckmann, 1903.

Chaucer, Geoffrey. *The Riverside Chaucer*. 3rd ed. Edited by Larry Benson. Oxford: Oxford University Press, 2008.

———. *The General Prologue*. Edited by Malcolm Andrew and Daniel J. Ransom. Norman: University of Oklahoma Press, 1993.

Chazan, Robert. *Medieval Jewry in Northern France: A Political and Social History*. Baltimore: Johns Hopkins University Press, 1973.

Cohen, Jeremy. *Living Letters of the Law: Ideas of the Jew in Medieval Christianity*. Berkeley: University of California Press, 1999.

Copeland, Deena. *The Insight of Unbelievers: Nicholas of Lyra and Christian Reading of Jewish Text in the Later Middle Ages*. Philadelphia: University of Pennsylvania Press, 2007.

Corrigan, Kathleen. *Visual Polemics in the Ninth-Century Byzantine Psalters*. Cambridge: Cambridge University Press, 1992.

Cronan, Todd. *Against Affective Formalism: Matisse, Bergson, Modernism*. Minneapolis: University of Minnesota Press, 2013.

Crouzel, H. *Théologie de l'image de Dieu chez Origène*. Paris: Aubier, 1954.

Curtius, Ernst Robert. *Europäische Literatur und lateinisches Mittelalter*. Berne: Francke, 1963.

Dagron, G. "Judaïser." *Traveaux et Mémoires* 11 (1991): 359–80.

Dahan, Gilbert. "L'exégèse de l'histoire de Caïn et Abel du XIIe au XIVe siècle en occident." *Recherches de théologie ancienne et médiévale* 49 (1982): 21–89.

Dán, Róbert. "Judaizare—the Career of a Term." In *Antitrinitarianism in the Second Half of the 16th Century*, edited by R. Dán and A. Pirnát, 25–34. Budapest: Brill, 1982.

Davis, Michael. *The Soul of the Greeks*. Chicago: University of Chicago Press, 2011.

Dawson, David. "Plato's Soul and the Body of the Text in Philo and Origen." In *Interpretation and Allegory: Antiquity to the Modern Period*, edited by Jon Whitman, 89–107. Leiden: Brill, 2000.

Degroote, G. "De poezia der rederijkers." *Dietsche warande en Belfort* 48 (1948): 292–301.

Déroche, Vincent. "Form and Function of Anti-Jewish Polemics: Polymorphy, Polysémy." In *Jews in Byzantium: Dialectics of Minority and Majority Cultures*, edited by R. Bonfil, O. Irshai, G. Stroumsa, and R. Talgam, 535–48. Leiden: Brill, 2012.

———. "La polemique anti-judaïque au VIe et au VIIe siècle: un memento inédit, les *Kephalaia*." *Travaux et Mémoires* 11 (1991): 275–311.

Derrida, Jacques. "A Testimony Given." In *Questioning Judaism: Interviews by Elizabeth Weber*. Translated by Rachel Bowlby. Stanford: Stanford University Press, 2004.

———. *The Truth in Painting*. Translated by Geoff Bennington and Ian McLeod. Chicago: University of Chicago Press, 1987.

Descartes, René. *Principia Philosophiae*. Amsterdam: 1644.

Deyermond, A. D. "Mester es sen Pecado." *Romanische Forschungen* 77 (1965): 111–16.

Dickey, Laurence. Hegel: Religion, Economics, and the Politics of Spirit, 1770–1807. Cambridge: Cambridge University Press, 1987.

Dillon, John. "An Ethic for the Late Antique Sage." In *The Cambridge Companion to Plotinus*, ed. Lloyd P. Gerson, 315–35. New York: Cambridge University Press, 1996.

Dixhoorn, A. van. *Lustige geesten: Rederijkers en hun kamers in het publieke leven van de Noordelijke Nederlanden in de vijftiende, zestiende en zeventiende eeuw*. Amsterdam: Proefschrift, 2004.

Doesborch, Jan van. *De Refreinenbundel van Jan van Doesborch*. Edited by C. Kruyskamp. Leiden: Brill, 1940.

Domínguez Rodriguez, Ana. "Imágenes de un rey trovador de Santa María (Alfonso X en Las Cantigas)." In *Il medio Oriente e l'Occidente nell'Arte del XIII secolo: Atti del XXIV Congresso Internazionale di Storia dell'Arte (Bologna, 1979)*, edited by Hans Belting, 229–39. Bologne: CLUEB, 1982.

Dutton, Brian. *El Cancionero del Siglo XV, c. 1360–1520*. 7 vols. Salamanca: Universidad de Salamanca, 1990–1991.

Eck, Johann. *See Ains Judenbuechlins verlegung: darin ain Christ, gantzer Christenhait zü schmach, will es geschehe den juden vnrecht in bezichtigung der Kristen kinder mordt*. Ingolstadt: Weissenhorn, 1542.

Edwards, Mark U. *Luther's Last Battles: Politics and Polemics, 1531–1546*. Ithaca: Cornell University Press, 1983.

Eisenstadt, Shmuel. "The Axial Age in World History." In *The Cultural Values of Europe*, edited by Hans Joas and Klaus Wiegandt, 22–42. Liverpool: Liverpool University Press, 2008.

Elslander, A. van. "Letterkundig leven in de Bourgondische tijd: de rederijkers." *Rederijkersstudien* 5 (1969): 3–20.

Engberg-Pedersen, Troels. *Cosmology and Self in the Apostle Paul: The Material Spirit*. New York: Oxford University Press, 2010.

———. *Paul and the Stoics*. Louisville: Westminster John Knox Press, 2000.

Ernout, A., and A. Meillet. *Dictionaire étymologique de la langue latine: histoire des mots*, 3rd ed. Paris: Klinksiek, 1939.

Espí Forcén, Carlos. *Recrucificando a Cristo: Los judíos de la Passio Imaginis en la isla de Mallorca*. Mallorca: Objeto Perdido, 2009.

Esposito, Roberto. *Bios: Biopolitics and Philosophy*. Minneapolis: University of Minnesota Press, 2008.

Evenepoel, W. "The Place of Poetry in Latin Christianity." In *Early Christian Poetry: A Collection of Essays*. Edited by Jan den Boeft and Antonius Hilhorst. Leiden: Brill, 1993.

Fichte, Johann Gottlieb. *Addresses to the German Nation*. Edited by George A. Kelly. New York: Harper, 1968.

Field Jr., L. *Liberty, Dominion, and the Two Swords*. Notre Dame: University of Notre Dame Press, 1998.

Fitzmyer, J. A. *First Corinthians*. Anchor-Yale Bible Commentaries. New Haven: Yale University Press, 2008.

Fontaine, Jacques. *Naissance de la poésie dans l'Occident chrétien: Esquisse d'une histoire de la poésie chrétienne du IIIe au Vie siècle*. Paris: Études Augustiniennes, 1981.

Foucault, Michel. "Il faut défendre la société." Cours au Collège de France, 1976. Paris: Gallimard/Seuil, 1997.

———. *The Order of Things: An Archaeology of the Human Sciences*. New York: Random House, 1994.

———. "Nietzsche, Genealogy, History." In *Language, Counter-Memory, Practice*, edited by D. Bouchard. Ithaca: Cornell University Press, 1977.

Foulché-Delbosc, R. *Cancionero Castellano del siglo XV*. Vol. 1. Nueva Biblioteca de Autores Españoles, vol. 19. Madrid: Bailly-Bailliere, 1912.

Fradenburg, Louise O. "Criticism, Anti-Semitism, and the 'Prioress's Tale.'" *Exemplaria* 1 (1989): 69–115.

Fraker, Charles. *Studies on the Cancionero de Baena*. Chapel Hill: University of North Carolina Press, 1996.

———. "Review of *El fraile trobador*." *Hispanic Review* 42, no. 3 (1974): 341–43.

Fredriksen, Paula. *Augustine and the Jews: A Christian Defense of Jews and Judaism*. New York: Doubleday, 2008.

Fricke, Beate. *Ecce fides: Die Statue von Conques, Götzendienst und Bildkultur im Westen*. Munich: Fink, 2007.

Fried, Michael. *The Moment of Caravaggio*. Princeton: Princeton University Press, 2010.

Friedländer, Max J. *Die altniederländische Malerei*. Berlin: P. Cassirer, 1929.

Frolow, A. *La relique de la vraie croix: recherches sur le développement d'un culte*. Paris: Institut français d'études Byzantines, 1961.

Fulda, Bernhard, and Aya Soika. "Emil Nolde and the National Socialist Dictatorship." In *Degenerate Art: The Attack on Modern Art in Nazi Germany, 1937*, edited by Olaf Peters, 186–95. New York: Prestel Publishing, 2014.

Gager, John G. *Reinventing Paul*. Oxford: Oxford University Press, 2000.

Gauer, Heinz. *Texte zum byzantinischen Bilderstreit: Der Synodalbrief der drei Patriarchen des Ostens von 836 und seine Verwandlung in sieben Jahrhunderten*. Frankfurt am Main: Peter Lang, 1994.

Gerli, E. Michael. "Antón de Montoro and the Wages of Eloquence: Poverty, Patronage, and Poetry in 15th-C. Castile." *Romance Philology* 48 (1994–1995): 265–76.

Gerli, E. Michael, and Julian Weiss, eds. *Poetry at Court in Trastamaran Spain: From the Cancionero de Baena to the Cancionero General*. Tempe: Medieval & Renaissance Texts & Studies, 1998.

Gestoso y Perez, J. *Ensayo de un diccionario de artifices que florecen en Sevilla durante el siglo XIII al XVIII*. 3 vols. Sevilla: En la oficina de la Andalucía moderna, 1899.

Godi, C. "La *Collatio laureationis* del Petrarca nelle due redazioni." *Studi petrarcheschi* 5 (1988): 1–56.

Goebbels, Joseph. *Michael: Ein deutsches Schicksal in Tagebuchblättern*. Munich: Franz Eher, 1929.

Gombrich, E. H. "The Father of Art History." In *Tributes: Interpreters of Our Cultural Tradition*, 51–69. Ithaca: Cornell University Press, 1984.

———. *Art and Illusion: A Study in the Psychology of Pictorial Representation*. Princeton: Princeton University Press, 1969.

Gomperz, Heinrich. "Asōmatos." *Hermes* 67 (1932): 155–67.

González Rolán, Tomás, and Pilar Saquero Suárez-Somonte. *De la* Sentencia-Estatuto *de Pero Sarmiento a la* Instrucción *del Relator*. Madrid: Aben Ezra Ediciones, 2012.

Gordon, Donald E. *Expressionism: Art and Idea*. New Haven: Yale University Press, 1987.

Gregory the Great. *The Letters of Gregory the Great*. Translated by John R. C. Martyn. Vol. 3. Toronto: Pontifical Institute of Mediaeval Studies, 2004.

———. *Registrum epistolarum*. Edited by Dag Norberg (CCSL 140–140A). Turnhout: Brepols, 1982.

Gregory of Tours. *Glory of the Martyrs*. Translated by Raymond van Dam. Liverpool: Liverpool University Press, 1988.

———. *History of the Franks*. Translated by Lewis Thorpe. Harmondsworth: Penguin, 1974.

Gross, Raphael. *Carl Schmitt und die Juden*. Frankfurt am Main: Suhrkamp, 2000.

Günther, Hans. *Rasse und Stil*. 2nd ed. Munich: J. F. Lehmann, 1927.

Hagemann, Karen. *Mannlicher Muth und Teutsche Ehre: Nation, Militär und Geschlecht zur Zeit der Antinapoleonischen Kriege Preußens*. Paderborn: Ferdinand Schöningh, 2002.

Halliwell, Stephen. *The Aesthetics of Mimesis: Ancient Texts and Modern Problems*. Princeton: Princeton University Press, 2002.

Hamacher, Werner. *Pleroma: Readings in Hegel*. London: Athlone Press, 1998.

Hamburger, Jeffrey F. "The Medieval Work of Art: Wherein the 'Work'? Wherein the 'Art'?" In *The Mind's Eye: Art and Theological Argument in the Middle Ages*, edited by J. Hamburger and A-M. Bouché, 374–412. Princeton: Princeton University Press, 2006.

———. "Body vs. Book: The Trope of Visibility in Images of Christian-Jewish Polemic." In *Kultbild 1: Ästhetik des Unsichtbaren: Bildtheorie und Bildgebrauch in der Vormoderne*, edited by D. Ganz and T. Lentes, 112–45. Berlin: Reimer, 2004.

Hanson, R. P. C. "The Christian Attitude to Pagan Religions up to the Time of Constantine the Great." In *Aufstieg und Niedergang der römischen Welt: Geschichte und Kultur Roms im Spiegel der neueren Forschung*. Edited by Hildegard Temporini and Wolfgang Haase. Berlin: Walter and Gruyter, 1980.

Harms, Wolfgang. *Deutsche illustrierte Flugblätter des 16. und 17. Jahrhunderts*. Tübingen: Max Niemeyer Verlag, 1980–1997.

Harris, H. S. *Hegel's Development: Towards the Sunlight, 1770–1801*. Oxford: Clarendon Press, 1972.

Haverkamp, Anselm. "Richard II, Bracton, and the End of Political Theology." *Law and Literature* 16 (2004): 313–26.

Heck, Eberhard. "Vestrum est—poeta noster: Von der Geringschätung Vergils zu seiner Aneignung in der frühchristlichen lateinischen Apologetik." *Museum Helveticum* 47 (1990): 102–20.

Heer, Friedrich. *Land in Strom der Zeit*. Vienna: Herold, 1958.

Hegel, Georg. *Philosophie der Kunst oder Ästhetik. Nach Hegel. Im Sommer 1826*.

Mitschrift Friedrich Carl Hermann Victor von Kehler. Edited by A. Gethmann-Siefert and B. Collenberg-Plotnikov. Munich: Wilhelm Fink Verlag, 2004.

———. *Mythologie der Vernunft*. Edited by C. Jamme and H. Schneider. Frankfurt: Suhrkamp, 1984.

———. *The Difference between Fichte's and Schelling's Systems of Philosophy*. Translated by H. S. Harris and Walter Cerf. Albany: State University of New York Press, 1977.

———. *Phenomenology of Spirit*. Translated by A. V. Miller. Oxford: Oxford University Press, 1977.

———. *Aesthetics, Lectures on Fine Art*. 2 vols. Translated by T. M. Knox. Oxford: Clarendon, 1975.

———. *Vorlesungen über die Philosophie der Religion*. 2 vols. Edited by Georg Lasson. Hamburg: Felix Meiner, 1975.

———. *Early Theological Writings*. Translated by T. M. Knox. Philadelphia: University of Pennsylvania Press, 1971.

———. *Wissenschaft der Logik*. Edited by Georg Lasson. Hamburg: Felix Meiner, 1971.

———. *Vorlesungen über die Ästhetik*. 3 vols. Edited by E. Moldenhauer and K. M. Michel. Frankfurt: Suhrkamp, 1970.

———. *Science of Logic*. Translated by A. V. Miller. Oxford: Oxford University Press, 1969.

———. "Differenz des Fichteschen und Schellingischen Systems der Philosophie." In *Gesammelte Werke*, vol. 4. Edited by Hartmut Buchner and Otto Pöggeler. Hamburg: Meiner, 1968.

———. *Lectures on the Philosophy of Religion*. 3 vols. Translated by E. B. Speiers and J. B. Sanderson. New York: Humanities Press, 1962.

———. *Hegels theologische Jugendschriften*. Tübingen: J. C. B. Mohr, 1907.

———. *The Philosophy of History, by G. W. F. Hegel*. Translated by J. Sibree, from the 2nd edition. New York: Collier & Son, 1902.

Heidegger, Martin. *Martin Heidegger: Letters to His Wife, 1915–1970*. Edited by Gertrud Heidegger and translated by R. D. V. Glasgow. London: Polity, 2010.

———. *"Mein liebes Seelchen": Briefe Martin Heideggers an seine Frau Elfride, 1915–1970*. Edited by Gertrud Heidegger. Munich: Deutsche Verlags-Anstalt, 2005.

Heine, Heinrich. "Ludwig Börne: Eine Denkschrift," Books 1 and 2. In *Ludwig Börne und Heinrich Heine, ein deutsches Zerwürfnis*, edited by Hans Magnus Enzensberger. Nördlingen: Franz Greno, 1986.

———. *Heines Werke*. Edited by Helmut Holtzhauer. Berlin: Aufbau Verlag, 1968.

———. "Shakespeare's Maidens and Women." *The Works of Heinrich Heine*, vol. 1. Translated by Charles Godfrey Leland. London: William Heinemann, 1906.

Herbert, George. *The Complete English Poems*. Edited by John Tobin. London: Penguin, 1991.

Herzog, Reinhart. *Die Bibelepik der lateinischen Spätantike: Formgeschichte einer erbaulichen Gattung*. Vol. 1. Munich: W. Fink, 1975.

Hibbard, Howard. *Caravaggio*. New York: Harper & Row, 1983.

Hodgson, Peter C. "Editorial Introduction." *Hegel's Lectures on the Philosophy of Religion*, 3 vols. Berkeley: University of California Press, 1984–1987.

Horace. *Satires, Epistles, and Ars Poetica*. Edited by H. Rushton Fairclough. Cambridge: Harvard University Press, 1966.

Horkheimer, Max, and Theodor W. Adorno. *Dialectics of Enlightenment*. New York: Continuum, 1972.

Hutcheson, Gregory S. "'Pinning Him to the Wall': The Poetics of Self-Destruction in the Court of Juan II." *Disputatio* 5 (2002): 87–102.

———. "Marginality and Empowerment in Baena's Cancionero." PhD diss., Harvard University, 1993.

Hutson, Lorna. "Imagining Justice: Kantorowicz and Shakespeare." *Representations* 106 (2009): 118–42.

Hyman, John. *The Imitation of Nature*. Oxford: Blackwell, 1989.

Isaacs, Marie E. *The Concept of Spirit: A Study of Pneuma in Hellenistic Judaism and Its Bearing on the New Testament*. London: Heythrop College, 1976.

Isidore of Seville. *Etymologiarum sive originum libri xx*. 2 Vols. Edited by W. M. Lindsay. Oxford: Clarendon Press, 1911/1985.

Jaspers, Karl. *A Way to Wisdom: An Introduction to Philosophy*. New Haven: Yale University Press, 1951.

Jay, Martin. *Downcast Eyes: The Denigration of Vision in Twentieth-Century French Thought*. Berkeley: University of California Press, 1993.

Joas, Hans. "The Axial Age Debate in Religious Discourse." In *The Axial Age and Its Consequences*, edited by Robert N. Bellah and Hans Joas, 9–29. Cambridge: Harvard University Press, 2012.

John of Damascus. *Three Treatises on the Divine Images*. Translated by Andrew Louth. Crestwood: St. Vladimir's Seminary Press, 2003.

Johnson, Eleanor. *Practicing Literary Theory in the Middle Ages: Ethics and the Mixed Form in Chaucer, Gower, Usk, and Hoccleve*. Chicago: University of Chicago Press, 2013.

Johnson, Willis. "Textual Sources for the Study of Jewish Currency Crimes in Thirteenth-Century England." *British Numismatic Journal* 66 (1997): 21–32.

Jordan, William C. *The French Monarchy and the Jews: From Philip Augustus to the Last Capetians*. Philadelphia: University of Pennsylvania Press, 1989.

Joyce, James. *Ulysses*. New York: Random House, 1934.

Kahn, Victoria. *The Future of Illusion: Political Theology and Early Modern Texts*. Chicago: University of Chicago Press, 2014.

Kaiser, Fritz. *Führer durch die Ausstellung Entartete Kunst*. Berlin: Verlag für Kultur- und Wirtschaftswerbung, 1937.

Kant, Immanuel. *The Critique of Judgment*. Translated by Werner S. Pluhar. Indianapolis: Hackett, 1987.

Kantorowicz, Ernst H. *The King's Two Bodies: A Study in Medieval Political Theology*. Princeton: Princeton University Press, 1997.

Kemp, Wolfgang. "Prakitsche Bildbeschreibung: Über Bilder in Bildern, besonders bei van Eyck und Mantegna." In *Beschreibungskunst—Kunstbeschreibung: Ekphrasis von der Antike bus zur Gegenwart*, edited by Gottfried Boem and Helmut Pfotenhauer, 99–120. Munich: Wilhelm Fin Verlag, 1995.

Kessler, Herbert L. "Shaded with Dust: Jewish Eyes on Christian Art." In *Judaism and Christian Art: Aesthetic Anxieties from the Catacombs to Colonialism*, edited by David Nirenberg and Herbert L. Kessler, 74–114. Philadelphia: University of Pennsylvania Press, 2011.

———. *Neither God nor Man: Words, Images, and the Medieval Anxiety about Art*. Freiburg im Breisgau: Rombach Verlag, 2007.

———. "Corporeal Texts, Spiritual Paintings, and the Mind's Eye." In *Reading Images and Texts: Medieval Images and Texts as Forms of Communication. Papers from the Third Utrecht Symposium on Medieval Literacy*, edited by M. Hageman and M. Mostert, 9–27. Utrecht: Turnhout Brepols Publishers, 2000.

———. *Spiritual Seeing: Picturing God's Invisibility in Medieval Art*. Philadelphia: University of Pennsylvania Press, 2000.

Kierkegaard, Søren. *Kierkegaard's Journals and Notebooks*. Vol. 3. Edited by Bruce H. Kirmmse. Princeton: Princeton University Press, 2007.

———. *Concluding Unscientific Postscript to "Philosophical Fragments."* Vol. 1. Edited and translated by Howard V. Hong and Edna H. Hong. Princeton: Princeton University Press, 1992.

Kirsch, Wolfgang. "Die Umstrukturierung des lateinischen Literatursystems im Zeichen der Krise des 3. Jahrhunderts." *Philologus* 132 (1988): 2–18.

Klein, Melanie. *The Writings of Melanie Klein: Envy and Gratitude and Other Works (1946–1963)*. Edited by Roger Morney-Kyrle, vol. 3. New York: Free Press, 1975.

Kligerman, Eric. *Sites of the Uncanny: Paul Celan, Specularity, and the Visual Arts*. Berlin: Walter de Gruyter, 2007.

Klopsch, Paul. *Einführung in die Dichtungslehren des lateinischen Mittelalters*. Darmstadt: Wissenschaftliche Buchgesellschaft, 1980.

Kohut, Karl. "La teoría de la poesia cortesana en el Prólogo de Juan Alfonso de Baena." In *Actas del coloquio hispano-aleman Ramón Menendez Pidal*, 120–37. Madrid: Niemeyer, 1982.

———. "Der Beitrag der Theologie zum Literaturbegriff in der Zeit Juans II von Kastilien: Alonso de Cartagena (1384–1456) und Alonso de Madrigal, genannt el Tostado (1400?–1455)." *Romanische Forschungen* 89 (1977): 183–226.

———. *Las teorías literarias en España y Portugal durante los siglos XV y XVI*. Madrid: Consejo Superior de Investigaciones Científicas, 1973.

———. "Zur Vorgeschichte der Diskussion um das Verhältnis von Christentum und antiker Kultur im spanischen Humanismus: die Rolle des *Decretum Gratiani* in der Übermittlung patristischen Gedankengutes." *Archiv für Kulturgeschichte* 55 (1973): 80–106.

Kretzenbacher, Leopold. *Das verletzte Kultbild: Voraussetzungen, Zeitschichten und Aussagewandel eines abendländischen Legendentypus*. Munich: Verlag der Bayerischen Akademie der Wissenschaften, 1977.

Küpper, Joachim. "Zu einigen Aspekten der Dichtungstheorie in der Frührenaissance." In *Renaissance: Konzepte einer Epoche im Dialog der Disziplinen*, edited by Andreas Kablitz and Gerhard Regn, 47–71. Heidelberg: C. Winter, 2005.

———. "'Uti' und 'frui' bei Augustinus und die Problematik des Genießens in der ästhetischen Theorie des Okzidents." In *Genuß und Egoismus: Zur Kritik ihrer geschichtlichen Verknüpfung*. Edited by Wolfgang Klein and Ernst Müller. Berlin: Verlag, 2002.

Lampert, Lisa. *Gender and Jewish Difference from Paul to Shakespeare*. Philadelphia: University of Pennsylvania Press, 2004.

Lange, Wolf-Dieter. *El fraile trobador: Zeit, Leben und Werk des Diego de Valencia de León (1350?–1412?)*. Frankfurt am Main: V. Klostermann, 1971.

Langmuir, Gavin. *Toward a Definition of Anti-Semitism*. Berkeley: University of California Press, 1990.

Lehman, Jürgen, ed. *Die Niemandsrose: Kommentar*. Heidelberg: Universitätsverlag C., 1996.

Leopold, J. "Philo's Vocabulary and Word Choice." In *Two Treatises of Philo of Alexandria: A Commentary on "De gigantibus" and "Quod Deus sit immutabilis,"* edited by D. Winston and J. Dillon. Chico: Scholars Press, 1983.

Levi, Neil. *Modernist Form and the Myth of Jewification*. New York: Fordham University Press, 2014.

Lichtenstein, Jacqueline. *The Eloquence of Color: Rhetoric and Painting in the French Classical Age*. Berkeley: University of California Press, 1993.

Lieberknecht, Otfried. *Allegorese und Philologie: Überlegungen zum Problem des vierfachen Schriftsinns in Dante's Commedia*. Stuttgart: Steiner, 1999.

Liebermann, Felix, ed. *Die Gesetze der Angelsachsen*. Halle: Niemeyer, 1903/2007.

Linehan, P. "The Spanish Church Revisited: The Episcopal *Gravamina* of 1279." In *Authority and Power: Studies on Medieval Law and Government Presented to Walter Ullmann on His Seventieth Birthday*, edited by Brian Tierney and Peter Linehan, 127–47. Cambridge: Cambridge University Press, 1980.

Lipton, Sara. *Dark Mirror: The Medieval Origins of Anti-Jewish Iconography*. New York: Henry Holt, 2014.

———. "The Temple Is My Body: Gender, Carnality, and Synagoga in the *Bible Moralisée*." In *Imagining the Self, Imagining the Other: Visual Representation and Jewish-Christian Dynamics in the Middle Ages and Early Modern Period*, edited by Eva Frojmavic, 129–63. Leiden: Brill, 2002.

Llorca, B. "La Inquisición española y los conversos judíos y marranos." *Sefarad* 8 (1942): 357–89.

Lloyd, G. E. R. *Polarity and Analogy: Two Types of Argumentation in Early Greek Thought*. London: Bristol Classical Press, 1992.

Lubac, Henri de. *Exégèse médiévale, les quatre sens de l'Écriture*. 4 vols. Paris: Éditions Montaigne, 1959–1964.

Lukács, Georg. "Expressionism: Its Significance and Decline." In *Essays in Realism*, translated by David Fernbach, 77–113. London: Lawrence and Wishart, 1980.

Lyna, F., and W. van Eeghem, eds. *Jan van Styevoorts Refreinenbundel anno 1524*. Antwerp: Z. J., 1929–1930.

Mackor, A. "Are Marinus' Tax Collectors Collecting Taxes?" *Bulletin de Musée National de Varsovie* 36 (1995): 3–13.

———. "Marinus van Reymerswaele: Painter, Lawyer, and Iconoclast?" *Oud-Holland* 109 (1995): 191–200.

Maitland, F. W., and F. Pollock. *History of English Law before the Time of Edward I*. 2 vols. Cambridge: University Press, 1952.

Mak, J. J. *De rederijkers*. Amsterdam: P. N. van Kampen and Zoon, 1944.

Mango, Cyril. *Art of the Byzantine Empire*. Toronto: University of Toronto Press, 1986.

Mann, Thomas. *Rede und Antwort*. Berlin: S. Fischer, 1922.

Mansi, J. D., ed. *Sacrorum Conciliorum Nova, et Omnium Amplissima Collectio*. Vol. 9. Florence: Expensis Antonii Zatta Veneti, 1763.

Mareel, S., and S. Bussels. "Strategieën van overtuiging in het rederijkerstoneel en de beeldende kunsten in de vijftiende- en zestiende-eeuwse Nederlanden." *Desipientia: Zin & Waan: Kunsthistorisch Tijdschrift* 15 (2008): 16–20.

Marin, Louis. *La critique du discours*. Paris: Minuit, 1975.

Márquez Villanueva, Francisco. "Jewish 'Fools' of the Spanish Fifteenth Century." *Hispanic Review* 50 (1982): 385–409.

Martin, Dale. *The Corinthian Body*. New Haven: Yale University Press, 1999.

Martínez Díez, Gonzalo, and Félix Rodríguez, eds. *La Colección Canónica Hispana*. Vol. 5: *Concilios Hispanos, Segunda Parte*. Madrid: CSIC, 1992.

Martyn, J. Louis. "Apocalyptic Antinomies in Paul's Letter to the Galatians." *New Testament Studies* 31 (1985): 410–24.

Marx, Karl. *Economic and Philosophical Manuscripts of 1844*. Translated by Martin Milligan. Mineola: Dover Publications Inc., 1961/2007.

Marx, Karl, and Friedrich Engels. *Karl Marx–Friedrich Engels Werke*. Vol. 1. Berlin: Dietz, 1957.

McLynn, N. B. *Ambrose of Milan: Church and Court in a Christian Capital*. Berkeley: University of California Press, 1994.

Meier, Heinrich. *The Lesson of Carl Schmitt: Four Chapters on the Distinction between Political Theology and Political Philosophy*. Expanded edition. Chicago: University of Chicago Press, 2011.

Meiss, Millard. *Painting in Florence and Siena after the Black Death: The Arts, Religion, and Society in the mid-Fourteenth Century*. Princeton: Princeton University Press, 1951.

Mendes-Flohr, Paul. "Martin Buber and Martin Heidegger in Dialogue." *Journal of Religion* 94 (2014): 2–25.

Messmer, E. "Laktanz und die Dichtung." Dissertation, Munich, 1974.

Michaud, Eric. *The Cult of Art in Nazi Germany*. Translated by Janet Lloyd. Stanford: Stanford University Press, 2004.

Middendorf, Ulrike. "Moralische Gesinnung." *Weltkunst* 75, no. 8 (2005): 73–75.

Milner, Jean-Claude. *De la syntaxe à l'interprétation: Quantités, insultes, exclamations*. Paris: Seuil, 1978.

Minnis, A. J., and Ian Johnson, eds. *The Cambridge History of Literary Criticism*. Vol. 2: *The Middle Ages*. Cambridge: Cambridge University Press, 2005.

Minnis, A. J., and A. B. Scott, eds. *Medieval Literary Theory and Criticism, 1100–1375: The Commentary Tradition*. Oxford: Clarendon, 2000.

Momigliano, Arnaldo. *Alien Wisdom: The Limits of Hellenization*. Cambridge: Cambridge University Press, 1975.

Mommsen, Theodore, ed. *Corpus iuris civilis*. 3 vols. Berolini: Apud Weidmannos, 1893.

Montoro, Antón de. *Cancionero de Antón de Montoro*. Edited by Emilio Cotarelo y Mori. Madrid: José Perales y Martínez, 1900.

Mothe-Fénelon, François de Salignac de la. *Oeuvres*. 2 vols. Edited by Jacques Le Brun. Paris: Gallimard, 1983.

———. *The Lettre à l'Académie*. Edited by Ernesta Calderini. Geneva: Droz, 1970.

Mundill, Robin R. *England's Jewish Solution: Experiment and Expulsion, 1262–1290*. Cambridge: Cambridge University Press, 1998.

Murray, Michele. *Playing a Jewish Game: Gentile Christian Judaizing in the First and Second Centuries CE*. Ontario: Wilfred Laurier University Press, 2004.

Murray, Penelope. *Plato on Poetry*. Cambridge: Cambridge University Press, 1996.

Nieto Soria, J.-M. "Los judíos de Toledo en sus relaciones financieras con la monarquía y la Iglesia (1252–1312)." *Sefarad* 41 (1981): 301–19.

Nietzsche, Friedrich. *Beyond Good and Evil*. Translated by Walter Kaufmann. New York: Vintage, 1989.

———. *The Gay Science*. Leipzig: E. W. Fritzsch Verlag, 1887.

Nirenberg, David. "Was There Race before Modernity? The Example of 'Jewish' Blood in Late Medieval Spain." In *Neighboring Faiths: Christianity, Islam, and Judaism in the Middle Ages and Today*, 169–90. Chicago: University of Chicago Press, 2014.

———. "'Judaism,' 'Islam,' and the Dangers of Knowledge in Christian Culture, with Special Attention to the Case of King Alfonso X, 'the Wise,' of Castile." In *Mapping Knowledge: Cross-Pollination in Late Antiquity and the Middle Ages*, Arabica Veritas, vol. 1, edited by C. Burnett and P. Mantas-España, 253–76. Cordoba: Oriens Academica, 2014.

———. *Anti-Judaism: The Western Tradition*. New York: W. W. Norton, 2013.

———. "Shakespeare's Jewish Questions." *Renaissance Drama* 38 (2010): 77–113.

———. "The Politics of Love and Its Enemies." *Critical Inquiry* 33, no. 3 (2007): 573–605.

———. "Figures of Thought and Figures of Flesh: 'Jews' and 'Judaism' in Late Medieval Spanish Poetry and Politics." *Speculum* 81 (2006): 398–426.

Nirenberg, Ricardo. "Metaphor: The Color of Being." In *Contemporary Poetics*, edited by Louis Armand, 153–74. Evanston: Northwestern University Press, 2007.

Nordau, Max. *Degeneration*. New York: Howard Fertig, 1968.

Osborne, Catherine. "The Repudiation of Representation in Plato's *Republic* and Its Repercussions." *Proceedings of the Cambridge Philological Society* 33 (1987): 53–73.

Ostrogorsky, Georg. *Studien zur Geschichte des byzantinischen Bilderstreites*. Breslau: M. and H. Marcus, 1929.

Paleotti, Gabriele. *Discourse on Sacred and Profane Images*. Translated by William McCuaig. Los Angeles: Getty Publications, 2012.

Panofsky, Erwin. *Early Netherlandish Painting*. Vol. 1. New York: Harper & Row, 1971.

———. *Idea: A Concept in Art Theory*. New York: Harper & Row, 1968.

Paris, Matthew. *Chronica majora*. 7 vols. Edited by Henry Richards Luard. London: Rolls Series, 1872–1884.

Pascual Argente, Clara. "'El Cabdal Sepulcro': Word and Image in the *Libro de Alexandre*." *La Corónica* 38 (2010): 71–98.

Patterson, Lee. "'Living Witnesses of Our Redemption': Martyrdom and Imitation in Chaucer's Prioress's Tale." *Journal of Medieval and Early Modern Studies* 31 (2001): 507–60.

Patton, Pamela. *Art of Estrangement: Redefining Jews in Reconquest Spain*. University Park: Pennsylvania State University Press, 2012.

———. "Constructing the Inimical Jew in the *Cantigas de Santa María*: Theophilus's Magician in Text and Image." In *Beyond the Yellow Badge: Anti-Judaism and Antisemitism in Medieval and Early Modern Visual Culture*, edited by Mitchell B. Merback, 233–56. Leiden: Brill, 2008.

Paviot, Jacques. "Les inscriptions grecques et hébraïques dans les tablexeaux eyckiens." *Revue belge d'archéologie et d'histoire de l'art* 75 (2006): 53–73.

Pereda, Felipe. "'Eyes That They Should Not See, and Ears That They Should Not Hear': Literal Sense and Spiritual Vision in the *Fountain of Life*." In *Fiction sacrée: Spiritualité et esthétique durant le premier âge moderne*, edited by Ralph Dekoninck, Agnès Guiderdoni, and Emilie Granjon, 113–56. Leuven: Peeters, 2013.

———. "Through a Glass Darkly: Paths to Salvation in Spanish Painting at the Outset of the Inquisition." In *Judaism and Christian Art: Aesthetic Anxieties from the Catacombs to Colonialism*, edited by Herbert L. Kessler and David Nirenberg, 263–90. Philadelphia: University of Pennsylvania Press, 2011.

———. *Las imagenes de la Discordia: Política y poética de la imagen sagrada en la España del 400*. Madrid: Marcial Pons, 2007.

———. "Le origini dell'architettura cubica: Alfonso de Madrigal, Nicola da Lira e la Querelle Salomonista nella Spagna del Quattrocento." *Annali di Architettura* 17 (2005): 21–52.

Pericolo, Lorenzo. "Visualizing Appearance and Disappearance: On Caravaggio's London Supper at Emmaus." *The Art Bulletin* 89 (2007): 519–39.

Peters, Olaf, et al., ed. *Degenerate Art: The Attack on Modern Art in Nazi Germany, 1937*. Munich: Prestel, 2014.

Peterson, Erik. *Der Monotheismus als politisches Problem*. Leipzig: Bai Jakub Hegner, 1935.

Petrarch. *Le familiari*. Edited by V. Rossi. Florence: Le Lettere, 1997.

———. *Opere latine di Francesco Petrarca*. Vol. 2. Edited by A. Bufano. Turin: Unione Tipografico-Editrice Torinese, 1975.

Petropoulos, Jonathan. *Art as Politics in the Third Reich*. Chapel Hill: University of North Carolina Press, 1996.

Petrus Cantor. *Petri Cantoris Parisiensis Verbum adbreviatum*. 3 vols. Edited by Monique Boutry. Turnhout: Brepols, 2012.

Philo of Alexandria. *On Abraham; On Joseph; On Moses*. Loeb Classical Library 289. Cambridge: Harvard University Press, 1935.

———. *On the Confusion of Tongues; On the Migration of Abraham; Who Is the Heir of Divine Things?; On Mating with the Preliminary Studies*. Loeb Classical Library 261. Cambridge: Harvard University Press, 1932.

Piccus, J. "El traductor español de *De genealogia deorum*." In *Homenaje a Rodríguez-Moñino*, vol. 2, 59–75. Madrid: Editorial Castalia, 1966.

Pichler, Wolfram. "Il dubbio e il doppio: le evidenze in Caravaggio." In *Caravaggio e il suo ambiente: Richerche e interpretazioni*, edited by Sybille Ebert-Schifferer and Elisabeth Kieven, 9–34. Milan: Silvana Editoriale, 2007.

Pop, Andrei. "Masks, Modernity and Egoism: Theatrical Practice in James Ensor and Maurice Maeterlinck." In *The Art of Theatre: Word, Image and Performance in France and Belgium, c. 1830–1910*, edited by Claire Moran, 287–305. Oxford: Peter Lang, 2013.

Prado Vilar, Francisco. "*Iudeus Sacer*: Life, Law, and Identity in the 'State of Exception' called 'Marian Miracle.'" In *Judaism and Christian Art: Aesthetic Anxieties from the Catacombs to Colonialism*, edited by Herbert L. Kessler and David Nirenberg, 115–42. Philadelphia: University of Pennsylvania Press, 2011.

Preimesberg, Rudolf. *Paragons and Paragone*. Los Angeles: Getty Research Institute, 2011.

———. "Zu Jan van Eycks Diptychon der Sammlung Thyssen-Bornemisza." *Zeitschrift für Kunstgeschichte* 54 (1991): 459–89.

Prodi, Paulo. *Ricerche sulla teorica delle arti figurative nella Riforma Cattolica*. Rome: Edizioni di storia e letteratura,1962.

Puymaigre, Théodore de. *La cour littéraire de don Juan II, roi de Castille*. Paris: A. Franck, 1873.

Rallo Grus, C. *Aportaciones a la técnica y estilística de la pintura mural en Castilla a final de la Edad Media: Tradición e influencia islámica*. Madrid: Universidad omplutense de Madrid, Servicio de Publicaciones, 2002.

Raynal, Maurice. "Conception and Vision." In *A Cubism Reader: Documents and Criticism, 1906–1914*, edited by Mark Antliff and Patricia Leighten, translated by Jane Marie Todd, 318–23. Chicago: University of Chicago Press, 2008.

Renehan, R. "On the Greek Origins of the Concepts Incorporeality and Immateriality." *Greek, Roman, and Byzantine Studies* 21, no. 2 (1980): 105–38.

Richter, Gerhard. *Writings, 1961–2007*. Edited by Dietmar Elger and Hans Ulrich Obrist, translated by David Britt. New York: D. A. P., 2009.

Roberts, Michael. *Poetry and the Cult of Martyrs*. Ann Arbor: University of Michigan Press, 1993.

———. *The Jeweled Style: Poetry and Poetics in Late Antiquity*. Ithaca: Cornell University Press, 1989.

———. *Biblical Epic and Rhetorical Paraphrase in Late Antiquity*. Liverpool: Francis Cairns, 1985.

Rodríguez Barral, Paulino. *La imagen del judío en la España medieval: El conflicto entre cristianismo y judaísmo en las artes visuales góticas*. Barcelona: Universitat Autonoma de Barcelona, 2008.

Rodríguez-Puértolas, Julio. *Poesía de protesta en la edad media castellana: historia y antología*. Madrid: Editorial Gredos, 1968.

Rose, Stanley. "Anti-Semitism in the 'Cancioneros' of the Fifteenth Century: The Accusation of Sexual Indiscretions." *Hispanófila* 26 (1983): 1–11.

———. "Poesía antijudía y anticonversa en la poesía artística del siglo XV en España." PhD diss., Catholic University of America, 1975.

Rothstein, Bret L. *Sight and Spirituality in Early Netherlandish Painting*. Cambridge: Cambridge University Press, 2005.

Rousseau, Jean-Jacques. *Politics and the Arts*. Edited and translated by Allan Bloom. Ithaca: Cornell University Press, 1968.

Rudolph, Conrad. "La resistenza all'arte nel Occidente." In *Arti e storia nel Medioevo*, vol. 3, 49–84. Turin: Einaudi, 2004.

———. *Artistic Change at St.-Denis: Abbot Suger's Program and the Early Twelfth-Century Controversy over Art*. Princeton: Princeton University Press, 1990.

———. *The "Things of Greater Importance": Bernard of Clairvaux's Apologia and the Medieval Attitude toward Art*. Philadelphia: University of Pennsylvania Press, 1990.

Runia, D. T. "'Verba Philonica,' 'Agalmatophorein' and the Authenticity of 'De Resurrectione' attributed to Athenagoras." *Vigiliae Christianae* 46 (1992): 313–27.

———. *Philo of Alexandria and the "Timaeus" of Plato*. Leiden: Brill, 1986.

Russo, Elena. *Styles of Enlightenment: Taste, Politics, and Authorship in Eighteenth-Century France*. Baltimore: Johns Hopkins University Press, 2007.

Sanders, K. O. "The Challenge of Homer: School, Pagan Poets and Early Christianity." In *Poetry and Exegesis in Premodern Latin Christianity: The Encounter between Classical and Christian Strategies of Interpretation*. Edited by W. Otten and K. Pollmann. Leiden: Brill, 2007.

Sansterre, Jean-Marie. "L'image blesse, l'image souffrante: quelques récits de miracles entre Orient et Occident (Vie–XIIe siècle)." In *Les images dans les societies médévales: Pour une histoire comparée. Actes du colloque international organize par l'Institut Historique Belge de Rome et l'Université Libre de Bruxelles*, 113–30. Brussels: Academia Belgica, 1999.

Santner, Eric L. *The Royal Remains: The People's Two Bodies and the Endgames of Sovereignty*. Chicago: University of Chicago Press, 2011.

———. *My Own Private Germany: Daniel Paul Schreber's Secret History of Modernity*. Princeton: Princeton University Press, 1996.

Schechter, F. I. "The Rightlessness of Medieval English Jewry." *Jewish Quarterly Review* 4 (1914): 121–51.
Schlegel, Friedrich. *Gemälde alter Meister*. Edited by Hans Eichner and Norma Lelless. Darmstadt: Wissenschaftliche Buchgesellschaft, 1984.
Schlie, Heike. *Bilder des Corpus Christi: sakramentaler Realismus von Jan van Eyck bis Hieronymus Bosch*. Berlin: Mann, 2002.
Schmitt, Jean-Claude. *La conversion de Hermann le Juif*. Paris: Seuil, 2007.
———. "Les dimensions multiples du voir: Les rêves et l'image dans l'autobiographie de conversion d'Hermann le Juif au XIIe siècle." *Micrologus* 4. Special issue. *Le vision e lasguardo nel Medio Evo*, 2 (1998): 1–27.
———. "La question des images dans les débats entre juifs et chrétiens au XIIe siècle." In *Spannungen und Widersprüche: Gedenkenschrift für Frantisek Graus*, 245–54. Sigmaringen: J. Thorbecke, 1992.
———. "Les idoles chrétiennes." In *L'idolâtrie (Rencontres de l'École du Louvre)*. Paris: La Documentation Française, 1990.
Schmitt, Carl. *Politische Theologie II, Die Legende von der Erledigung jeder Politischen Theologie*. Berlin: Dunker and Humblot, 1970.
———. *Der Nomos der Erde im Völkerrecht des Jus Publicum Europaeum*. Cologne: Greve, 1950.
———, ed. *Das Judentum in der Rechtswissenschaft: Ansprachen, Vorträge und Ergebnisse der Tagung der Reichsgruppe Hochschullehrer des NSRB am 3. und 4. Oktober 1936*. Berlin: Deutscher Rechts-Verlag, 1936.
———. *Der Begriff des Politischen*. Berlin: Duncker and Humblot, 1932.
———. *Politische Theologie: Vier Kapitel zur Lehre von der Souveränität*. Munich: Duncker and Humblot, 1922.
Schneider, Norbert. *Die rhetorische Eigenart der paulinischen Antithese*. Tübingen: J. C. B. Mohr, 1970.
Schnitzler, Norbert. "Faules Holz—Toter Stein: Thesen zum Bilderkult des Mittelaters aus ikonoklastischer Perspektive." In *Pictura quasi fictura: die Rolle des Bildes in der Erforschung von Alltag und Sachkultur des Mittelalters und der frühen Neuzeit*, edited by Jaritz Gerhard, 175–90. Vienna: Österreichischen Akademie der Wissenschaften, 1996.
———. *Ikonoklasmus—Bildersturm: Theologischer Bilderstreit und ikonoklastishes Handeln während des 15. a und 16. Jahrhunderts*. Munich: Wilhelm Fink, 1996.
Schöner, Petra. *Judenbilder im deutschen Einblattdruck der Renaissance: ein Beitrag zur Imagologie*. Saecula Spiritualia, vol. 42. Baden-Baden: Valentin Koerner, 2002.
Schulte, Christoph. *Psycopathologie des Fin de Siècle: Der Kulturkritiker, Arzt und Zionist Max Nordau*. Frankfurt am Main: Fischer, 1997.
Schultze-Naumburg, Paul. *Kunst und Rasse*. Munich: J. H. Lehmann, 1928.
Schuster, Peter-Klaus, ed. *Die "Kunststadt" München 1937: Nationalsozialismus und "Entartete Kunst."* Munich: Prester-Verlag, 1987.
Schwartz, Benjamin I. "The Age of Transcendence." *Daedalus* (Spring 1975): 1–7.

Sedulius. *Sedulii Opera Omnia*. CSEL 10. Edited by Johann Huemer. Vienna: Apud C. Geroldi filium, 1885.

Seelig, Rachel. "Between Center and Periphery: Transnational Jewish Literature in Weimar Berlin." PhD diss., University of Chicago, 2011.

Sergius the Stylite. *The Disputation of Sergius the Stylite against a Jew*. CorpusSCO 338, *Scriptores Syri* 152. Edited by A. P. Hayman. Louvain: Secretariat du CorpusSCO, 1973.

Serrano Reyes, Jesús L., and Juan Fernández Jiménez, eds. *Juan Alfonso de Baena y su Cancionero: actas del I Congreso Internacional sobre el Cancionero de Baena, Baena, del 16 al 20 de febrero de 1999*. Córdoba: M. I. Ayuntamiento de Baena, Delegación de Cultura, 2001.

Shachar, Isaiah. *The Judensau: A Medieval Anti-Jewish Motif and Its History*. London: Warburg Institute, 1974.

Shearman, John. *Only Connect . . . : Art and the Spectator in the Italian Renaissance. The A. W. Mellon Lectures in the Fine Arts, 1988*. Princeton: Princeton University Press, 1992.

Siegfried, M. *Abkehr vom Subjekt: Zum Sprachdenken bei Heidegger und Buber*. Freiburg im Breisgau: Verlag Karl Alber, 2010.

Silver, Larry. *The Paintings of Quinten Massys: With Catalogue Raisonné*. Montclair: Allanheld and Schram, 1984.

Silvestris, Bernardus. *Commentary on the First Six Books of Virgil's "Aeneid."* Translated by Earl Schreiber and Thomas Maresca. Lincoln: University of Nebraska Press, 1979.

———. "Power and Pelf: a New-Found Old Man by Massys." *Simiolus* 9 (1977): 63–92.

Šmahel, František. *Husitské čechy: Struktury—procesy—ideje*. Prague: Lidové noviny, 2001.

Solovieva, Olga. "Epiphanius of Salamis between Church and State: New Perspectives on the Iconoclastic Fragments." *Zeitschrift für Antikes Christentum / Journal of Ancient Christianity* 16, no. 2 (2012): 344–67.

———. "Epiphanius of Salamis and His Invention of Iconoclasm in the Fourth Century AD." *Fides et Historia* 42, no. 1 (2010): 21–46.

Speck, P. *Ich bin's nicht, Kaiser Konstantin ist es gewesen: Die Legenden vom Enfluss des Teufels, des Juden, und des Moselm auf den Ikonoklasmus*. Bonn: Poikila Byzantina, 1990.

Stacey, Robert. "Anti-Semitism and the Medieval English State." In *The Medieval State: Essays Presented to James Campbell*, edited by John Robert Maddicott and David Michael Palliser, 163–77. London: Hambledon Press, 2001.

———. "Parliamentary Negotiation and the Expulsion of the Jews from England." In *Thirteenth-Century England VI*, edited by Michael Prestwich, Richard H. Britnell, and Robin Frame, 93–94. Woodbridge: Boydell Press, 1997.

Stauff, Philipp. *Semi-Kürschner, oder Literarisches Lexicon*. Berlin: self-published, 1913.

Stijevoort, Jan van. *Refreinenbundel: Anno 1524*. 2 vols. Edited by F. Lyna and W. van Eeghem. Antwerp: De Sikkel, 1930.

Stoichita, Victor I. *A Short History of the Shadow*. London: Reaktion Books, 1997.

Strauss, Ludwig. *Gesammelte Werke in vier Bänden*. Edited by Tovia Rübner and Hans Otto Horch. Göttingen: Wallstein Verlag, 1998.

Suger of St. Denis. "De Administratione." In *Abbot Suger on the Abbey Church of St. Denis and Its Art Treasures*. 2nd ed. Edited and translated by Erwin Panofsky, second edition edited by Gerda Panofsky-Soergel. Princeton: Princeton University Press, 1979.

Summers, David. *The Judgment of Sense: Renaissance Naturalism and the Rise of Aesthetics*. Cambridge: Cambridge University Press, 1990.

Talavera, Hernando de. "Invectivas contra el médico rudo e parlero." In *Petrarca: Obras*, I: *Prosa*, edited by F. Rico et al., 369–410. Madrid: Alfaguara, 1978.

———. *Católico Impugnación*. Barcelona: Floris, 1961.

Taylor, Anna Lisa. *Epic Lives and Monasticism in the Middle Ages, 800–1050*. Cambridge: Cambridge University Press, 2013.

Teyssèdre, Bernard. *Roger de Pile et les débats sur le coloris au siècle de Louis XIV*. Lausanne-Paris: Bibliotheque des Arts, 1964.

Theodulf, Bishop of Orléans. *Opus Caroli regis contra Synodum*. Edited by Ann Freeman and Paul Meyvaert. Hannover: Hahnsche Buchhandlung, 1998.

Tronsarelli, Ottavio. *L'Apollo*. Rome: Francesco Corbelletti, 1634.

Tsvétayeva, Marina. *Marina Tsvétaeva: Selected Poems*. Translated by David McDuff. Newcastle upon Tyne: Bloodaxe Books Ltd., 1987.

Tyler, Royall, ed. *Calendar of State Papers, Spanish (1550–1552)*. London: Institute of Historical Research, 1914.

Unglaub, Jonathan. "Caravaggio and the 'Truth in Pointing.'" In *Caravaggio: Reflections and Refractions*, edited by David Stone and Lorenzo Pericolo, 149–76. Burlington: Ashgate, 2012.

Valpy, F. E. J. *An Etymological Dictionary of the Latin Language*. London: Baldwin and Longman, 1828.

Vasiliev, A. A. "The Iconoclastic Edict of the Caliph Yazid II, AD 721." In *Dumbarton Oaks Papers* 9–10 (1956): 23–47.

Vocht, H. de "Rodrigo Manrique's Letter to Vives." In *Texts and Studies about Louvain Humanists in the First Half of the Sixteenth Century*, Monumenta Humanistica Lovaniensia, vol. 4, 427–58. Louvain: Librairie universitaire, 1934.

Ward, H. L. D., and J. A. Herbert, eds. *Catalogue of Romances in the Department of Manuscripts in the British Museum*. London: British Museum, 1883.

Watt, John A. *The Jews, the Law, and the Church: The Concept of Jewish Serfdom in Thirteenth-Century England*. Studies in Church History, Subsidia 9. Oxford: Ecclesiastical History Society, 1991.

Wedderburn, A. J. M. *Baptism and Resurrection: Studies in Pauline Theology against Its Graeco-Roman Background*. Tübingen: Mohr, 1987.

Weiss, Julian. "Álvaro de Luna, Juan de Mena and the Power of Courtly Love." *Modern Language Notes* 106 (1991): 241–56.

———. *Poet's Art: Literary Theory in Castile, c. 1400–60*. Oxford: Oxford University Press, 1990.

Weissberger, Barbara F. "'Deceitful Sects': The Debate about Women in the Age of Isabel the Catholic." In *Gender in Debate from the Early Middle Ages to the Renaissance*, edited by Thelma S. Fenster and Clare A. Lees, 207–35. New York: Palgrave Macmillan, 2002.

Werveke, H. van. "Aantekeningen bij de zogenaamde Belastingpachters en Wisselaers van Reymerswaele." *Gentsche Bidragen tot de Kunstgeschiedenis* 12 (1949–1950): 43–58.

Whitford, Frank. "Radical Art and Radical Politics." In *Germany in Ferment: Exhibition of Paintings, Prints, Sculpture, 1900–1935*. Durham: Durham University Press, 1970.

Wilson, Jean C. "Self-Representation and the Evolution of the Northern European Occupational Portrait: The Metropolitan Museum's Man Weighing Gold, ca. 1515." *Dutch Crossing* 23, no. 2 (1999): 29–55.

Winston, D., ed. and trans. "Philo and the Contemplative Life." In *Jewish Spirituality from the Bible through the Middle Ages*, edited by Arthur Green, 198–231. New York: Crossroads, 1988.

Winston, D., and J. Dillon. *Two Treatises of Philo of Alexandria: A Commentary on "De gigantibus" and "Quod Deus sit immutabilis."* Chico: Scholars Press, 1983.

Wölfflin, Heinrich. *The Sense of Form in Art: A Comparative Psychological Study*. Translated by A. Muehsam and N. Shatan. New York: Chelsea Publishing Co., 1958.

———. *Italien und das deutsche Formgefühl*. Munich: F. Bruckmann, 1931.

Wulf, Joseph, ed. *Die Bildenden Künste im Dritten Reich: eine Dokumentation*. Gütersloh: Sigbert Mohn Verlag, 1963.

Žižek, Slavoj. *In Defense of Lost Causes*. London: Verso, 2009.

INDEX

Page numbers in *italics* refer to illustrations.